Genocide

University of Pennsylvania Press
Pennsylvania Studies in Human Rights
Bert B. Lockwood, Jr., Series Editor

A complete listing of the books in this series appears at the back of this volume

Genocide: Conceptual and Historical Dimensions

Edited by George J. Andreopoulos

UNIVERSITY OF PENNSYLVANIA PRESS

Philadelphia

This volume was prepared under the auspices of the Orville H.
Schell Center for International Human Rights.

Copyright © 1994 by the University of Pennsylvania Press
All rights reserved
Printed in the United States of America

Library of Congress Cataloging-in-Publication Data
Genocide: conceptual and historical dimensions / edited by George J. Andreopoulos.
    p.   cm. — (Pennsylvania studies in human rights)
  Includes bibliographical references (p.   ) and index.
  ISBN 0-8122-3249-6
  1. Genocide.   2. Genocide—History—20th century—Case studies.
I. Andreopoulos, George J.   II. Series.
HV6322.7.G45   1994
304.6'63—dc20   93-44384
                                                 CIP

To Yanni and Pari

Contents

Preface

This volume is the result of written papers, informal presentations, and a most lively series of exchanges at a one-day conference entitled *Genocide: The Theory—the Reality,* which was held on 16 February 1991 at Yale Law School under the auspices of the Orville H. Schell Center for International Human Rights. The purpose was to bring together both scholars who have examined the conceptual dimensions of genocide and case studies specialists in order to analyze (1) the relevance of various definitions of genocide in law and social theory for the interpretation of a wide range of situations often generically labeled as genocide; (2) the evaluative criteria used in classifying different types of mass killings as genocide; (3) the implications of the conceptual misuse to which the term genocide is prone; and (4) the extent to which specific case studies can credibly highlight the strengths and weaknesses of the aforementioned definitions.

This book is divided into two parts. In the first part, contributors debate the conceptual dimensions of genocide and the implications of varying definitions. In the second part, contributors focus on the relevance of the main theoretical insights to the analysis and evaluation of their respective case studies, which center on the Armenians in the Ottoman Empire and beyond, the Kurds in Turkey and Iraq, the East Timorese after the Indonesian invasion, and the Cambodians under the Khmer Rouge.

This book could not have come into being without the assistance of a number of people. In particular, I would like to thank Drew S. Days, former director of the Schell Center and current U.S. Solicitor General, for his encouragement and support throughout this project, and Bert Lockwood of the University of Cincinnati College of Law, the Series Editor of the Pennsylvania Studies in Human Rights, for his strong interest in the project and his indispensable advice. The success of our conference owed much to the invaluable help we received from our administrative assistants Joan Paquette-Sass and Louise Koch. A special note of thanks must go to my secretary, Marge Camera, for the preparation of the finished manuscript. At the University of Pennsylvania Press, it was a great pleasure to work with Tim Clancy, Associate Director of the Press, and Mindy Brown, Project Editor.

Above all, my thanks go to the contributors to this volume, who brought this project to fruition. I sincerely hope that the end result lives up to their endorsement.

George J. Andreopoulos
New Haven, June 1993

Introduction: The Calculus of Genocide

George J. Andreopoulos

No crime matches genocide in the moral opprobrium that it generates. It is a crime which, despite its well-documented destructive impact on societies and the progressive enforcement of human rights norms in the international community, has more than a historical relevance. The massacres committed by the Khmer Rouge in Cambodia in the late 1970s, those committed by Idi Amin in Uganda during his rule (1971–79), the Tutsi massacre of the Hutu in Burundi in the 1960s and 1970s, the Iraqi massacres of the Kurds in the late 1980s, and most recently the killings of Muslims in Bosnia-Herzegovina are troubling reminders of genocide's staying power. Hence any study of genocide, whether legal, historical, or sociological, has an unavoidable contemporary dimension.

Initially, the debate on the nature of genocide was predominantly the terrain of international lawyers. After all, Raphael Lemkin, the man who coined the term, was a jurist. It was during the Fifth International Conference for the Unification of Criminal Law in Madrid (in 1933) that Lemkin submitted a proposal "to declare the destruction of racial, religious or social collectivities a crime under the law of nations,"[1] an idea he developed further in his seminal work, *Axis Rule in Occupied Europe.*[2] A key component in the calculus of genocide was, in Lemkin's own words, "the criminal intent to destroy or to cripple permanently a human group. The acts are directed against groups, as such, and individuals are selected for destruction only because they belong to these groups."[3] Lemkin's definition, which was to form the backbone of the UN Convention on the Prevention and Punishment of the Crime of Genocide (hereinafter the "Genocide Convention" or "Convention"), focused on the legal task of defining a crime, and thus placed the emphasis on intention and on the individual and/or collective responsibility of a well-defined set of actors (the perpetrators).

The concern over the persecution of specific groups also became an issue during the drafting process of the Charter of the International Military Tribunal for the trial of the major war criminals of the European Axis Powers at Nuremberg. Under Article 6 of the Charter, defendants were indicted for committing crimes against the peace, war crimes, and crimes against humanity. Crimes against the peace referred to *jus ad bellum* violations, while war crimes and crimes against humanity to *jus in bello* violations. More than anything else, it was the latter term that reflected concerns similar to the ones expressed by Lemkin. The Charter defined crimes against humanity as

murder, extermination, enslavement, deportation, and other inhumane acts committed against any civilian population, before or during the war, or persecutions on political, racial or religious grounds in execution of or in connection with any crime within the jurisdiction of the Tribunal, whether or not in violation of the domestic law of the country where perpetrated.[4]

The Charter's definition did not allow for the conceptual autonomy of "crimes against humanity"; on the contrary, by attaching it to that of war crimes, it contributed to considerable conceptual overlap. Despite these problems, however, the establishment of "crimes against humanity" as a crime under international law paved the way, in the words of one scholar, "for subsequent development of other offenses of international concern" (those of genocide and apartheid, among others).[5] There is no doubt that the efforts of Lemkin and those who drafted the Nuremberg Charter contributed substantively, first, to the passage of General Assembly Resolution 96-I on the crime of genocide (December 1946), and then to the passage of General Assembly Resolution 260-III (December 1948), which, among other things, approved the text of the Genocide Convention.[6]

In the last twenty years or so, however, genocide has come under increasing scrutiny from social scientists. Armed with different tools and objectives, their input has sharpened the focus on the definitional shortcomings of the Genocide Convention. Moreover, their contributions have launched a long overdue inquiry into the origins and unfolding of genocide as a social process.[7]

The shortcomings of the Genocide Convention have been commented upon by numerous scholars, including the contributors to this volume. The main criticisms usually center on (1) the exclusion of political and social groups from those deemed worthy of protection; (2) the exact meaning of the intentionality clause in the Convention (Article II); and (3) the absence of an international enforcement mechanism in the form of an international penal tribunal that would punish the perpetrators of genocidal activities. However, the most fundamental problem remains, as Fein observes, "its unenforceability, as the perpetrator of genocide, the state, is responsible for its prosecution."[8] In a comprehensive overview destined to elicit a healthy dose of cynicism, Kuper demonstrated the political bargains to which the Convention's provisions were subjected, as the various proposals moved from one draft of the convention to the next.[9] The United Nations, being an international organization composed of sovereign states and committed to the principles of sovereignty and territorial integrity, is hardly the place to generate proceedings against fellow member states. Even if there were provisions for an international penal tribunal, it is highly unlikely that the system would be of much use as long as only governments could take cases to court.

The international community is currently experiencing this frustrating impasse in the case of the Khmer Rouge in Cambodia. As Kiernan notes in his chapter, the record of the Pol Pot regime, which ruled the country from 1975 to 1979, is an open and shut case of genocidal activities on at least four fronts: the extermination of a religious group, the Buddhist monks ("out of a total of 2,680 Buddist monks from eight of Cambodia's monasteries, only 70 monks were found to have survived in 1979")[10]; and the persecution of three ethnic groups, including the Vietnamese community ("in more than a year's research in Cambodia after 1979, it was not possible to find a Vietnamese resident who had survived the Pol Pot years there"),[11] the Chinese community (reduced by half by 1979), and the Muslim Chams (reduced by 36 percent, from 250,000 to 160,000, by 1979).[12] Kiernan makes a cautious case for the inclusion of the decimated Eastern Zone Khmers as part of the Khmer national group; it is this group whose persecution has been termed as "auto-genocide."[13] Regardless of whether the Eastern Zone Khmers are included, few would dispute the solid case against the Khmer Rouge. Yet not only has no government expressed interest in taking the case against the Khmer Rouge to the International Court of Justice,[14] but the Cambodian mission in New York is still partially staffed by Pol Pot supporters.[15] It has been argued that cases like the Cambodian one demonstrate that the problem is not one of definitions but one of enforcement. This argument reflects a false dilemma. The quest for a comprehensive definition and the quest for an enforceable mechanism are indicative of complementary rather than conflictual processes.

The quest for a comprehensive definition would enable us first to "map out" the area within which the concept is to operate; an analytically rigorous definition could then be developed which would avoid conceptual overstretch. Because the concept refers to a social process, a good definition has a critical functional value: to assist in the detection of early signs of an impending crisis and, provided the appropriate mechanisms are in place, devise preventive measures. Thus a good definition can be instrumental in the creation of an early warning system for the detection of genocide-prone situations. Finally, a proper conceptual framework should be able to explain nonevents: In particular, it should provide insights into why genocide-prone situations did not develop into full-scale genocides, and why societies that had witnessed large-scale genocidal massacres[16] in the past managed to achieve relative stability without any structural changes in the perpetrator regime. Northern Ireland, South Africa, and Cyprus are good examples of the former,[17] while the Soviet Union under Stalin and Khrushchev exemplifies the latter.[18]

This is indeed a tall order for any conceptual undertaking. I do not intend to highlight the impossibility of achieving it, but rather the necessity of approximating it. While the quest for a comprehensive definition addresses primarily the social-scientific concern for analytical rigor, early detection, and (hopefully) prevention, the complementary quest for an enforceable mechanism addresses primarily the juridical concern for punishment. To give one example: If the definition of genocide, as provided in Article II of the Convention, were to be revised so as to highlight the state's role in the commission of the crime, it would necessitate a corresponding revision of Article VI, providing for the establishment of international criminal jurisdiction.[19] Otherwise, the only way that a genocidal regime could be brought to justice would be following its overthrow. If history offers any lesson, it is that such an outcome is as rare as it is desirable.

Any discussion on the conceptual dimensions of genocide has as its starting point the definition of the Genocide Convention. Kuper, although critical of the Convention's definition (in particular because of its exclusion of political and social groups), believes that "it provides a workable definitional core for interdisciplinary analysis and application."[20] In addition, he credits the Convention's definition with "some possibilities for preventative action"[21] at a time when the incidence of genocide shows no signs of abatement.

Fein is likewise critical of the Convention's definition and attempts to broaden it so as to include "all nonviolent collectivities who have or may become victims."[22] She defines genocide as "sustained purposeful action by a perpetrator to physically destroy a collectivity directly or through interdiction of the biological and social reproduction of group members, sustained regardless of the surrender or lack of threat offered by the victim."[23]

Despite their criticisms, both Kuper and Fein consider the Convention's definition as a fundamentally working one. This is not the case with Frank Chalk and Israel Charny, who view the same definition as deeply flawed. Chalk, in his study on *The History and Sociology of Genocide* (coauthored with Kurt Jonassohn), cites the exclusion of political groups and social classes as one of the main reasons for rendering the definition "of little use to scholars."[24] Chalk believes that this exclusion led the International Commission of Jurists to exonerate both Macias in Equatorial Guinea and the Pakistani leadership in Bangladesh from charges of genocidal killings. He defines genocide as "a form of one-sided mass killing in which a state or other authority intends to destroy a group, as that group and membership in it are defined by the perpetrator."[25]

The authors' differences regarding the conceptual dimensions of genocide are reflective of the evaluative criteria used in classifying different types of mass killings as genocide. Among the most important differences are the authors' views on the connection between state terror and war crimes with genocide.

Fein has proposed a paradigm for the detection and tracing of genocide which includes the following conditions:

1. There was a sustained attack or continuity of attacks by the perpetrator to physically destroy group members;
2. The perpetrator was a collective or organized actor (usually the state) or commander of organized actors;
3. The victims were selected because they were members of the collectivity;
4. The victims were defenseless or were killed regardless of whether they surrendered or resisted; and
5. The destruction of group members was undertaken with intent to kill and murder was sanctioned by the perpetrator.[26]

On the basis of this paradigm, Fein argues that despite the similarities between state terror and genocide, there is a major difference: "victims of terror are selected because they are believed to have committed 'subversive' acts or they are chosen arbitrarily rather than as members of a group as are victims of genocide."[27] Fein is critical of Chalk and Jonassohn's conception, which places the emphasis for the definition of the victimized group on the perpetrator's criteria for victimization rather than on a set of well-defined criteria for group membership. Although placing the emphasis on the mind of the perpetrator is not problem-free, particularly in the case of preventive measures,[28] there are two very valid reasons for pursuing this line of inquiry: (1) Regimes that have persecuted imaginary groups (i.e., groups that are defined arbitrarily by the perpetrator) have also persecuted real groups, and (2) the intersections between the targeted groups do not allow for clear-cut distinctions.

It is difficult, for example, to understand the persecution of the Ukrainians in the 1932–33 period without examining the contextual persecution of the "hostile peasantry" as enemies of collectivization in the late twenties and early thirties. And although the Ukraine and the Ukrainian-speaking area of the North Caucasus bore the brunt of persecution during that period, they were by no means the exclusive targets. Other groups in the North Caucasus and the Lower Volga were equally victimized, groups who shared with the Ukrainians the generic label "enemies of collectivization."[29]

Another area of disagreement is the connection between war crimes and genocide. Kuper has argued that the atomic bombing of Hiroshima and Nagasaki, the pattern bombing of Hamburg and Dresden, and the firebombing of Tokyo constituted genocide.[30] Kuper believes that the targeting of civilians as a result of the changing nature of warfare "and the technological means for the instantaneous annihilation of large populations, creates a situation conducive to genocidal conflict."[31] Civilian populations, be they German or Japanese, were targeted for being German or Japanese with the intention of destroying them; thus, their intended victimization falls under the provisions of the Genocide Convention. Kuper's assertions are problematic. As both Fein and Chalk argue, such a perspective conflates the concept of war crimes and genocide. The civilian populations were targeted as enemies in warfare and not as groups to be destroyed irrespective of a challenge or threat posed to the perpetrator. The critical distinction to bear in mind here is the extent to which the killing would have continued had the war ended and had the Japanese and Germans no longer been considered enemies.[32] It is obvious that had Japan capitulated before August 1945, neither Hiroshima nor Nagasaki would have been bombed. This does not mean that what took place in Japan in August 1945 was consistent with international legal principles. However, for any violation of these principles one should look for guidance to the provisions of the 1907 Hague Conventions regulating the conduct of warfare. While in my view both sides violated the laws of war during World War II, the labeling of the aforementioned bombings as genocide is indicative of moral outrage at the outcome, rather than of an analytical perspective on the process.

A Note on Intentionality

One of the key elements in the Convention's definition of genocide is the perpetrator's intent to destroy a certain group as such. As mentioned earlier, the precise meaning of the intentionality clause has stirred considerable debate among specialists: in particular, the way in which the intent of the perpetrator can be demonstrated as opposed to the motive, "the perpetrator's social accounting for its action."[33] The confusion usually stems from the universal reluctance of genocidal regimes to admit that their repressive policies were aimed at destroying the targeted group; rather, a set of explanations is usually offered ranging from the reestablishment of law and order (the Iraqi chemical warfare against the Kurds) to the classification of the victims as casualties of war (one of the explanations offered by the Turkish government for the Armenian Genocide).

For Fein, intent can be demonstrated by "showing a pattern of purposeful action"[34] leading to the destruction of a significant part of the targeted group, regardless of the reasons offered by the perpetrator for his actions. Other scholars have proposed definitions that do away with the intentionality criterion. Israel Charny, in his chapter, proposes a generic definition of genocide with numerous subcategories ranging from genocidal massacres, to genocide as a result of ecological destruction (ecocide), and all the way to accomplices of genocide and cultural genocide (ethnocide). For Charny, the intentionality criterion is irrelevant; he uses the term genocide indiscriminately to refer to the "mass killing of substantial numbers of human beings, when not in the course of military action against the military forces of an avowed enemy, under conditions of the essential defenselessness and helplessness of the victims."[35] According to him the quest for discriminatory definitions cannot but lead "into assigning hierarchical value to different kinds of mass death."[36] While Charny properly cautions against some of the dangers of excessive "definitionalism," his generic labeling of most mass killings as genocide will raise questions concerning its analytical value.

The intentionality criterion has come under attack from another group of scholars, who advocate a structuralist perspective on the origins of the genocidal process. According to Isidor Wallimann and Michael Dobkowski, it is becoming increasingly difficult to locate the issue of intentionality on the societal level "because of the anonymous and amorphous structural forces that dictate the character of our world."[37] They argue that since we are living in a world in which "individuals are dominated by anonymous forces such as market mechanisms, bureaucracies, and distant decision making by committees and parliaments, the emphasis on intentionality appears anachronistic."[38] Without ignoring the role of individuals and of the choices they make, Wallimann and Dobkowski believe that such a perspective forces us "to probe more deeply and fundamentally into the nature of social structures and systems," and "it must be investigated which forms of social organization are more likely to guarantee the preservation rather than the systemic destruction of lives through structural violence."[39]

Wallimann and Dobkowski's perspective refers to the well-known debate in the social sciences between those who in their analysis of societal developments place primary emphasis on the role of individual and collective actors and those who place primary emphasis on depersonalized processes or institutional structures and assess their impact on society's functional requirements. Both perspectives have adherents among the Marxist and non-Marxist traditions alike; the former is reflective of certain conflict theories and the "voluntarist" school of Marxism (Gyorgy Lukacs, Edward Thompson), while the latter is reflective of the functionalist school (Talcott Parsons) and the structuralist school of Marxism (Louis Althusser).[40] While the former perspective offers interesting insights into the manner in which the choices that individual and collective actors make have a critical impact and sometimes can lead to institutional transformation, the latter offers interesting insights into the systemic constraints within which these actors operate. From their respective strengths emerge their respective weaknesses. The former, by placing too much emphasis on actors, does not take into proper consideration the systemic constraints that often provide a limited range of available options for the actors concerned. The latter, by placing too much emphasis on structures, views the actors as passive vehicles for the system's values and goals; hence the actors can only mechanically reflect and never shape the system. Its greatest weakness is the inability to explain change.

Given this rather elliptical presentation of the two main traditions, it is obvious that Wallimann and Dobkowski's perspective (and that of some of the contributors to their volume) shares both the strengths and weaknesses of the structuralist tradition. In an essay on the genocidal fate that befell the Aborigines in Australia, Tony Barta refers to the *relation of destruction* between colonizers and Aborigines to explain the outcome. According to him, "It was not 'an exclusively good or bad will on either side' which caused the destruction of the Aborigines but 'the objective nature of the relationships' between (white) capitalist wool producers and (black) hunter-gatherers."[41]

Tony Barta draws selectively from the writings of Marx that emphasize the systemic constraints that structure human relationships. ("Selective" is used here because the more historical writings of Marx are clearly voluntarist.) He proposes without any further theoretical elaboration the term relations of destruction. Such terminology is reflective of Marx's use of the terms "forces of production" and "relations of production" in his analysis and discussion of the capitalist mode of production. Marx's analysis has generated a similar discussion among scholars who study those forces and relations in society that are of a strictly political nature and thus cannot be reduced to the economic level, the key term here being *forces and relations of domination*. However, more work is needed before these concepts can provide the analytical insights on the political and social level that the corresponding concepts of *forces and relations of production* have provided on the economic level.

Despite the problems associated with the systemic approach (some of them highlighted in Chalk's chapter), it is a constructive reminder of the role of impersonal forces in shaping group and individual choices. However, this perspective offers no convincing argument for doing away with the intentionality criterion, and no insights whatsoever on the feasibility of preventive measures against genocide. Its main claim that genocide is coextensive with the reproductive needs of a certain system suggests the normalization of the genocidal process and the concomitant impossibility of devising preventive measures against a process that is part of everyday life.

The contributors to the second part of this volume focus on the contextual factors of the genocidal process, and analyze its key characteristics with reference to the arguments generated by the Convention's definition. Hovannisian and Kiernan argue that their cases (Armenia and Cambodia, respectively) are covered by the definition. On the other hand, Dunn and van Bruinessen (Kurds and East Timor, respectively) make a cautious argument that what transpired in their cases was most probably ethnocide (see, however, van Bruinessen's postscript).

Hovannisian argues that all aspects of the Convention's definition apply in the case of the Armenian Genocide that took place during the First World War. Reports on the number of Armenians killed cite variously from 600,000 to 2 million, while "the rest were forcibly driven from their ancestral homeland."[42] Despite these mass killings, none of the perpetrators was ever punished and the international community quickly forgot the Armenian tragedy. In an overview of the Armenian effort to keep the collective memory alive and to set the historical record straight, Hovannisian gives a disturbing account of the systematic campaign conducted by the Turkish government to relativize and rationalize the events in Armenia. This campaign culminated with the successful effort to defeat the passage in Congress of resolutions commemorating the Armenian Genocide.

What were the factors contributing to the unleashing of the genocidal process? According to Hovannisian, they include:

1. The existence of a plural society (Ottoman Turkey) with clearly defined racial, religious, and cultural differences;
2. A sense of deprivation/danger felt by the perpetrator groups (Turks);
3. The relative social and economic upward mobility of the victim group (Armenians);
4. The espousal and propagation by the perpetrators of an ideology/belief system (Pan-Turkism) emphasizing the mobility and distinctiveness of its own group as opposed to the exploitative nature of the intended victims (the need to subhumanize the intended victim); and
5. The determination to establish a new regional order and in that process eliminate elements posing real, potential, or perceived threats.[43]

The painful memories of the 1915–18 events have acquired a contemporary relevance as a result of the interethnic strife in Azerbaijan between Armenians and Azerbaijanis. In Hovannisian's view, the recent killings in the industrial city of Sumgait have reawakened the collective fear of another genocidal cycle in the Armenian experience: "Historical memory forcefully shapes contemporary outlook. The past is present."[44]

The recycling of a tradition of victimization is by no means a uniquely Armenian phenomenon. As van Bruinessen argues in his essay, the Kurds have had to practice the art of survival politics in an increasingly volatile region. Confined within countries that "collectively repress their culture and aspirations,"[45] the Kurds had to hone—depending on the occasion—their diplomatic and military skills to deal with the repressive policies of Turkey, Syria, Iran, and Iraq.[46] Van Bruinessen examines two cases of military operations against the Kurds: Turkey's suppression of the rebellious Kurdish district of Dersim in 1937–38, and the Iraqi government's use of chemical weapons against the Kurds in 1988. While the latter has received wide coverage in the West, the former is a relatively unknown massacre "gracefully passed over in silence or deliberately misrepresented by most historians, foreign as well as Turkish."[47]

As in the Armenian case, it was the transition from a plural, multiethnic society to a unidimensional Turkish nation-state that generated the policies of forced assimilation and/or destruction vis-à-vis those groups perceived to be obstacles to the grand goal of national unity. A key component of the turkification process was the policy of massive population resettlement. Referring to the main policy document in this context, the 1934 Law on Resettlement, van Bruinessen demonstrates that it provided "the legal framework for a policy of ethnocide,"[48] a policy targeting the region of Dersim as one of its first test cases, with disastrous consequences for the local population.

The recurring destruction of Kurdish villages and the resulting forced resettlements are also an integral part of the Iraqi government's policies vis-à-vis the Kurds. And although the Kurds are recognized as a separate ethnic group in Iraq (which is not the case in Turkey), their treatment at the hands of the Iraqi government has been equally (if not more) brutal. According to van Bruinessen, the Iraqi government's Kurdish policies were the outgrowth of the Baath Party's self-image as the sole embodiment of the Arab nation; hence the policy of Arabization became an indispensable component of the Iraqi government's quest to fulfill its "historic mission." There are some intriguing parallels in the language of power used by the Turkish and Iraqi governments to justify their policies toward the Kurds. The Turkish government presented its assimilationist policies as an effort to abolish feudalism, tribalism, and religious reaction. The Kurds stood in the way of a policy that sought to replace Islam and the cleavages inherent in a multiethnic unit, with a secular, Turkish-based nationalism. Likewise, the Iraqi government has often sought to portray its policy as one of state-led modernization. In this context, the Kurds, with their demands for autonomy and the desire to sustain their own culture, are viewed as a security threat capable of undermining the Baathist conception of Iraq's historic role in the Arab world. In both cases, the discourse of modernization/civilizing mission has been employed as a rationalization for exterminist policies.

Can we characterize the Turkish and Iraqi policies toward the Kurds as genocidal ones? Van Bruinessen refrains from passing final judgment on this issue, although he repeatedly refers to these policies as ethnocidal. To be sure, some have argued that ethnocide (that is, the suppression of the culture, religion, and language of the targeted group leading to its forced assimilation with the dominant group) is a form of genocide; this, however, is a minority view among specialists. Van Bruinessen acknowledges that on at least two occasions the Kurds were deliberately wiped out: during the suppression of the Dersim rebellion by the Turkish government and during the resettlement of eight thousand Barzani Kurds by the Iraqi government in August 1983. In the latter case, all eight thousand disappeared. Thus, according to van Bruinessen, in an overall pattern of ethnocidal policies, there are "instances" of genocidal activities.

However, such compartmentalization within a pattern of consistently repressive policies is problematic. On the other hand, if one were to disassociate the notion of intent from that of motive and examine whether the Turkish and Iraqi policies show a pattern of purposeful action leading to the destruction of the Kurdish minority irrespective of the official reasons offered by these two governments, then it can be argued that these policies bear the characteristics of genocide.[49]

The relevance of ethnocidal policies is also at the center of Dunn's treatment of the case of East Timor. A former Portuguese colony, East Timor was invaded by Indonesian forces on 7 December 1975 in order to derail Fretilin's unilateral declaration of independence. Dunn shows that a whole year before the invasion a group of Indonesian generals set up a covert operation code-named "Operasi Komodo." Its aim was "to bring about the integration of East Timor at any cost."[50] The Indonesians lived up to their policy with remarkable consistency. Dunn chronicles the brutality of the invading forces and the ensuing destruction from the continuing occupation, especially during the 1975–82 period. In addition, he highlights the embarrassing lack of international outcry at the governmental level. Despite the sympathetic attention that the East Timorese case has received in the U.S. Congress and the European Parliament, Western governments—with the notable exception of the Netherlands—have shown little concern about the invasion and its impact. Moreover, some of these governments have refused to support UN resolutions favoring self-determination and humanitarian assistance to East Timor.[51]

Did the Indonesian forces commit genocide in East Timor? Although Dunn refrains from calling it genocide and instead opts for the term cultural genocide (that is, ethnocide), he admits that the strategy pursued by Indonesian forces in their quest for total control and eventual integration was of genocidal proportions. As in the Kurdish case, one can detect a pattern of purposeful action on the part of the Indonesian authorities aimed at the destruction of the distinct identity of the East Timorese; in the process, the Indonesian authorities have used a mixture of violence, forced resettlements, and aggressive promotion of Indonesian cultural identity. At a time when the pro-independence movement poses no military challenge to the Indonesian forces, the progressive "Indonesianization" of East Timor constitutes the greatest challenge to the survival of the indigenous group.

None of this ambivalence concerning the genocidal nature of the regime's policies exists in the case of Cambodia. As Kiernan argues, the exterminist policies of the Khmer Rouge fit the provisions of the Genocide Convention in the cases of the Buddhist monks, of the Vietnamese and Chinese communities, and of the Muslim Chams, while he admits that the legal case for the Eastern Zone Khmers is weaker. According to Kiernan's figures, the Pol Pot regime is responsible for the death of more than 1.6 million people out of a population of almost 8 million, or approximately 21 percent of the total population of the country.

Efforts to understand the genocidal process have primarily focused on the nature of the Pol Pot regime. A debate has ensued on the extent to which Pol Potism should be viewed as an indigenous peasant movement responding to needs generated by the social and political evolution of the country, or whether it should be seen as a product of diffusionism, with Stalinism and/or Maoism providing the model that was to be uncritically adopted by the Khmer Rouge elite. A related argument has centered on whether the exterminist nature of the Pol Pot regime was the product of a peasant revolution run amok, which in the process left the leadership behind, or the product of a ruthlessly executed plan of social engineering, masterminded by the Stalinist leadership of the Khmer Rouge. Kiernan suggests that there is no evidence to support the thesis of a peasant revolution that transcended its leadership; instead, he views the Khmer Rouge regime as a highly centralized dictatorship whose ideology consisted of an amalgam of various intellectual traditions, including most prominently Khmer elite chauvinism, but also Stalinism, Maoism, and Third World nationalism. In a comprehensive overview of the failure of international action against the Pol Pot forces, Kiernan presents a disturbing picture of the cynical geopolitical use of the Khmer Rouge as an anti-Vietnamese instrument. In an unprecedented collusion, China and several Western nations, including the United States, supported the Khmer Rouge as the legitimate representative of the Cambodian people in the United Nations. It was the beginning of a multifaceted policy of support which included the United States' semipublic approval of Chinese and Thai aid for the Khmer Rouge—a policy of support that has persisted until the recently concluded Paris Peace Agreement. To this very day, the reluctance to deal with what the chairman of the United Nations Human Rights Subcommission has called "the most serious [human rights violations] to have occurred anywhere since Nazism"[52] is a reminder of the international community's mere lip service to human rights enforcement.

Conclusion: Genocide and the New World Order

The Gulf War and its aftermath have generated much discussion concerning the lessons to be drawn from that experience. Coming shortly

TABLE 1. Case Studies.

Case Study	Perpetrator	Victim	Crime	Ideological vehicle of perpetrator	Code words in the language of power*
Ottoman Empire/ Armenians (1915–18)	Ottoman Government (Young Turks)	Armenians	Genocide	Pan-Turkism	*Communal warfare/war casualties.* The Ottoman government claimed that Armenians were victims of communal warfare and that the Turks and Armenians had suffered alike during World War I.
Turkey/ Kurds (1937–38)	Turkish government	Kurds	Ethnocide, genocide	Pan-Turkism	*Abolition of feudalism, tribalism, and religious reaction.* The Turkish government claimed that tribal chieftains and mischievous religious leaders were oppressing the people and fomenting discord.
Iraq/Kurds (1988)	Iraqi government	Kurds	Ethnocide, genocide	Arab nationalism	*Modernization/enhancing national security.* The Iraqi government claimed that its policies were aimed at the economic development of a "backward" mountainous people; hence their relocation to "new model villages." In cases of internal unrest, troublemakers were relocated to "strategic villages."

Indonesia/East Timor (1975–82)	Indonesian government	East Timorese	Ethnocide, genocide	Anti-communism/Indonesian nationalism	*Integration/neutralization of subversion.* The Indonesian government claimed that East Timor's integration was essential to foster stability and welfare in the region. The covert operation "Operasi Komodo" focused on, among other things, highlighting the dangers of "communist subversion," and fabricating links between the Fretilin leaders and Peking and/or Hanoi.
Cambodia (1975–79)	Khmer Rouge	Chams, Vietnamese community, Chinese community, Buddhist monks, Eastern Zone Khmers	Genocide	Stalinism, Maoism, Khmer elite chauvinism, Third World nationalism	*National sovereignty.* The Khmer Rouge argued that for the first time in its history Cambodia became a sovereign nation. To achieve this, the regime had to neutralize all internal and external opponents. They did not try to create a rationalizing discourse for their internal policies. They pursued a policy of total denial and viewed any queries as interference and an attempt to undermine the newly founded sovereignty. In recent years, the Khmer Rouge leadership has admitted that mistakes were committed which they attribute to the unpunished "Vietnamese agents."

*Key words and expressions used by perpetrators to rationalize their activities and render them acceptable domestically and internationally. The list is by no means exhaustive.

after the demise of communist rule in Central and Eastern Europe, the Gulf War presented what appeared to be the first truly collective action against aggression undertaken by the UN Security Council. Has the United Nations' reliance on a collective security approach been finally vindicated, albeit with a forty-five-year delay? President Bush seemed to think so when he proudly proclaimed that the Gulf War was about "a new world order." Ever since that statement was made, much energy has been expended on deciphering the president's oracular pronouncements and identifying the constitutive elements of this new "concept." In this brief concluding note, I do not intend to provide a full-scale analysis of the concept; rather, I would like to explore the relevance of some of the issues that it has raised to the question of genocide.

In international politics, there are two different approaches on the subject of world order. As Joseph Nye has pointed out,

> Realists, in the tradition of Richard Nixon and Henry Kissinger, see international politics occurring among sovereign states balancing each others' power. World order is the product of a stable distribution of power among the major states. Liberals, in the tradition of Woodrow Wilson and Jimmy Carter, look at relations among peoples as well as states. They see order arising from broad values like democracy and human rights, as well as from international law and institutions such as the United Nations.[53]

The realists have always had less of a problem with their own conception of order because it correlated with the (tangible) distribution of power among states rather than with the (lofty) ideals of "rule of law," "democracy," and "human rights." The liberals, on the other hand, had to live with the creative tension between the state-centered and the society-centered conceptions of order. This distinction is also evident in the related issue of security. Realists have traditionally focused on security threats posed by external enemies of the state, while liberals have sought to balance traditional security concerns with concerns resulting from the failure of societies to provide for basic human needs and concerns resulting from repression by the state itself. Thus, while realists have paid lip service to the creative tension between *regime security* and *societal security*,[54] liberals not only have acknowledged that tension, but have sought to incorporate it (not always successfully) into their policy-making.

Although the Gulf War has rekindled discussion about collective security, the rule of law, and human rights, "it also exposed an important weakness in the liberal conception. The doctrine of collective security enshrined in the UN Charter is state-centric, applicable when borders are crossed but not when force is used against peoples within a state."[55] The Gulf War has also exposed the inconsistency in the application of the state-based notion of collective security. On what grounds can the international community punish the Iraqi aggression and remain oblivious to continuing cross-border violations in other parts of the world, like the Indonesian occupation of East Timor? And how can one expect the international community to become more sensitive toward people-centered aggression when it has systematically failed to guard against the more easily identifiable and punishable state-centered aggression? This concern is of direct relevance to any discussion about the prevention and punishment of genocidal massacres; since 1945, these massacres have—with very few exceptions—occurred as a result of intra-state rather than inter-state conflicts.

What can the United Nations contribute to the containment of genocidal conflicts? The UN has emerged from the Gulf War experience with a mixed record at best. On the positive side, the war witnessed the unprecedented cooperation of the major powers in pursuit of collective security, a goal that the Cold War had rendered elusive for the past forty-five years. The series of Security Council resolutions issued with the concurring votes of the five permanent members between 2 August and 25 August 1990 seemed to signal the beginning of "a new era of internationalism" and reinforced the notion that "the UN Security Council might at last begin to live up to the role as set forth in the Charter."[56] In addition, the wide support among Third World countries for the resolutions seemed to indicate that the traditional north/south cleavages would not stand in the way of the newly found consensus.

On the negative side, the Gulf War witnessed the Security Council's being drawn into approving "the shift from sanctions to military measures without the sort of finding evidently contemplated by the language of Article 42"[57] of the UN Charter. Article 42 clearly states that action by air, sea, or land forces to maintain or restore international peace and security can take place only after the Security Council has concluded that nonmilitary actions have failed. Such a Security Council finding was never issued;[58] on the contrary, the Security Council was clearly pressured (primarily by the U.S.) into endorsing Resolution 678, thus authorizing the coalition to go to war on its behalf. Concerning the conduct of the war, the Security Council exercised no control whatsoever over the nature and scope of the mission. To the very end, Desert Storm remained substantively a U.S.-U.K. military operation under formal UN auspices. Thus, in certain ways, the UN role during the Gulf War bore a striking resemblance to its role during the Korean War[59]—that of an important bystander rather than the harbinger of a new world order.

If the Gulf War experience offers any constructive lessons, they point to the need for certain long-overdue UN reforms. Such reforms would address the need for preventive as well as coercive measures. And although preventive measures are a crucial component of the new calculus, the overall credibility of the UN would hinge on its capability to mobilize forces for peacekeeping and enforcement purposes under genuine international control.

The first step in this direction would be the reactivation of the Military Staff Committee of the UN as provided in Article 47 of the UN Charter. That provision was consigned—as were many others—to oblivion during the Cold War era. The second step would require bringing into being the special agreements provided for in Article 43 of the Charter. According to Article 43, at the initiative of the Security Council, special agreements are to be concluded with the member states, so as to make available to the Security Council "armed forces, assistance, and facilities. . . . necessary for the purpose of maintaining peace and security." To be sure, such forces would be most effective against small-scale military challenges. However, they could also have an important deterrent effect, since all potential aggressors would be aware of the fact that, as a result of these agreements, the Security Council is endowed with a credible means of response.[60]

It is a sign of the times that some of these suggestions have been endorsed by the Secretary-General of the UN in his report to the General Assembly, entitled *An Agenda for Peace*.[61] In fact, on the issue of the UN forces, the Secretary-General provides an additional suggestion concerning peace-enforcement units: these units would be "available on call and would consist of troops that have volunteered for such service." Their task would be to "restore and maintain the cease-fire" under the command of the Secretary-General. The report considers "such peace-enforcement units to be warranted as a provisional measure under Article 40 of the Charter."[62]

These suggestions are indicative of a serious effort to begin the process of transforming the UN into an entity that would be more than the sum of its parts. However, such a transnationalist approach can gather momentum seriously only if it is prepared to tackle the thorny issues associated with the primacy of state sovereignty. And in the context of the prevention and punishment of genocide, this implies a serious rethinking of the concept of humanitarian intervention—a rethinking that would establish a set of clearly defined criteria for UN endorsement.

The Secretary-General's report acknowledges the growing permeability of national boundaries: "National boundaries are blurred by advanced communications and global commerce, and by the decisions of States to yield some sovereign prerogatives to larger, common political associations. . . . The time of absolute and exclusive sovereignty . . . has passed. . . . It is the task of leaders of States today to understand this and to find a balance between the needs of good internal governance and the requirements of an even more interdependent world."[63] A few pages later, however, this carefully worded appeal for balance is grounded by the exigencies of a ritualistic reaffirmation of sovereignty. Discussing the issue of preventive deployment in conditions of crisis within a country, the report emphasizes that "the United Nations will need to respect the sovereignty of the State . . . [and] that humanitarian assistance must be provided in accordance with the principles of humanity, neutrality and impartiality; that the sovereignty, territorial integrity and national unity of States must be fully respected in accordance with the Charter of the United Nations; and that, in this context, humanitarian assistance should be provided *with the consent of the affected country and, in principle, on the basis of an appeal by that country*" (emphasis added).[64] Thus, if a government engages in massive repression of its own population, only the very same perpetrator government can appeal for humanitarian assistance—hardly a "visionary" perspective for the new world order!

To be sure, no one expected the Secretary-General to urge the taming of sovereignty in a document addressed to member states. However, since this is the first conceptual document on the issues of peace and security to have emerged from his office since the end of the Cold War, one would have expected a more creative presentation, coupled with a few bold suggestions for further discussion.

Any serious discussion of humanitarian intervention should focus, first, on identifying the circumstances under which it can be undertaken and, second, on the relevant organizational framework. In a recent study, Bazyler identified five relevant criteria:

- Commission of large-scale atrocities
- Overriding humanitarian motive
- Preference for joint action
- Limited intervention (application of the principles of relativity and proportionality)
- Exhaustion of other remedies.[65]

Two of the five criteria—overriding humanitarian motive and limited intervention—should be excluded because they only lend themselves to an ex post facto assessment. If the relevant criteria are to be codified in a legal instrument authorizing humanitarian intervention, those that lend themselves to an ex post facto assessment are of limited value concerning the authorization; they are more relevant in passing moral judgment on the intervention.

The remaining three—commission of large-scale atrocities, preference for joint action, and exhaustion of other remedies—can constitute a workable starting point for a comprehensive reassessment of the doctrine of humanitarian intervention.[66] The organizational framework for this reassessment should be the United Nations. The office of the Secretary-General should offer these "baseline criteria" as talking points to the General Assembly for the possibility of amending the UN Charter in accordance with the relevant provisions of Articles 108 and 109. Thus humanitarian intervention would be authorized by the UN and governed by the relevant provisions of Chapter VII. This would be a lengthy and difficult procedure, however, since it would impact the explosive issue of sovereignty. But if the UN is to play a meaningful role in shaping a new world order, it can only do so by reconsidering the linkages between the protection and promotion of international human rights norms and the maintenance of international peace and security.

The conflict currently unfolding in the territory of the former Yugoslavia poses one of the biggest challenges to the UN's efforts to link grave human rights violations with threats to international peace and security. Numerous reports of large-scale massacres and the practice of ethnic cleansing led the Security Council to adopt Resolution 771, which called upon

States and, as appropriate, international humanitarian organizations to collate substantiated information . . . relating to the violations of humanitarian law, including grave breaches of the Geneva Conventions, being committed in the territory of the former Yugoslavia and to make this information available to the Council.[67]

In addition, the Commission on Human Rights requested its chairman to appoint a special rapporteur "to investigate firsthand the human rights situation in the territory of the former Yugoslavia, in particular within Bosnia and Herzegovina."[68] The appointed special rapporteur, Tadeusz Mazowiecki, and his team made two visits to the territory of the former Yugoslavia: the first on 21–26 August 1992, and the second on 12–22 October 1992.[69]

The results of the missions were published in two separate reports. Both reports confirmed the widespread use of ethnic cleansing and "massive and grave violations of human rights" throughout the territory of Bosnia-Herzegovina. While all parties to the conflict were both perpetrators and victims, the reports singled out the plight of the Muslims. In the words of the first report, "the situation of the Muslim population is particularly tragic: they feel that *they are threatened with extermination.*"[70] Perhaps the most disturbing conclusion was that "*ethnic cleansing does not appear to be the consequences of the war, but rather its goal.*"[71] And it was this realization that led to one of the key recommendations of the first report: "The need to prosecute those responsible for mass and flagrant human rights violations and for breaches of international humanitarian law and to deter future violators requires the systematic collection of documentation on such crimes and of personal data concerning those responsible."[72]

Following this recommendation and Resolution 771, the Security Council adopted Resolution 780, which requested that the Secretary-General

establish, as a matter of urgency, an impartial Commission of Experts to examine and analyze the information submitted pursuant to resolution 771 (1992) . . . with a view to providing the Secretary-General with its conclusions on the evidence of grave breaches of the Geneva Conventions and other violations of international humanitarian law.[73]

In accordance with Resolution 780, the Secretary-General appointed a five-member Commission of Experts which proceeded with the investigation of the situation in the former Yugoslavia.[74] In an interim report submitted to the Secretary-General (who then forwarded it to the president of the Security Council), the Commission concluded that "grave breaches and other violations of international humanitarian law had been committed . . . including willful killing, 'ethnic cleansing,' mass killings, torture, rape, pillage and destruction of civilian property, destruction of cultural and religious property and arbitrary arrests."[75] In addition, the report noted that if the Security Council were to create an ad hoc international tribunal, "such a decision would be consistent with the direction of its work."[76]

After further deliberations, the Security Council adopted Resolution 808, which provided for the establishment of an international tribunal and requested a report on the appropriate options for its effective implementation.[77] Finally, with Resolution 827, the Security Council decided

to establish an international tribunal for the sole purpose of prosecuting persons responsible for serious violations of international humanitarian law committed in the territory of the former Yugoslavia between 1 January 1991 and a date to be determined by the Security Council upon the restoration of peace.[78]

The same resolution adopted the Statute of the International Tribunal, which was included in the Secretary-General's report to the Security Council.[79]

It is too early to assess the possible impact of these developments. It can be argued that all this activity centering on the international tribunal reflects the international community's reluctance to deal decisively with the more pressing issue of reversing the outcome of aggression, namely the acquisition of territory by force. At a time when the headlines are being captured by the controversial "safe havens" policy and the questionable commitment of the sponsoring powers to its enforcement,[80] questions are being raised concerning the international community's will to resist, let alone reverse, the forcible dismemberment of Bosnia-Herzegovina.

On the other hand, it can be argued that irrespective of whether, at this juncture, the value of the tribunal is symbolic or substantive, it does create some interesting precedents. In particular, two issues need to be highlighted: the legal basis for the establishment of the tribunal and the subject-matter jurisdiction.

Concerning the legal basis, it should be noted that the General Assembly was bypassed in the drafting and review processes of the Statute of the International Tribunal. The reason for this, according to the Secretary-General, was that the involvement of the General Assembly "would not be reconcilable with the urgency expressed by the Security Council in resolution 808 (1993)."[81] Thus, the International Tribunal was established "by a decision of the Security Council on the basis of Chapter VII of the Charter of the United Nations."[82] What this means is that for the first time in its history the Security Council is establishing as an enforcement measure *a subsidiary organ of a judicial nature* in accordance with Article 29 of the Charter. And for the first time a judicial organ's life-span is directly linked to the restoration and maintenance of international peace and security.[83]

Concerning the subject-matter jurisdiction, the Secretary-General's report included the Genocide Convention as embodying rules of international humanitarian law applicable in the current Yugoslav conflict. In fact, Article 4 of the statute empowers the tribunal to prosecute perpetrators of genocidal activities. If the tribunal were to prosecute persons under Article 4, it would be the first time that the provisions of the Genocide Convention were invoked in judicial proceedings since the Convention's entry into force in 1951.[84] In addition, the Secretary-General's report reaffirmed that the Genocide Convention, the Geneva Conventions for the Protection of War Victims of 12 August 1949, the Hague Convention (IV) Respecting the Laws and Customs of War on Land of 18 October 1907 and the regulations annexed thereto, and the Charter of the International Military Tribunal of 8 August 1945 have become part of international customary law.

As noted at the beginning of this chapter, genocide regrettably has more than a historical relevance. Despite the formal protestations of the international community, precious little has been done so far toward its punishment, let alone its prevention. The recent efforts at the United Nations to reconsider the linkages between the protection and promotion of international human rights norms and the maintenance of international peace and security are a step in the right direction, although it is too early to assess their potential impact. The foregoing discussion by no means exhausts this complicated issue, and I must admit that any attempts to transcend the realist parameters (as in the case of a comprehensive reassessment of the doctrine of humanitarian intervention) will be utopian in character. However, the realist parameters have consistently grounded the whole undertaking. This does not mean that any vision of a "new world order" will necessarily be more successful. This vision does indicate, however, a willingness to rethink the creative tension between state-centered and people-centered security or, to put it differently, a willingness to admit that the price of inaction may at times be higher than the risks associated with utopian endeavors.

Notes

1. Raphael Lemkin, "Genocide as a Crime Under International Law," *American Journal of International Law (AJIL)* 41 (1947): 146.

2. It was published in 1944 under the auspices of the Carnegie Endowment for International Peace.

3. Lemkin, "Genocide as a Crime Under International Law," 147; see also his "Genocide," *The American Scholar* 15, no. 2 (April 1946): 227–30

4. Adam Roberts and Richard Guelff, eds., *Documents on the Laws of War* (Oxford: Clarendon Press, 1989), 155. The term "crimes against humanity" first appeared in the joint declaration by the governments of Great Britain, France, and Russia (28 May 1915) in response to the unfolding massacres of the Armenian population by the Ottoman Turkish troops; see Roger S. Clark, "Crimes Against Humanity at Nuremberg," in *The Nuremberg Trial and International Law,* ed. George Ginsburgs and V. N. Kudriavtsev (Netherlands: Martinus Nijhoff Publishers, 1990), 177–78; and Vahakn N. Dadrian, "Genocide as a Problem of National and International Law: The World War I Armenian Case and Its Contemporary Legal Ramifications," *Yale Journal of International Law* 14, no. 2 (1989): 226.

5. Clark, "Crimes Against Humanity at Nuremberg," 199. For an overview of the development of the concept during the drafting of the Charter, see 181–92; see also, Iu. A. Reshetov, "Development of Norms of International Law on Crimes Against Humanity," in *The Nuremberg Trial and International Law,* 199–212.

6. For the text of Resolution 96-I, see Leo Kuper, *Genocide: Its Political Use in the Twentieth Century* (New Haven, CT: Yale University Press, 1982), 23.

7. Among others, see Kuper, *Genocide: Its Political Use in the Twentieth Century,* esp. 19–39; Helen Fein, "Genocide: A Sociological Perspective," *Current Sociol-*

ogy 38, no. 1 (1990): esp. 8–31; Frank Chalk and Kurt Jonassohn, *The History and Sociology of Genocide: Analyses and Case Studies* (New Haven, CT: Yale University Press, 1990), esp. 3–43; Isidor Wallimann and Michael Dobkowski, eds., *Genocide and the Modern Age* (Westport, CT: Greenwood Press, 1987); and Helen Fein, ed., *Genocide Watch* (New Haven, CT: Yale University Press, 1992).

8. See Helen Fein's chapter, "Genocide, Terror, Life Integrity, and War Crimes: The Case for Discrimination," in this volume.

9. See Kuper, *Genocide: Its Political Use in the Twentieth Century*, 19–39.

10. See Ben Kiernan's chapter, "The Cambodian Genocide: Issues and Responses," in this volume.

11. Ibid.

12. Ibid.

13. Ibid. I personally do not think that it fits under the provisions of the Convention. Only if the Convention were to be revised to include political and social groups could such a case stand. The term "auto-genocide," defined as "internal mass destruction of a significant part of the members of one's group," was used in the report prepared by Benjamin Whitaker in 1985 under the auspices of the UN Commission on Human Rights; see UN Economic and Social Council, Commission on Human Rights, *Revised and Updated Report on the Question of the Crime of Genocide*, UN Doc. E/CN.4/Sub.2/1985/6 (1985).

14. The feasibility of action in the International Court of Justice against the Khmer Rouge is explored in Gregory Stanton's "International Legal Options," paper presented at the Schell Center Conference on Genocide and Democracy in Cambodia, Yale Law School, New Haven, CT, 22 February 1992.

15. At the time of this writing, there is concern that the Khmer Rouge may disrupt the voting in the upcoming elections; see *The Economist*, 22–28 May 1993, 38.

16. I am using the expression "genocidal massacres" in the same sense as Kuper's *Genocide: Its Political Use in the Twentieth Century*, although sometimes he uses it interchangeably with genocide, as for example when he discusses the cases of Rwanda, Burundi, Zanzibar, and Algeria. Barbara Harff and Ted Gurr, on the other hand, use the term "politicides" in "Genocides and Politicides since 1945: Evidence and Anticipation," *Internet on the Holocaust and Genocide* 13 (1987): 1–7.

17. The South African and Northern Ireland examples are analyzed by Kuper, *Genocide: Its Political Use in the Twentieth Century*, 186–209. The Cyprus example is closer to that of Northern Ireland. Although there are several differences, the main one is on the nature of the cleavage: In Cyprus, the fundamental cleavage is of a predominantly ethnic rather than religious nature.

18. See Robert Conquest, *The Great Terror: A Reassessment* (New York: Oxford University Press, 1990), 445–89.

19. During the UN debates for the successive drafts of the Convention, the French delegation proposed an amendment to the definition stating that "it is committed, encouraged or tolerated by the rulers of a State." The proposal was defeated; see Kuper, *Genocide: Its Political Use in the Twentieth Century*, 37.

20. See Leo Kuper's chapter, "Theoretical Issues Relating to Genocide: Uses and Abuses," in this volume.

21. Ibid.

22. Fein, "Genocide, Terror, Life Integrity, and War Crimes," in this volume.

23. In her introduction to *Genocide Watch*, 3.

24. Chalk and Jonassohn, *The History and Sociology of Genocide,* 10–11. See

also, Frank Chalk's chapter, "Redefining Genocide," in this volume; and Kurt Jonassohn, "What Is Genocide?" in Fein, ed., *Genocide Watch,* 17–18.

25. Chalk, "Redefining Genocide," in this volume.

26. Fein, "Genocide, Terror, Life Integrity, and War Crimes," in this volume.

27. Ibid.

28. To be sure, it is difficult to devise preventive measures to protect a group that is not recognizable by an outside observer and is exclusively defined by the perpetrator.

29. Conquest, *The Great Terror,* 19–20. The classic study of these events is Robert Conquest, *The Harvest of Sorrow: Soviet Collectivization and the Terror-Famine* (New York: Oxford University Press, 1986); see also James E. Mace, "The American Press and the Ukrainian Famine," in Fein, *Genocide Watch,* 113–32.

30. Kuper, *Genocide: Its Political Use in the Twentieth Century,* 46; and "Theoretical Issues Relating to Genocide," in this volume.

31. Kuper, *Genocide: Its Political Use in the Twentieth Century,* 46.

32. This is Telford Taylor's view quoted in Kuper's chapter, "Theoretical Issues Relating to Genocide" ("The Convention Definition").

33. Fein, "Genocide, Terror, Life Integrity, and War Crimes," in this volume.

34. Ibid.

35. See Israel Charny's chapter, "Toward a Generic Definition of Genocide," in this volume.

36. Israel Charny, in his review of Helen Fein's *Genocide: A Sociological Perspective,* in *Internet on the Holocaust and Genocide,* nos. 30–31 (February 1991): 6.

37. Wallimann and Dobkowski, eds., *Genocide and the Modern Age,* xvi.

38. Ibid.

39. Ibid., xvii.

40. N. Mouzelis, *Modern Greece: Facets of Underdevelopment* (New York: Holmes and Meier, 1979), 52.

41. Tony Barta, "Relations of Genocide: Land and Lives in the Colonization of Australia," in Wallimann and Dobkowski, eds., *Genocide and the Modern Age,* 247.

42. See Richard Hovannisian's chapter, "Etiology and Sequelae of the Armenian Genocide," in this volume.

43. Hovannisian, "Etiology and Sequelae," in this volume.

44. Ibid.

45. Vera Beaudin Saeedpour, "Establishing State Motives for Genocide: Iraq and the Kurds," in Fein, ed., *Genocide Watch,* 66.

46. On the policies of the Syrian and Iraqi governments vis-à-vis the Kurds, see Middle East Watch, *Syria Unmasked: The Suppression of Human Rights by the Assad Regime* (New Haven, CT: Yale University Press, 1991), 95–99, and *Human Rights in Iraq* (New Haven, CT: Yale University Press, 1990), 69–96.

47. See Martin van Bruinessen's chapter, "Genocide in Kurdistan?" in this volume.

48. Ibid.

49. See my earlier discussion on intentionality. Although using a slightly different phrasing, Middle East Watch reaches a similar conclusion concerning the Iraqi policies vis-à-vis the Kurds (*Human Rights in Iraq,* 94). Vera Saeedpour, in her study of the 1988 chemical weapons attacks against the Kurds, effectively debunks the Iraqi government's official explanations for its actions ("Establishing State Motives for Genocide," 66–69). The objectives of Iraq's

policy toward the Kurds, in particular those of the notorious *al-Anfal* operation, which extended from February to September 1988, have recently come under close scrutiny. The reason for this scrutiny is the availability of official Iraqi documents seized by Kurdish rebels during their uprising against Baghdad in the immediate aftermath of the Gulf War. These documents are reported to describe in great and disturbing detail the campaign of terror waged by the Iraqi government against the Kurds. The documents are currently being studied by Middle East Watch "with logistical help from the United States Defense Intelligence Agency"—an unprecedented collaboration between a human rights group and an intelligence agency. The purpose of this collaborative undertaking is to gather enough evidence to bring a case of genocide against the Iraqi government before the International Court of Justice. For more details, see Judith Miller, "Iraq Accused: A Case of Genocide," *The New York Times Magazine*, 3 January 1993, esp. 12–17.

50. See James Dunn's chapter, "East Timor: A Case of Cultural Genocide?" in this volume.

51. A typical example is Canada, whose businessmen are among the most important foreign investors in Indonesia; see Chalk and Jonassohn, *The History and Sociology of Genocide*, 411.

52. Quoted in Michael J. Bazyler, "Reexamining the Doctrine of Humanitarian Intervention in Light of the Atrocities in Kampuchea and Ethiopia," *Stanford Journal of International Law* 23, no. 2 (1987): 552.

53. Joseph Nye, Jr. "What New World Order?" *Foreign Affairs* 71, no. 2 (Spring 1992): 84.

54. Richard Ullman has an interesting discussion on this distinction in his "Some Notes on the Continuing Problem of Security" (unpublished paper, 26 August 1991).

55. Nye, "What New World Order?" 90.

56. Richard Falk, "Reflections on the Gulf War Experience: Force and War in the United Nations System," (unpublished paper, 28 May 1991), 19.

57. Ibid., 20. See Falk's discussion at 15–22.

58. A closer look at the text of all the Gulf War resolutions would confirm this; see UN Department of Public Information, *United Nations Security Council Resolutions Relating to the Situation Between Iraq and Kuwait* (no date), 9–18.

59. The main difference in the UN authorization of the Korean and the Gulf Wars was that consensus was achieved in the former because of the Soviet Union's temporary absence from the Security Council, while in the latter because of China's abstention. However, the extent to which both the Soviet Union's absence and China's abstention can be treated as satisfying the provisions of Article 27, Section 3, of the UN Charter concerning the "concurring votes" of the permanent members on all nonprocedural matters is debatable. Also, in the Korean War, there was a "unified command" under the UN flag; this was not the case in the Gulf War.

60. See remarks by Sir Brian Urquhart, "After the Cold War: Learning from the Gulf," in *Toward Collective Security: Two Views,* Occasional Paper no. 5, The Thomas J. Watson Jr. Institute for International Studies, Brown University, Providence, RI, 1991, 18–19; and Stanley Hoffmann, "Delusions of World Order," *The New York Review of Books,* 9 April 1992, 40.

61. UN General Assembly, Report of the Secretary-General on the Work of the Organization, *An Agenda for Peace. Preventive Diplomacy, Peacemaking and Peace-Keeping,* UN Doc. A/47/277/S/24111, 17 June 1992, 12–13.

62. Ibid., 13; see also the relevant remarks in Boutros Boutros-Ghali, "Empowering the United Nations," *Foreign Affairs* 71, no. 5 (Winter 1992/93): 93–94.

63. *An Agenda for Peace,* 3 and 5.

64. Ibid., 8–9. Quotations are from page 9.

65. Bazyler, "Reexamining the Doctrine of Humanitarian Intervention," 598–607.

66. To be sure, these "baseline" criteria are open to modifications. For example, humanitarian intervention may be justified not only in the case of large-scale atrocities, but also "when weapons of mass destruction are used against domestic enemies, or when a state remains indifferent to natural or man-made disasters on its territory," as Hoffmann has suggested; see "Delusions of World Order," 41. In addition, the criterion of preference for joint action can be modified to render collective action mandatory.

67. UN Department of Public Information, *The United Nations and the Situation in the Former Yugoslavia,* S/RES/771, 13 August 1992, 38.

68. UN General Assembly, *Human Rights Questions: Human Rights Situations and Reports of Special Rapporteurs and Representatives. The Situation of Human Rights in the Territory of the Former Yugoslavia,* UN Doc. A/47/418 S/24516, 3 September 1992, at 3.

69. Ibid.; and UN General Assembly, *Human Rights Questions: Human Rights Situations and Reports of Special Rapporteurs and Representatives. The Situation of Human Rights in the Territory of the Former Yugoslavia,* UN Doc. A/47/635 S/24766, 6 November 1992.

70. Emphasis added; UN Doc. A/47/418 S/24516, 3 September 1992, at 13.

71. Emphasis added; UN Doc. A/47/635 S/24766, 6 November 1992, at 4.

72. UN Doc. A/47/418 S/24516, 3 September 1992, at 15.

73. UN Security Council, Resolution 780 (1992), S/RES/780, 6 October 1992.

74. UN Department of Public Information, Press Release, SG/A/508, BIO/2718, 26 October 1992.

75. UN Security Council, *Report of the Secretary-General Pursuant to Paragraph 2 of Security Council Resolution 808 (1993),* S/25704, 3 May 1993, at 4.

76. Ibid.

77. UN Security Council, Resolution 808 (1993), S/RES/808, 22 February 1993.

78. UN Security Council, Resolution 827 (1993), S/RES/827, 25 May 1993.

79. The full text of the Statute can be found in S/25704, 3 May 1993, 36–48; see note 75.

80. At the time of this writing, of the five cosponsors of the recent Security Council resolution concerning the protection of the designated safe havens for the Muslims, only Russia has indicated a willingness to send ground troops to defend these havens. The United States, France, Great Britain, and Spain have declared that they are only prepared to provide support for air strikes against Serbian forces that attack the designated safe havens ("UN Starts Plans for Bosnia Force Tomorrow," *New York Times,* 6 June 1993, p. 13).

81. S/25704, 3 May 1993, at 7.

82. Ibid.

83. Ibid., 8.

84. On 20 March 1993, the Republic of Bosnia and Herzegovina instituted proceedings against the Federal Republic of Yugoslavia in the International

Court of Justice. In its application to the Court, the Republic of Bosnia-Herzegovina argued that former members of the Yugoslav People's Army and Serb military and paramilitary forces had engaged—with assistance from Yugoslavia—in acts that amounted to breaches of the Genocide Convention and asked the Court to declare that Yugoslavia had breached its legal obligations under the Convention. In a follow-up request filed the very same day, Bosnia-Herzegovina requested that the Court indicate a series of provisional measures, including Bosnia-Herzegovina's exemption from the UN arms embargo, so as to exercise its inherent right of individual or collective self-defense. In its ruling issued on 8 April 1993, the Court dealt only with the genocide issue. It did not issue a finding on whether genocide was being committed in Bosnia; rather, in a cautiously phrased ruling, it asked the government of the Federal Republic of Yugoslavia to "ensure that any military, paramilitary or irregular armed units which may be directed or supported by it . . . do not commit any acts of genocide, of conspiracy to commit genocide, of direct and public incitement to commit genocide, or of complicity in genocide, whether directed against the Muslim population of Bosnia and Herzegovina or against any other national, ethnical, racial or religious group." International Court of Justice, *Order on Request for the Indication of Provisional Measures in Case Concerning Application of the Convention on the Prevention and Punishment of the Crime of Genocide* (Bosnia and Herzegovina v. Yugoslavia (Serbia and Montenegro)), April 8, 1993, 32 I.L.M.888 (1993). This ruling can at best be considered an "early warning" to the Federal Republic of Yugoslavia—an early warning whose value was mostly symbolic.

Part I
The Conceptual
Dimensions of Genocide

Theoretical Issues Relating to Genocide: Uses and Abuses

Leo Kuper

Many definitions of genocide circulate in contemporary discourse and academic analysis, motivated by diverse theoretical perspectives or by ethnocentric preoccupations. They range from at one extreme the objective categorizing of the murder of identifiable groups to the opposite extreme of an exclusionary, ethnocentric emphasis on the unique suffering of one's own group as the target of total annihilatory intent.

In this bewildering array of definitions, there are sound reasons for working with the definition of the United Nations Convention on the Prevention and Punishment of the Crime of Genocide. It provides a workable definitional core for interdisciplinary analysis and application, and it is the legally accepted definition that has been incorporated in a convention ratified by the great majority of the member states of the United Nations. Moreover, it provides some possibilities for preventative action, and it incorporates the original concept of Raphael Lemkin, whose dedication promoted the framing and adoption of the Genocide Convention. The preventive provisions, however much neglected and abused in the past, are of particular significance at the present time, which is witnessing a continuing incidence of genocide and the threat of an imminent increase.

The Convention Definition

Problems in the interpretation of the Genocide Convention might readily have been resolved by recourse to the International Court of Justice. But appeal to the Court by member states seems to be virtually taboo; the only recourse so far concerned the validity of specific reservations relating to the ratification of the Convention. Presumably, member states are restrained by the fact that most genocides are committed by or with the condonation of governments. This avoidance is carried to such extremes that not a single member state was prepared to sponsor a carefully prepared memorandum to the International Court which would have declared Democratic Kampuchea to have breached its obligations under Articles I–V of the UN Genocide Convention, and this at a time when there was the threat of a return to power by the annihilatory Khmer Rouge regime.

The Convention definition of genocide may be summarized briefly as the intent to destroy *in whole or in part* a racial, ethnic, religious, or national group *as such,* by killing members of the group or imposing conditions inimical to survival. The inclusion of mental harm among the acts constituting genocide seems incongruous, but it must be read in the overall context of the intent to destroy the victim group.

The phrase *in whole or in part* raises a problem. One can dismiss as pedantry the discussion in the UN Legal Committee as to whether the murder of an individual should be considered genocide if it took place "with a connecting aim," that is to say, if it was directed against a person of the same race, or nationality, or ethnic, or religious group.[1] And I will assume that "in part" denotes an *appreciable part,* while recognizing the imprecision of the phrase.

A major difficulty is presented, however, by ambiguity in the phrase "as such," and this, in my view, has contributed significantly to abuse in the defense against charges of genocide.

The original draft of the Convention defined genocide as deliberate acts committed with intent to destroy a national, racial, religious, or political group *on grounds of the national or racial origin, religious belief, or political opinion of its members.* This introduced motive as an essential element in the commission of the crime, and touched off a conflict in legal perspectives; the British representative maintained that the intent to commit the crime was the crucial defining characteristic, whatever the reasons the perpetrators of the crime might allege. Including the motives "was not merely useless, for its limitative nature would enable those who committed a crime of genocide to claim that they had not committed that crime 'on grounds of' one of the motives listed in the article."[2]

In the ensuing argumentative caldron, the Venezuelan representative proposed the substitution of the phrase "as such." This compromise was accepted, but it transpired that the participants in the debate had different conceptions of the meaning of the phrase. Presumably whatever else "as such" signifies, it cannot be interpreted as a shorthand for the rejected statement of motives. But it is precisely this interpretation that is advanced as a defense. For example, the permanent UN representative of Brazil, in reply to charges of genocide against Indians in the Amazon river region, stated that this could not "be characterized as genocide since the criminal parties involved never eliminated the Indians as an ethnic or cultural group," the crime being "committed for exclusively economic reasons, the perpetrators having acted solely to take possession of the land of their victims."[3]

A more significant application of this defense was used by General Telford Taylor, a former special assistant to the U.S. attorney general and representative at the Nuremberg trials. In my book *Genocide*, I described the atomic bombing of the Japanese cities of Hiroshima and Nagasaki by the United States and the pattern bombing of Hamburg and Dresden by the Allies as genocide. I should have added the fire-bombing of Tokyo. General Taylor, in rejecting this view, relied on the original formulation in interpreting "as such." He argued that "Berlin, London and Tokyo were not bombed because their inhabitants were German, English or Japanese, but because they were enemy strongholds. Accordingly, the killing ceased when the war ended and there was no longer any enemy."[4]

It is difficult to know what is implied by the phrase "enemy strongholds." It cannot really suggest with plausibility that these cities, civilian populations and all, were totally involved in war-related activities and hence legitimate targets. In any event, in current discourse, the defense is that the inhabitants of the Japanese and German cities were destroyed not as Japanese or Germans, but as enemies, and when the war was over the annihilation ceased.

This is indeed a curious argument. Since the annihilatory bombs were deliberately dropped on the German and Japanese inhabitants of these cities, there was clearly the intent to destroy them.

But the inhabitants were not only Germans and Japanese; they were also enemies. Hence, the defense reduces itself to the contention that in destroying Japanese and Germans, the target was only the enemy within them—a sort of magical exorcism, though also regrettably entailing their physical destruction.

The more general problem raised by this controversy is the relationship between war crimes and genocide.

War Crimes and Genocide

Under Article I of the UN Convention, the contracting parties confirm that genocide, whether committed in time of peace or in time of war, is a crime under international law. This cannot be interpreted as equating genocides in time of peace with those committed during war. It is only at a very general level of abstraction that genocide is a uniform phenomenon. Its manifestations and processes and contexts are quite varied and need to be distinguished. I draw a basic distinction between "domestic" genocides and genocides committed in the course of international war.[5]

The domestic genocides are those which arise on the basis of internal divisions within a single society. They are a phenomenon of the plural society, with its marked divisions between racial, ethnic, and/or religious groups. Plural society theory deals with the relations between these groups, and the conditions promoting peaceful cohabitation, integration, or violent polarization leading to genocide.[6] It has no application to the genocides of international war, committed in armed conflict between separate states.

Genocide in international war is by no means an exclusive category. It may also be a war crime, as the international jurist Antonio Cassese argues in his analysis of the Sabra and Shatila massacres. These were committed against the inhabitants of two Palestinian camps in Beirut by Christian Phalangists during Israel's military occupation of the area, and, accordingly, responsibility attaches to Israel as an occupying army. The Phalangists had entered the camps "under the aegis and control of the Israelis," and the army did not stop the massacre immediately after it discovered the indiscriminate slaughter.[7] An Israeli judicial commission of inquiry drew a distinction between direct and indirect responsibility, attributing direct responsibility to the Phalangists, and indirect responsibility to members of the Israeli cabinet and army.

So too, the incendiary pattern bombing of Hamburg, Dresden, and Tokyo, and the atomic bombings of Hiroshima and Nagasaki may constitute both genocides and war crimes. The distinctive feature of pattern bombing is that the entire population of a city becomes the target of annihilatory assault. Thus Lifton and Markusen comment that the "four furious assaults on Hamburg in late July and early August 1943 had resulted in the first great firestorm of the war and abandonment of even a pretense of industrial targeting in the systematic bombing of residential areas, so that any destruction of factories was only a 'bonus.'"[8]

The city of Coventry, in which for three years after the war I worked on research connected with the planning of urban neighborhoods, was not subjected to pattern bombing. The small medieval center, including the cathedral, was destroyed, and some five hundred civilians were killed, but the city itself was left largely intact. In London, the Nazi bombers had followed the course of the Thames to the port, and in the process destroyed the financial center. There was also the destruction of a residential area, described by Lifton and Markusen as accidental,[9] and the terroristic rocket attacks on civilians toward the end of the war.

London had been a target throughout the war years, and there were bomb craters and destruction in many parts of the city. Some thirty thousand were killed in the earlier raids and eight thousand by V-1 and V-2 rockets. But again, London had not been subjected to pattern bombing. Nor was Rotterdam the target of pattern bombing, though the German Luftwaffe had destroyed the city center and much of the port area, killing about nine hundred people and rendering approximately 78,000 homeless.[10]

The massacres in the pattern bombings were far more lethal. In Dresden at least 40,000 people were killed (with other estimates going as high as 250,000); in Hamburg, "it is also believed that more than 40,000 Germans died"; and in Tokyo as many as 130,000 were victims, exceeding even the casualties in the atomic bombings of Hiroshima and Nagasaki.[11]

The pattern bombings were a significant step in the movement toward total war, attaining their apotheosis in the atomic bombings. Destruction was not limited to war-related targets, and noncombatants became the innocent victims of indiscriminate annihilation in contravention of the humanitarian laws governing international war.

Are these humanitarian laws now being abrogated by current practice and by technological advances for the deployment against distant targets of high-powered missiles conveying nuclear, incendiary, chemical, and biological bombs of devastating lethal power, all weapons of indiscriminate effect and of mass murder? Has technological invention rendered international warfare inevitably genocidal?

Meanwhile, the United Nations' record, in either times of war or of peace, hardly encourages confidence in its ability or its commitment to restrain genocide.

United Nations—Uses and Abuses

With the adoption of the United Nations Genocide Convention, the concept of genocide gained currency as a most horrendous crime. It was, therefore, to be expected that the charge of genocide would become a weapon in the defense against discrimination and injustice and oppression. Experiencing the indifference of the outside world to their suffering, disadvantaged groups sought to gain a sympathetic hearing by dramatic denunciation.

Hence birth control clinics, for example, were interpreted as instruments of genocide. This presumably relied on Article II(d) of the Convention, which specified as one of the acts constituting genocide the imposition of measures "intended to prevent births within [a] group," but ignored the overall context for commission of the crime, namely the intent to destroy the victim group in whole or in part. More generally, violations of human rights, or a pattern of violations, were denounced as genocide.

The resultant abuse of the concept proved counterproductive in the United Nations, which turned a deaf ear to these extravagant charges. In fact, in some situations, the avoidance of extreme charges and rhetoric might contribute to a favorable response. Thus, the representatives of the Bahais, threatened with the violent eradication of their religion in Iran and subjected to systematic discrimination reminiscent of the persecution of Jews by the Nazis in the 1930s, were advised to avoid the charge of genocide, a strategy they successfully followed.

The resistance of the United Nations to charges of genocide is not simply a reaction to the trivializing abuse of the concept. A significant factor is that genocide is usually, though not exclusively, a crime committed by governments or with governments' condonation or complicity. And, as Franck and Rodley comment, the United Nations is a professional association of governments which cannot be counted upon to act in any way likely to undermine the authority of—and, by implication, all of—the member regimes.[12]

This supportive stance is reflected in the primacy accorded by the UN to norms protective of the status quo, such as its emphasis on sovereignty, on territorial integrity, and on nonintervention in the internal affairs of member states. It is also reflected in the UN's failure to respond to valid charges of genocide and to emergency situations of mass murder.

Examples of the UN's reluctance to respond abound, though there has been a continuing incidence of genocide since the adoption of the Genocide Convention. Offending regimes might be protected during years of annihilatory violence by regional and ideological alliances, as in the case of Uganda under Amin in the 1970s. Or the Cold War, with veto-empowered superpowers divided in their support for the contending parties, might frustrate the efforts of the Secretary-General to convene the Security Council and ensure United Nations intervention, as in the case of Bangladesh. Some regimes, such as the Khmer Rouge in Democratic Kampuchea, were so intransigent, and so contemptuous of outside involvement, that war and invasion were the only effective measures against genocide.

In contrast to the protective stance toward member states, and the failure to take action against genocide or even to invoke the assistance of the International Court of Justice, certain vilified states, and notably Israel, are vulnerable to charges of genocide. This availability of a scapegoat state in the UN restores to members with a record for murderous violence against their subjects a self-righteous sense of moral purpose as principled members of "the community of nations." I recall the representative of Uganda during the Obote regime denouncing the Sabra and Shatila massacres in extravagant terms, with comparative reference to the atrocities of the Nazi regime.

Estimates of the numbers killed in the Sabra-Shatila massacres range from about four hundred to eight hundred—a minor catastrophe in the contemporary statistics of mass murder. Yet a carefully planned UN campaign found Israel guilty of genocide, without reference to the role of the Phalangists in perpetrating the massacres on their own initiative. The procedures were unique in the annals of the United Nations.

The General Assembly initiated the campaign by a resolution declaring the massacres to be an act of genocide. This was preceded by reference to the Genocide Convention and the Fourth Geneva Convention of 1949 Relative to the Protection of Civilian Persons in Time of War. The resolution was carried by 123 votes, with 22 abstentions (by the Western democracies and four Third World countries). The Commission on Human Rights followed with a resolution condemning "in the strongest terms the large scale massacres of civilians in the Sabra and Shatila refugee camps for which the responsibility of the Israeli Government has been established." All that then remained was for the Human Rights Sub-Commission to combine the resolutions in a judgment against the Israeli government. A suggestion by the director of the British Minority Rights Group that the role of the Phalangists as perpetrators of the massacre should be included in the resolution was rejected.[13]

A more startling denunciation, with no vestige of justification, resulted in the convening of the Security Council on a charge by the Palestine Liberation Organization that Israeli soldiers had carried out a massacre in a Palestinian refugee camp. In fact, the director of the United Nations Relief and Works Agency had cabled the Secretary-General that the Israeli force had not killed anyone in their search of the camp. But the Security Council, nevertheless, met with the PLO representative, who charged that Israeli "Judeo-Nazi troops" had committed a "racist genocidal crime," and who secured support from members of the Council.[14] This abuse needs to be set against the failure of the Security Council to meet on Bangladesh, in a case where millions of lives were imperiled.

The committee's condemnation of Israel as guilty of the crime of genocide is in strong contrast to the careful phrasing of its decision on South African apartheid at the same session. International concern over South Africa's gross violations of the rights of subject races goes back to the very inception of the United Nations, a reminder that the infrastructure of racial oppression was already firmly established prior to the Nationalist Party's apartheid regime. From the time of the first meeting of the General Assembly in 1946, the monitoring of South Africa's performance on human rights has become a major UN industry, with a vast proliferation of reports.

Inevitably the issue of genocide would be raised, given the close resemblance of the key apartheid statutes to the Nuremberg laws, the brutality of the systematic deprivation of human rights, and the implementation of a policy designed to ensure the perpetuity of a hierarchy of racial domination, with each race encouraged (forced) "to develop in its own way." And in 1967, the Commission on Human Rights had appointed the Ad Hoc Working Group of Experts, who extended their mandate to investigate torture and ill-treatment into a sort of preparatory examination of the South African government on charges of genocide.

After taking the testimony of witnesses who had been victims of persecution, the group concluded that the intention of the government to destroy a racial group in whole or in part was not established in law. This showed surprising integrity, given the pariah status of South Africa.

Two later reports dealt with the relationship between apartheid and genocide and with crimes against humanity, and the group finally recommended that the Genocide Convention be amended to make punishable inhuman practices resulting from apartheid. This was not accepted. Instead the United Nations introduced a new Convention on the Suppression and Punishment of the Crime of Apartheid.[15] Provisions for punishment include universal jurisdiction in contrast to the Genocide Convention. Whereas the governments of member states are by no means immune to the temptations of genocide, apartheid is a uniquely South African phenomenon.

At the same session at which the commission found Israel guilty of genocide, it decided that the Ad Hoc Working Group of Experts should continue to study the policies and practices that violate human rights in South Africa and Namibia, bearing in mind the effects of apartheid on black women and children and the group's conclusion that the "criminal effects of apartheid amount to a policy bordering on genocide."

Thus, in United Nations' discourse and resolutions, South Africa continued to be associated with genocide.

International Human Rights: Theory and Practice

Self-determination might conceivably have assisted in the prevention of genocide, but the doctrine has been appreciably modified in the

United Nations and rejected in practice by member states. And the doctrine of humanitarian intervention, also relevant for the prevention of genocide, is in considerable disrepute.

At the Treaty of Versailles, and following the disintegration of the Austro-Hungarian and Ottoman Empires, the principle of self-determination was applied by the victorious Allies in the redivision of Europe.[16] In the United Nations Charter, two articles (1 and 55) refer to respect for the principle of equal rights and self-determination of peoples as a basis for developing friendly relations among nations and creating conditions of stability and well-being.

In the preamble to the General Assembly's *Declaration on the Granting of Independence to Colonial Countries and Peoples,*[17] the right to self-determination is reaffirmed in the following terms: "All peoples have the right to self-determination; by virtue of that right they freely determine their political status and freely pursue their economic, social and cultural development." The right appears again in the same terms, in the first article of both the International Covenant on Economic, Social and Cultural Rights and the International Covenant on Civil and Political Rights. In both covenants, it has pride of place, indicating its status as a fundamental human right.

In a chapter devoted to the issues raised by the secession of Bangladesh, I wrote that

self determination in its original conception was a liberating revolutionary doctrine, and it has served this function in the decolonizing process. Indeed, it may be viewed as the "Marseillaise" of decolonization. But in other contexts, the doctrine has been domesticated to serve the interests of ruling classes. Its present state, in United Nations practice, is a bewildering complex of radicalism and conservatism.[18]

There is an inherent contradiction in the cardinal principles of international law as described in the General Assembly's *Declaration Concerning Friendly Relations and Co-operation Among States.* The preamble declares that "the subjection of peoples to alien subjugation, domination and exploitation constitutes a major obstacle to the promotion of international peace and security." It then reaffirms the principle of equal rights and self-determination as being of "paramount importance for the promotion of friendly relations among States, based on respect for the principle of sovereign equality." But at the same time, the preamble emphasizes the contradictory principle "that any attempt aimed at the partial or total disruption of the national unity and territorial integrity of a State or country or at its political independence is incompatible with the purposes and principles of the Charter."[19]

The contradiction arises from the fact that many of the member states are in fact plural societies, composed of a variety of ethnic or national groups. This is appreciably a heritage of colonization with its often arbitrary grouping of peoples in a single administrative entity. As a result, claims for self-determination by former subject peoples in the form of secession from the now independent state, or claims for greater autonomy, or indeed for freedom from discrimination, conflict with concern for national unity, territorial integrity, or political independence.

Movements for independence, for secession, are most likely to evoke an extreme response from the state to the threat of a diminution in territory and power. Notable examples are the West Pakistan genocidal assault on East Pakistan (Bangladesh), and the Nigerian federal government assault on the Ibos, with its deliberate use of starvation as a weapon in the final stages of the civil war.

In the debate on Bangladesh, the Pakistan representative warned delegates that the pluralistic structure of many of their societies rendered them equally vulnerable to fragmentation.

Today you may rejoice over what is happening to us. But if you think that today you are going to dismember Pakistan and the germs of dismemberment are not going to spread to your country, you are sadly mistaken. And where is this Pandora's box going to be closed? Is it going to be closed in Yugoslavia? Why not Czechoslovakia? . . . And Brittany, the Basque country, Morocco, Algeria, all the countries in Africa? Can it not happen in any single country in Africa and Asia? If there is Bangladesh in Africa, there must be Bangladesh everywhere. . . . Let us open the floodgates, because if sovereign States are going to be mutated in this fashion, let the deluge come.[20]

His warning had a prophetic quality, as we witnessed the dismemberment of the Soviet Empire, and the resultant lethal conflicts, not only in the movements for independence, but also between the plural sections in different societies.

Indeed, movements for independence or for a restructuring of relations have been a major source of lethal and often genocidal conflict. Africa is particularly vulnerable. Currently there is a long-standing and deadly conflict between the Sudanese Islamic government and the African peoples in the south as a result of the casual, almost indifferent, incorporation of these peoples into the Sudan upon decolonization. Eritrea still struggles for independence from Ethiopia,* with starvation deployed as a weapon in the conflict. Rwanda and Burundi have not yet achieved conciliation between Hutu and Tutsi. Ethnic conflicts persist in Angola and now complicate the racial struggle in South Africa.

In this situation of widespread and destructive conflict, the Organization of African Unity has been of little assistance. Its charter

---

*Since this piece was written, Eritrea has gained independence.—ED.

safeguards the independence, sovereignty, and territorial integrity of African states; members proclaim their adherence to the principle of respect for the sovereignty and territorial integrity of each state. And the United Nations has radically modified the principle of self-determination, domesticating the doctrine to serve the interests of the independent member states of the United Nations.

Though in theory it remains relevant under the *Declaration of the Principles of International Law,* which provides for the protection of the territorial integrity and political unity of sovereign and independent states that conduct themselves "in compliance with the principle of equal rights and self-determination of peoples . . . and thus possessed of a government representing the whole people belonging to the territory without distinction as to race, creed or colour,"[21] in UN practice, the right of self-determination has little relevance for the internal relations of groups within sovereign and independent states.

The only successful secession is that of Bangladesh,* achieved however with a loss of some three million Bengalis, an exodus of ten million refugees, and the intervention of the Indian army in a war with Pakistan. For all practical purposes, secession is not available as an option in defusing conflicts between racial, ethnic, and religious groups.[22]

In fact, "the right of self-determination has been limited to colonial situations . . . it is the principle of national unity that has been almost universally followed by the international community . . . which, after all, is composed of states whose interest is to maintain themselves."[23] But if a powerful state is adamant in its colonization of a conquered territory, the annexation becomes increasingly a *fait accompli* in the course of time, as in the Indonesian colonization of East Timor. And it would seem that the same fate is likely to overtake Tibet.

It is difficult to see how the doctrine of self-determination can be effective at the present time for the prevention of genocide. But it does provide a normative guideline or incentive in the search for constitutional solutions to the conflicts between the constituent groups of plural societies.

Humanitarian Intervention Against Genocide

The doctrine of humanitarian intervention may be defined as "the right of one nation to use force against another nation for the purpose of protecting the inhabitants of that other nation from inhumane treat-

---

*Since this piece was written, we have witnessed the secession of the Baltic States and of the other former Soviet Republics, as well as those of Croatia, Slovenia, the Former Yugoslav Republic of Macedonia, and Bosnia-Herzegovina from Yugoslavia.—ED.

ment by their governing sovereign."[24] It is clearly in conflict with the cardinal principles of respect for national unity, territorial integrity, and political independence. To the extent that these principles are emphasized, humanitarian intervention is excluded.

Further objections cite the impurity of motives in humanitarian intervention. In this connection, Bazyler refers, for example, to Hitler's annexation of Czechoslovakia, justified as a humanitarian intervention on behalf of the maltreated ethnic Germans. But the occurrence of totally altruistic intervention must be a rarity. Conceptions of national self-interest guide diplomacy and foreign relations. This is surely routine.

However, is impurity of motive a valid objection? For example, applications to the World Bank for aid are doubtless often motivated by the expectation of the availability of funds for personal fortunes. And consideration of strategic goals or other interests are by no means foreign to the policies of the bank. Is this then to be a ground for the total denial of aid, or should the response be to control these "impurities" as far as possible? So too, in the case of humanitarian intervention, the strategy should be to impose conditions to reduce, in some measure, the outright abuse of the doctrine.

A further objection is that humanitarian intervention by individual countries is now redundant, having been superseded by the collective security of the United Nations. But this assumes that the United Nations is an effective international organization for the prevention of crimes against humanity. In fact, to the contrary, the United Nations, which protects its member states, is an obstacle to effective preventive action against genocide.

The obstacle might be in the form of disagreement between the veto superpowers, or in the powerful vote of "non-aligned" Third World countries, oil-rich Arab states, and, in former times, the Communist bloc. And when there is an appreciable consensus, this may lead to abuse by acts of commission—the vote—and acts of omission—abstention—as in the case of Israel. Or the sheer enormity of action required to intervene against a powerful offending state might inhibit forceful intervention.

Meanwhile many cases call for urgent international intervention. In the Sudan, for example, the war between the ruling Islamic north and the rebel African south continues to take a tragic toll of lives and suffering, with starvation deployed as a weapon against civilians. The present policies of the Sudanese government threaten an estimated five to seven million inhabitants with agonizing death by starvation. The campaign by Eritrea in the exercise of its legitimate right to self-determination is still unresolved in the war with Ethiopia; and here too starvation has been a weapon deployed by the warring parties. And the dissolution of the Soviet Empire, the struggle for independence, and the internal conflicts in many of the constituent units overwhelm with genocidal potentiality.

In these circumstances, humanitarian intervention could improve the situation in only a few cases. But even this is significant, and conditions could be imposed to restrain abuses. Bazyler proposed the following prerequisites for humanitarian intervention:

1. Large-scale atrocities must be occurring or contemplated;
2. Overriding humanitarian motive of the intervening power;
3. Collective intervention by a group of states;
4. Limited intervention to stop the killing, and, if necessary, to remove the responsible despot; and
5. Exhaustion of other peaceful remedies.[25]

The views of distinguished scholars are often cited in developing standards of international law. And it would certainly contribute to the prevention of genocide if lawyers could suggest a set of objective criteria that would render the doctrine of humanitarian intervention operational.

Domestic Jurisdiction and the Prevention of Genocide

The failure of the United Nations to take effective action against genocide renders necessary the search for alternate structures and processes. Networks of international organizations that have proliferated in recent years may provide an effective structural base for monitoring UN performance and exerting pressure, and for independent action. So too, the extension of domestic jurisdiction to the prevention and punishment of genocide could perhaps make some contribution.

Article VI of the Genocide Convention provides that "[p]ersons charged with genocide . . . shall be tried by a competent tribunal of the State in the territory of which the act was committed, or by such international penal tribunal as may have jurisdiction with respect to those Contracting Parties which shall have accepted its jurisdiction." By contrast the International Convention on the Suppression and Punishment of the Crime of Apartheid stipulates that states parties undertake to punish, "in accordance with their jurisdiction," persons responsible for, or accused of the crime of apartheid, whether such persons reside in the territory of the state in which the acts are committed or are nationals of that state or of some other state or are stateless persons

(Article IV), and any state party to the Convention may try accused persons over whom they acquire jurisdiction. This explicitly confers universal jurisdiction in contrast to Article VI of the Genocide Convention, presumably because apartheid is so specifically a South African crime that its punishment is not threatening to member states of the UN. No international penal court has as yet been established.

The provisions of Article VI have different significance in domestic genocides and genocides in times of war. The domestic genocides are generally committed by governments or with their complicity or condonation. Hence, governments would be required in most cases to institute prosecutions relating to their own crimes. The only situation in which this is likely to occur is when the government has been overthrown, as in Equatorial Guinea and Cambodia.

When genocide is committed in other countries during the course of international war, jurisdiction vests in competent tribunals of the state where the crime was committed. This may impose quite insuperable obstacles to extradition or result in trials before courts protectively inclined toward the accused.

However, the omission of reference to universal jurisdiction in the Genocide Convention does not necessarily exclude this possibility. Nigel Rodley writes that "while the Convention *requires* jurisdiction only by the state in which the genocide was committed, and also envisages a future international penal jurisdiction, it is reasonably certain that international law *permits* the exercise of jurisdiction on a universal basis."[26] Earlier, he commented "that universality was certainly the most convincing claim to jurisdiction that could be made by the court in Jerusalem that tried Adolf Eichmann."[27]

Given the controversies relating to the reliance on universal jurisdiction, the extension of domestic jurisdiction to crimes of genocide or the threat of genocide might be a more promising approach. The 1980 decision of the Second Circuit Court of Appeals in *Filartiga v. Peña-Irala*[28] set an interesting precedent in the award of damages in a civil suit against a Paraguayan torturer then present in the United States (on a visitor's visa which had expired). The court's unanimous decision played an important role in the progressive application of internationally defined human rights norms by national courts. In particular, it made clear that the United States would not constitute a safe haven for alien violators of international human rights norms who could be held liable for damages before a U.S. court. The more difficult issue of criminal jurisdiction has yet to be tested.[29]

Mass murderers normally seek refuge in friendly countries. Thus Amin found refuge from Uganda in Libya and thereafter in Saudi Arabia. And Obote fled to Zambia. But under domestic jurisdiction there would be possibilities for civil actions against, say, multinational corporations with headquarters in the United States whose projects threaten the survival of indigenous peoples in the Amazon region, or against individual members of the World Bank who must have known, or should have known, that they were supporting governments engaged in genocidal conflict. Or application might be made to restrain a U.S. administration from supplying weapons to a government with a record of annihilatory action against its subjects.

A simpler approach would be to initiate precedents by class action suits in democratic countries with liberal court systems. The creative use of civil suits in many parts of the world against individual key actors might conceivably effect a radical change in the lethal availability of genocidal technology and support.

Notes

1. See UN Legal Committee, 7 October 1948, 62, and 13 October 1948, 90–93.
2. UN Legal Committee, 15 October 1948, 118–21.
3. United Nations, H.R. Communication No. 478, 29 September 1969.
4. *New York Times Book Review,* 28 March 1982, 9, 18, and 19.
5. See my typology of genocides in *International Action Against Genocide* (London: Minority Rights Group, 1984), 5–7.
6. Leo Kuper and M. G. Smith, eds., *Pluralism in Africa* (Los Angeles: University of California Press, 1969), chap. 14; also Leo Kuper, *The Pity of It All* (London: Duckworth, 1977).
7. Antonio Cassese, "Genocide and the International Community: The Case of Sabra and Shatila," in *New Directions in Human Rights,* ed. Ellen L. Lutz, Hurst Hannum, and Kathryn J. Burke (Philadelphia: University of Pennsylvania Press, 1987), chap. 5, 99 ff.
8. Robert Jay Lifton and Eric Markusen, *The Genocidal Mentality: Nazi Holocaust and Nuclear Threat* (New York: Basic Books, 1988).
9. Ibid.
10. *Encyclopedia Britannica,* 1959, vol. 19, 578–79.
11. Lifton and Markusen, *The Genocidal Mentality,* 21.
12. Thomas M. Franck and Nigel S. Rodley, "The Law, United Nations and Bangladesh," *Israel Yearbook on Human Rights* 2 (1972): 165.
13. Cassese, "Genocide and the International Community," 102–13, and Leo Kuper, *The Prevention of Genocide,* (New Haven, CT: Yale University Press, 1985), 168–69.
14. June Rosen, "The P.L.O.'s Influential Voice at the U.N," *The New York Times Magazine,* 16 September 1984, 59.
15. For a fuller discussion of this inquiry, see Leo Kuper, *South Africa: Human Rights and Genocide,* Eleventh Annual Hans Wolff Memorial Lecture, African Studies Program (Bloomington: Indiana University, 1981).
16. But see in this connection the comments of Hurst Hannum in "The Limits of Sovereignty and Majority Rule: Minorities, Indigenous People and the Right to Autonomy" in Lutz, et al., *New Directions in Human Rights,* 7–9.

17. UN General Assembly, Resolution 1514 (XV), dated 14 December 1960.

18. Kuper, *The Prevention of Genocide*, 63.

19. UN General Assembly, Resolution 2625 (XXV), dated 24 October 1970 (entitled Declaration on Principles of International Law Concerning Friendly Relations and Co-operation among States in Accordance with the Charter of the United Nations).

20. S/PV 1611, 21.

21. UN General Assembly, Resolution 2625 (XXV), dated 24 October 1970.

22. For an outstanding analysis of these issues, see Lee C. Buchheit, *Secession: The Legitimacy of Self-Determination,* (New Haven, CT: Yale University Press, 1978).

23. Hannum, "The Limits of Sovereignty," 9.

24. Michael J. Bazyler, "Reexamining the Doctrine of Humanitarian Intervention in Light of the Atrocities in Kampuchea and Ethiopia," *Stanford Journal of International Law* 23, no. 2 (1987): 547–48.

25. Bazyler, "Reexamining the Doctrine of Humanitarian Intervention," 598–607.

26. Nigel Rodley, "The International Legal Consequences of Torture, Extra-Legal Execution and Disappearance," in Lutz et al., *New Directions in Human Rights,* 183.

27. Ibid., 181.

28. *Filartiga v. Peña-Irala,* 630 F. 2d 876 (2d Cir. 1980).

29. Rodley, "The International Legal Consequences of Torture," 181.

Redefining Genocide

Frank Chalk

> In Lwov University, where I enrolled for the study of law, I dis-
> cussed . . . with my professor[s] [the assassination of Talat on
> March 15, 1921 by Soghoman Tehlirian, who was a survivor of the
> murder of approximately one million Armenians in Turkey, and
> Tehlirian's acquittal by a German court]. They invoked the argu-
> ment about sovereignty of states. "But sovereignty of states," I
> answered, "implies conducting an independent foreign and inter-
> nal policy, building of schools, construction of roads, in brief, all
> types of activity directed towards the welfare of people. Sover-
> eignty," I argued, "cannot be conceived of as the right to kill
> millions of innocent people."
> —From the manuscript autobiography of Raphael Lemkin
> (chapter 1, page 26, deposited at the New York Public Library,
> Main Branch)

Early Definitions of Genocide

International lawyers and scholars in the social sciences have their own
legitimate sets of objectives when laying out the boundaries of a subject. For international lawyers, defining genocide means defining a
crime. Like any criminal offense, the definition of genocide must be
appropriate for legal prosecution, and it must withstand review by
judges and lawyers for the accused. Social scientists have a different set
of objectives. When defining genocide, they are outlining the boundaries of a set of cases which they want to study for the purpose of
discovering their common elements and analyzing the processes that
brought them about. Perhaps these differences in objectives account
for the differences in breadth and focus which one finds in the several
definitions of genocide that have appeared since the concept was first
elaborated by Raphael Lemkin in 1944.[1]

Lemkin, a Polish Jewish jurist, defined genocide as the coordinated and planned annihilation of a national, religious, or racial group by a variety of actions aimed at undermining the foundations essential to the survival of the group as a group. For a time, the General Assembly of the United Nations seriously debated adding a new category of victims—"political and other groups"—to Lemkin's list, but it gave up the effort when delegates from Great Britain and the Soviet bloc argued that "because of their mutability and lack of distinguishing characteristics" the inclusion of political groups would blur and weaken the whole convention.[2]

On 9 December 1948, the United Nations adopted the Genocide Convention, incorporating the following definition in Article II:

In the present Convention, genocide means any of the following acts committed with intent to destroy, in whole or in part, a national, ethnical, racial or religious group, as such:
  (a) Killing members of the group;
  (b) Causing serious bodily or mental harm to members of the group;
  (c) Deliberately inflicting on the group conditions of life calculated to bring about its physical destruction in whole or in part;
  (d) Imposing measures intended to prevent births within the group;
  (e) Forcibly transferring children of the group to another group.[3]

The narrow definition of the victim groups which lies at the heart of the UN definition of genocide was the direct result of a political compromise designed to preserve the remainder of the Genocide Convention. It answered the practical needs of governments as well as the strictures of international lawyers. Since 1944, several alternative definitions of genocide have been advanced by social scientists. Among the most important for the field are those advanced by Pieter N. Drost, Irving Louis Horowitz, and Helen Fein.[4]

In 1959, Pieter N. Drost, a Dutch law professor with extensive experience in the Dutch East Indies, wrote a major work assessing the UN Convention. Drost assailed the omission of political and other groups from the UN definition of genocide, accurately predicting that governments would thoroughly exploit the obvious loophole in the convention. Rejecting the notion that the victims of genocide were limited to racial, religious, national, and ethnic groups, Drost proposed that the United Nations redefine genocide as "the deliberate destruction of physical life of individual human beings by reason of their membership of any human collectivity as such."[5]

In the early 1970s, Hervé Savon voiced his skepticism about the utility of the UN definition as a tool for sociologists, noting that it really belongs to the language of law and ethics, not the realm of sociological analysis.[6] In 1976, the sociologist Irving Louis Horowitz addressed this same issue, but proposed to view genocide as a fundamental policy employed by the state to assure conformity to its ideology and to its model of society. He amended the UN definition to emphasize that genocide was "a structural and systematic destruction of innocent people by a state bureaucratic apparatus."[7] Since then, Horowitz has concluded that a totalitarian society is a necessary precondition for the genocidal process, but it is not a sufficient one. Horowitz believes that national culture plays a much more important role in genocide than the ideology of the state. A totalitarian ideology may make class, race, or religion lethal sins, he contends, but the decision to eradicate these sins by committing genocide is largely a function of culture.[8]

In the 1980s, Helen Fein focused her attention on developing a broader and deeper sociological definition of genocide. She arrived at the conclusion that

Genocide is sustained purposeful action by a perpetrator to physically destroy a collectivity directly or indirectly, through interdiction of the biological and social reproduction of group members, sustained regardless of the surrender or lack of threat offered by the victim.[9]

Fein's explanation of her definition shows that she has decided to include political and social groups as victims and to exclude deaths resulting from warfare.

Leo Kuper has contributed more to the comparative study of the problem of genocide in the twentieth century than anyone since Raphael Lemkin. In *Genocide* (1981) and *The Prevention of Genocide* (1985),[10] Kuper presents a comprehensive analysis of genocidal processes and motivations and confronts the difficulties of defining genocide. After delivering a devastating critique of the UN definition, the political compromises that shaped it, and the organization's morally bankrupt record of nonenforcement, Kuper reluctantly accepts the UN handiwork on the grounds that its definition is internationally recognized and may one day become the basis for more effective preventive action by the United Nations. Kuper does not ignore the groups excluded by the UN definition. He discusses the victims of state-organized, politically-motivated mass killings in Stalin's Soviet Union, in Indonesia, and in Cambodia under the heading "related atrocities." He suggests that each of these cases would have been labeled a genocide if the UN definition had included political groups.

The Importance of Protecting Political and Social Groups

When defining a field for research, the needs of social scientists and historians differ from those of international legal authorities. In the case of genocide, the well-known United Nations definition has a number of widely recognized defects.[11] In the work which I have been doing for the past ten years with my friend and colleague, sociologist Kurt Jonassohn, we have found it most useful to use a broad definition of genocide which permits us to analyze many cases of mass killing in so far as they fall within the definition. We see the job of the social scientist as examining the history of mass killings and identifying any underlying patterns and common elements that may reveal the processes at work. Clearly, whichever definition of genocide scholars choose will have important implications for the measures we can take to predict and prevent genocides.

One of our major disagreements with the definition of genocide in the United Nations Convention on the Prevention and Punishment of the Crime of Genocide is the exclusion of political and social groups from that definition. Acceptance of the UN definition for our research on the history and sociology of genocide implied continuing the traditional silence in the social science literature about the assault on certain victimized social groups of the past. It meant, for example, ignoring the 15 to 20 million Soviet civilians liquidated as "class enemies" and "enemies of the people" between 1920 and 1939. It meant neglecting the roughly 300,000 mentally impaired and mentally ill Germans and others murdered by the Nazis as "life unworthy of life." It meant overlooking the thousands of homosexuals killed by the Nazis because of their sexual orientation. And it meant disregarding the million or more Khmer murdered by the state and the Communist party of Kampuchea in the years from 1975 to 1978. David Hawk and Hurst Hannum have offered an innovative argument that the Kampuchean case actually is covered by the UN definition because the Khmer Rouge were actually seeking to destroy the existing Khmer national group and to replace it with a purified populace cleansed of any remaining loyalty to "propertyism" or "privateness."[12] In my opinion, their argument exceeds anything that the architects of the Genocide Convention intended. But even if Hawk and Hannum are correct, the UN definition would still exclude perpetrators who sought the annihilation of the mentally ill, the mentally handicapped, homosexuals, and others who were not murdered because of their membership in national, ethnic, racial, or religious groups.

With these cases in mind, we felt that our research must be based on a definition that included social groups. Within living memory, the governments of the Soviet Union, Germany, and Cambodia had defined class, mental and physical condition, and sexual preference as primary classifications in their societies. In the hands of rulers who claimed a monopoly on truth and of a bureaucracy which did their bidding, membership in these social categories had proven lethal to millions of human beings. It seemed obvious to us that researchers on genocide must investigate the destruction of such social groups or surrender any hope of explaining the modern world in all its complexity.[13]

Equally problematic for us was the omission of political groups from the UN definition. The killing of some 500,000 Indonesian communists in 1965–66; the murder of members of the Awami League in 1970–71 during the breakaway of Bangladesh; the planned annihilation by the Khmer Rouge from 1975 to 1978 of opposition politicians in Cambodia—these were only a few of the political groups whose destruction merited study.

As David Hawk has noted, "The absence of 'political groups' from the coverage of the Genocide Convention has unfortunately had the effect of diverting discussion from what to do to deter or remedy a concrete situation of mass killings into a debilitating, confusing debate over the question of whether a situation is 'legally' genocide."[14] Many international human rights activists would agree with him. It was the exclusion of political groups from the definition of genocide in the Convention which led the International Commission of Jurists to rule that neither the killings in Equatorial Guinea under Macias nor Pakistan's murder of members of the Awami League and the educated elite in Bangladesh were genocide.[15] In the case of the Hindu dead, regarded as victims of genocide by the Commission, Pakistani officials had declared that they were not killed as members of a religious group, but as "enemies of the state."

The Khmer Rouge regime in Cambodia epitomized the complex mixture of delusions and annihilatory aims common to ideologically motivated perpetrators of genocide who have sought the destruction of political and social groups. The Khmer Rouge defined social class and political background as if they were biological traits that could be passed down from parents to children. "It is possible that some compositions can correct themselves," wrote a top level Khmer Rouge official in an important directive appearing in 1976, "but many of them can not. If they die, they will have instructed their children to keep struggling against communists."[16] For this reason, the regime frequently took the lives of all family members. Teachers and students who were products of pre-Khmer Rouge Cambodia were regarded as hopelessly polluted by their educations and as extremely dangerous. They were hounded through round after round of security checks fueled by the autobiographies demanded of everyone by the Khmer Rouge until they could be caught and killed. Not only former government soldiers down to the rank of private and their families, but all former civil servants, all public health officials, and even foresters and their families were searched out for execution.[17] Like the Nazis, the Khmer Rouge regime killed to purify and cleanse society, to rid it of all sources of social and political pollution, to make it "clean, tough and strong."[18]

A Research Definition of Genocide

Our research on more than thirty cases of genocide stretching from ancient times to the present has convinced us of the need to define the boundaries for research in the field rather broadly. We use the following definition:

Genocide is a form of one-sided mass killing in which a state or other authority intends to destroy a group, as that group and membership in it are defined by the perpetrator.[19]

In addition to incorporating the social and political groups listed above, our definition of genocide emphasizes that the initiative in defining the boundaries and membership of a victim group always lies in the hands of the perpetrator, and that the perpetrator will quite often affirm the existence of malevolent "groups" that are patently imaginary, a fact that offers little solace to those who are killed as a consequence of the delusion. As the editors of the *Wall Street Journal* pointed out when the U.S. Senate finally ratified the Genocide Convention in 1986:

[L]ike so many of the fine words issued from the U.N., these are worse than toothless. The convention actually manages to *exempt* every contemporary act of genocide. . . . Stalin's men insisted that "political genocide" be struck off the list of outlawed practices. Under the treaty, the Kremlin can send political dissidents to Siberia without having committed genocide. Likewise, Ethiopia's Mengistu can starve and relocate Tigreans and Eritreans, Nicaragua's Ortega can decimate Miskito Indians, Cambodia's Pol Pot could kill a third of his countrymen, and Uganda's Amin could butcher his opponents. Even where the victims are of one ethnic or religious group, the tormentors can claim that this is merely political genocide.[20]

Since 1985, a consensus has emerged among students of genocide and among the leaders of international human rights groups—a consensus urging protection of social and political groups by the UN Convention and supporting further research on attempts to destroy such groups. The roots of the current consensus tap several sources:

- The 1946 report of the UN's Ad Hoc Committee on Genocide which included political groups among the human groups to be protected in the Convention;[21]
- The arguments advanced in 1959 by the Dutch jurist Pieter N.

Drost, assailing the exclusion of political and other groups from the UN definition of genocide;[22]

- The recommendations of the International Commission of Jurists in 1973 that the definition of genocide be expanded to include political groups;[23]
- The recommendations advanced in 1985 by Benjamin Whitaker, the UN rapporteur on genocide, in his *Revised and Updated Report on the Question of the Prevention and Punishment of the Crime of Genocide;*[24]
- And, in that same year, the publication of Leo Kuper's arguments on political mass murder in his book, *The Prevention of Genocide.*

Thus, it is not surprising that in 1986, when the U.S. Senate finally approved the Genocide Treaty 83 to 11, it also voted 93 to 1 to direct the president to try to get a change in the treaty to cover political genocide.

It is increasingly common for investigators to include political and social groups in contemporary research on genocide. It is vital that social and political groups should be incorporated if the debate is not to revolve around old fixed arguments. It is imperative that we now get on with the job of exploring the dynamics of genocidal processes and the possibilities of humanitarian intervention.

Issues in the Definition of Genocide

In the course of the past five years, publications and conference papers on genocide have appeared in larger numbers than ever before. Several new issues have been raised by scholars and activists in the field which bear on the prediction and prevention of genocide.

Intentionality and the Distinctiveness of Genocide

An important issue in the recent literature concerns the distinctiveness of genocide and the importance assigned to intentionality. For several scholars, the line between genocide and its precursors is too blurred to specify and the suggestion that a clear line of divisibility exists is misleading. A genocidal society exists when a government and its citizens persistently pursue policies which they know will lead to the annihilation of the aboriginal inhabitants of their country. Intentionality is demonstrated by persistence in such policies whether or not the intent to destroy the aboriginal groups is verbalized.[25]

For Isidor Wallimann and Michael N. Dobkowski, respectively a sociologist and a researcher in religious studies, intentionality itself is increasingly problematic. They argue that:

In a world that historically has moved from domination based primarily on the will of given individuals (in the Middle Ages, for example) to one in which individuals are dominated by anonymous forces such as market mechanisms, bureaucracies, and distant decision making by committees and parliaments, the emphasis on intentionality almost appears anachronistic. . . . [In] the modern age, the issue of intentionality on the societal level is harder to locate because of the anonymous and amorphous structural forces that dictate the character of our world.[26]

The idea that "only intentional or planned massive destruction of human lives should be called genocide," Wallimann and Dobkowski contend, leads to:

the neglect of those processes of destruction which, although massive, are so systematic and systemic, and that therefore appear so "normal" that most individuals involved at some level of the process of destruction may never see the need to make an ethical decision or even reflect upon the consequences of their action.[27]

They would remedy these deficiencies in current research by focusing on new questions such as "Which forms of social organization . . . make it less likely for a massive genocide to occur?"[28]

Wallimann and Dobkowski's tentative questioning of the salience of intentionality is carried a step further by another author who argues against the crucial role of intent in the definition of genocide. Tony Barta is a historian who studies the impact of colonization on the native peoples of Australia. Barta advocates "a conception of genocide which embraces *relations* of destruction and removes from the word the emphasis on policy and intention which brought it into being."[29] The destruction of many peoples, he concludes, was "the result of complex and only obscurely discerned causes, and in that respect genocide should properly lose its uniqueness—the uniqueness of having intentionality as its defining characteristic."[30]

It is but a short jump from the arguments of Dobkowski, Wallimann, and Barta to those of Seamus Thompson, a sociologist studying Northern Ireland, for whom genocide is "inherently a continuous variable." In Thompson's view, "the search for a clear dichotomous definition of genocide may be a manifestation of . . . [the] general phenomenon of avoidance."[31] Our definitional attempt to mark the boundary between "genocide" and "not genocide" is intellectually unprofitable, he asserts, because:

It renders impossible a research finding that incremental steps, involving much normal behavior, and quite conceivable deviations from conventional ideals, can move us to genocide. In short, it cuts us off from the possibility of the understanding that we so earnestly claim to seek through it.[32]

Thompson's conviction that there is a genocidal component in the Northern Ireland conflict leads him to analyze events since 1800 as steps toward a future genocide. I am not able to debate whether this will happen in the future, but there is no evidence in past cases that genocide is a continuous variable.

Each of the authors considered in this section, in varying degrees, questions definitions of genocide that emphasize intent and proposes that genocide can take place without anyone consciously willing it. The focus in their essays is on structural violence, systemic conditions, and social and political structures. The underlying foundations of their perspectives appear clearly in their remedies and their proposals for future research on the prediction and prevention of genocide. For Wallimann and Dobkowski "freedom from structural violence and the anonymous forces that dominate modern man seems to be one precondition for overcoming our age of genocide." They seek "a society that can provide an equal access to power and resources for all with a minimum degree of personal or structural coercion."[33]

Tony Barta is inspired by Karl Marx's attempt "to establish the sets of relationships structuring historical reality as the proper object of historical enquiry, rather than only the intentions and actions of individuals." Pursuing "the objective nature of the relationships,"[34] he discovers the "key relationship" in the Australian settlers' appropriation of the land. This systemic relationship is "fundamental to the type of society rather than to the type of state." Barta conceives of a *genocidal society* as:

one in which the whole bureaucratic apparatus might officially be directed to protect innocent people but in which a whole race is nevertheless subject to remorseless pressures of destruction inherent in the very nature of society.[35]

He disagrees with Irving Louis Horowitz who, "misleadingly" in his view, "calls Germany 'a genocidal society' because during one terrible period of political aberration the 'state bureaucratic apparatus' was used for 'a structural and systematic destruction of innocent people.' "[36] In Barta's configuration, Australian society is genocidal for taking the lives of more than 20,000 Aborigines, but German society, whose victims number in the millions, is not. Barta makes no attempt to explain the significance for his analysis of Germany's devastation of the Herero people of South-West Africa in the years from 1904 to 1907.[37]

Seamus Thompson's view of the genocidal process has led him to undertake two interdependent studies, the first a time-series analysis of political violence in Northern Ireland from 1800 to 1985, the second a cross-societal, strategic comparison of Northern Ireland with England and the United States, and Israel and the Republic of Ireland. In the second case, a crucial question is, "Are members of more peaceful societies prepared to endorse the same killings as people in Northern Ireland, but fortunate enough to live in societies whose social and political structures do not present them with this type of decision?"[38]

*   *   *

The appearance of a group of researchers emphasizing their questions about the role of the state and intentionality as necessary elements in defining genocide marks a departure from earlier work in the field and requires comment. On the positive side, their approach bespeaks a serious concern with the underlying social dynamics of genocide and a refusal to settle for oversimplifying generalization. By calling attention to the impersonal factors in capitalism conducive to genocide, they remind those who emphasize individuals and their existential decisions that larger circumstances and contexts are also important.

These potential gains are won, however, at an enormous cost in the rigor of the analysis. If modern genocide is primarily a matter of social structures and relationships, why does genocide occur in some countries and not in others with the same structures and relationships? To take just one example, why did the native peoples of Canada fare so much better during the invasion by Europeans than the original populations of the United States or of Tasmania?

Another problem of the systemic approach is that it downplays the influence of the individuals who initiate genocides and ignores the capacity of individual interveners to deter or to halt them. Systemic variables facilitate genocide, but it is people who kill. It is our awareness of the very important role of existential decisions by individuals in genocide which encourages us to invest our energies in predicting and preventing future cases.

The overloading of the impersonal power of societies in Barta's notion of a genocidal society illustrates this problem. His image of a society in which the whole bureaucratic apparatus stands by helplessly while a race is destroyed begs the question. Historians and anthropologists know of cases in which powerful government departments have stymied a weaker department's efforts to save a group from destruction, but we do not know of any cases in which the energetic efforts of an entire government to rescue a group were overcome by the anonymous pressures of society. One of the flaws in Barta's assertion is illuminated by de Tocqueville's observations on the United States in 1831: it was the hand-in-glove pressure of American settlers and the military might deployed by the government of the United States that destroyed large numbers of the American Indians, not the nature of the American society.

Knowledge of these nineteenth-century American events is so widespread today that no modern government should be immune from condemnation if it fails to vigorously protect its aboriginal peoples. As Canada and other countries have demonstrated, the destruction of capitalism is not an essential prerequisite for the protection of native peoples. Indeed, Marxist states eschewing capitalism—the Soviet Union, China, and Cambodia—have perpetrated genocides of their own against ethnic groups, political parties, and social classes. Capitalist, socialist, and fascist states have all been responsible for genocides. By treating genocide as if it is purely a problem of capitalism, Barta neglects its occurrence in a number of social systems.

Still another, larger set of concerns arises from a consideration of these new definitions of genocide: they confuse genocide with other violations of human rights and other forms of killing. If the spontaneous acts of self-aggrandizing individuals are defined as acts of genocide, this trivializes the responsibility of governments when their acts of commission or of advertent omission threaten the survival of whole peoples; if genocide in the twentieth century is primarily the consequence of impersonal forces and social systems, then there is little that we can do to prevent it; and if perpetrator intent is not crucial to the definition of genocide, then all sorts of unintended lethal consequences of human action would be classified as genocide.

Arguments which minimize the importance of the role of the state and of intentionality in genocide also distract our attention from the role of absolutist or utopian or uncompromisingly idealistic doctrines or ideologies in the great mass killings of the twentieth century. What Armenians, Ukrainians, Jews, Gypsies, and Khmer know better than any other peoples is the lethal power of a certain set of ideas adopted by a government or party as part of its search for a perfect future. In my view, the Holocaust belongs to that category of genocides deeply rooted in the urge to purify the world through the annihilation of some category of human beings imagined as agents of corruption and incarnations of evil. Hitler's war against the Jews exemplifies the triumph of one of several myths in history by which powerful states have consigned whole categories of innocent human beings to annihilation.

Norman Cohn has written extensively on this subject,[39] and Sir Isaiah Berlin spoke of it when he talked of the search for a perfect society as a recipe for bloodshed, even if it is demanded by "the sincerest of idealists" and "the purest of heart."[40] Of "the possibility of a final solution—even if we forget the terrible sense that these words acquired in Hitler's day," Berlin warns:

surely no cost would be too high to obtain it: to make mankind just and happy and creative and harmonious forever—what could be too high a price to pay for that? To make such an omelette, there is surely no limit to the number of eggs that should be broken—that was the faith of Lenin, of Trotsky, of Mao, for all I know, of Pol Pot.[41]

The consequences of past searches for a perfect society and their implication for the future are just as clear for Berlin:

Some armed prophets seek to save mankind, and some only their own race be-cause of its superior attributes, but whichever the motive, the millions slaugh-tered in wars or revolutions—gas chambers, gulag, genocide, all the monstrosi-ties for which our century will be remembered—are the price men must pay for the felicity of future generations. If your desire to save mankind is serious, you must harden your heart, and not reckon the cost.[42]

Raphael Lemkin sensed these commonalities when he formulated the concept of genocide. He would have agreed, I think, with the scholars who argue that the uniqueness of the Holocaust inheres in its detailed planning aimed at the destruction of a biologically defined group and in its implementation using administrative and industrial means by a highly civilized and culturally renowned nation. I believe he would also have insisted on the place of the Holocaust within the category of ideologically motivated genocides. And with the experi-ence of the great genocides of the post-World War II era—Indonesia, Bangladesh, Burundi, and Cambodia—it is probable that he would have supported revision of the UN Genocide Convention to protect political and social groups.

The Salience of the State in Genocide

A second major issue which emerges in the recent literature concerns the identity of the perpetrator: Are genocides committed when small, relatively isolated aboriginal groups are destroyed by perpetrators acting "as individuals—peasants, ranchers, miners and land specula-tors—and are permitted by governments that either cannot or will not stop the process"?[43] A step in this process is described in a recent news dispatch from São Paulo, Brazil:

Fifteen Indians, including six children, were shot dead by white timber exploit-ers in a remote Amazonian border region, a survivor of the massacre said yesterday. The witness told Reuters news agency by telephone that a group of whites with rifles and sub-machine guns, fatally shot the Indians, from the Tukuna tribe, in an attack Monday. The Tukuna are the biggest tribe of Indians in Brazil, numbering about 20,000.[44]

Should cases such as this challenge us to refine our concept of genocide? In a recent paper, Jason Clay of Cultural Survival distinguishes two types of genocide. The first type is "official genocide, carried out by states and directed at groups that, although distinct, had long been part of the society." The second type is "the elimination of small relatively isolated groups on the frontiers of expanding political, social and economic systems." It is the second type, Clay argues, that is far more common in the twentieth century and is exemplified by cases such as the one cited above.[45]

There is more at stake here than at first meets the eye. From its inception as a concept in international law, genocide has been seen mainly as a crime of states. The emphasis on the state as a perpetrator is one of the characteristics which helps to distinguish genocide from culpable homicides committed by individuals. Killings by individuals acting on private motives are covered by the criminal codes of most countries. The United Nations created an international convention against genocide because governments themselves had attempted to destroy groups of human beings who in many cases were their own citizens.

In cases in which governments do nothing to prevent or punish killings that threaten to destroy groups of their own nationals, it is because they condone such killings or give a low priority to the acquisition of the means to stop them.[46] Neglect of these acts of omission is one of the defects of the present UN Genocide Convention that Benjamin Whitaker, the special rapporteur on genocide, hopes to remedy. He proposed in 1985 that Article II of the Convention should be amended to add to the list of acts of genocide those "acts of advertent omission [which] may be as culpable as an act of commission."[47]

Efforts to prevent genocide should be directed at states and other authorities. Only governments have the power to stop genocides and to alter the development policies which facilitate and encourage the killing of aboriginal peoples. Certain aspects of the situation in Latin America are reminiscent of the United States in the nineteenth century, when native peoples suffered a drastic decline in their numbers due to the impact of frontier settlement. The behavior of settlers and government officials bespoke an implicit understanding that it was desirable to reduce the numbers of the native peoples to the level at which they could no longer block "progress."

Today's government-sanctioned programs for the development of the Amazon basin and other remote areas of Latin America are re-creating nineteenth-century United States' frontier conditions in Brazil, Paraguay, and other countries promoting the opening of virgin lands for mining, timbering, ranching, and commercial farming in areas inhabited by small hunting and fishing tribes. The Tupi, the Kreen-Akrore, and similar tribes in these once remote areas face the ravages of predatory settlers backed by government reprisals if they resist the destruction of their traditional way of life. And like the American Indians in the nineteenth century, their numbers are being drastically reduced by their contact with new microbes and alcohol. It is primarily governments in Latin America who must be held responsible for opening up the interior without developing the means to protect their Indian inhabitants, not the settlers who are pawns in the game. The rulers of these nations are powerful and educated persons who understand the inevitable consequences of their actions. When they persist in a development process that annihilates native peoples, they are the major perpetrators of genocide. The forcible evacuation in 1993 by the Brazilian police and military of three thousand gold miners trespassing on land reserved for the Yanomani people of the Amazon and the arrest of forty-five Brazilian gold miners who had crossed into Yanomani land on the Venezuelan side of the border shows what Latin American governments are capable of doing to protect native people when they accept their responsibilities.[48]

I have discussed a number of arguments advanced in several recent essays on genocide. The authors of these essays insist that genocide need not be intentional and that it does not require the support of the state. I strongly disagree with their arguments. Let me state my position concisely:

1. Killings by individuals are murder, not genocide;
2. Genocide is primarily a crime of state and empirically it has not been true that it appears without intent;
3. Neither is there any evidence that genocide is a continuous variable; and
4. If we include every form of war, massacre, or terrorism under genocide, then what is it that we are studying?

Anticipation and prevention of genocide require a broadly based definition which emphasizes the role of the state, underscores the intent of the perpetrator, and respects the crucial role that ideological motivation plays in modern genocides. The need for pressure on governments who violate human rights and endanger the survival of their aboriginal populations is great, but while attending to these concerns we must never forget that the great genocides of the past have been committed by perpetrators who acted in the name of absolutist or utopian ideologies aimed at cleansing and purifying their worlds. It is that insight which sparked Raphael Lemkin's lonely crusade for a UN Convention on the Prevention and Punishment of the Crime of Genocide. And it is that insight which eventuated for the first time in history in a decision by the International Court of Justice—in the case of *Bosnia and Herzegovina versus Yugoslavia (Serbia and Montenegro)*—ordering a sovereign state to ensure that armed units that may be directed or supported by it do not commit genocide.[49]

Notes

1. Raphael Lemkin, *Axis Rule in Occupied Europe* (Washington, DC: Carnegie Endowment, 1944), chap. 9.
2. Leo Kuper, *Genocide: Its Political Use in the Twentieth Century* (New Haven, CT: Yale University Press, 1982), 26, quoting the Polish delegation.
3. United Nations, *Convention on the Prevention and Punishment of the Crime of Genocide*, 9 December 1948 (London: Her Majesty's Stationery Office, March 1966).
4. Frank Chalk and Kurt Jonassohn, *The History and Sociology of Genocide: Analyses and Case Studies* (New Haven, CT: Yale University Press, 1990), 9–23.
5. Pieter N. Drost, *The Crime of State*, vol. 2, *Genocide* (Leyden: A. W. Sythoff, 1959), 125.
6. Hervé Savon, *Du cannabalisme au génocide* (Paris: Hachette, 1972), chap. 1.
7. Irving Louis Horowitz, *Taking Lives: Genocide and State Power* (New Brunswick, NJ: Transaction Books, 1980), 17.
8. Irving Louis Horowitz, "Genocide and the Reconstruction of Social Theory: Observations on the Exclusivity of Collective Death," *Armenian Review* 37 (1984): 1–21.
9. Helen Fein, "Genocide: A Sociological Perspective," *Current Sociology* 38 (Spring 1990): 23–25.
10. Leo Kuper, *Genocide: Its Political Use in the Twentieth Century* (New Haven, CT: Yale University Press, 1982) and *The Prevention of Genocide* (New Haven, CT: Yale University Press, 1985).
11. See Drost, *The Crime of State*, vol. 2; Kuper, *Genocide: Its Political Uses in the Twentieth Century;* and Kuper, *The Prevention of Genocide.* The substance of this argument and of those which follow was first presented at the conference on "Remembering for the Future," Oxford, 10–13 July 1988, and in Frank Chalk, "Definitions of Genocide and Their Implications for Prediction and Prevention," *Holocaust and Genocide Studies* 4 (1989): 149–60. They are presented here in slightly revised form.
12. See Hurst Hannum, "International Law and the Cambodian Genocide: The Sounds of Silence," *Human Rights Quarterly* 11 (1989): 82–138, and Hurst Hannum and David Hawk, *The Case Against the Standing Committee of the Communist Party of Kampuchea* (New York: Cambodia Documentation Commission, 1986). A parallel argument about Afghanistan is proposed in W. Michael Reisman and Charles H. Norchi, "Genocide and the Soviet Occupation of Afghanistan," *Institute for the Study of Genocide Newsletter* 1 (Spring 1988): 4–6.
13. The flavor of the attacks on classes is epitomized in the statement of M. Y. Latsis, a Cheka official, who declared: "We are not carrying out war against individuals. We are exterminating the bourgeoisie as a class. We are not looking

for evidence or witnesses to reveal deeds or words against the Soviet power. The first question we ask is—to what class does he belong, what are his origins, upbringing, education or profession. These questions define the fate of the accused." Quoted in Harrison Salisbury, *Black Night, White Snow: Russia's Revolutions, 1905–1917* (Garden City, NY: Doubleday, 1978), 565.

14. Institute of the International Conference on the Holocaust and Genocide, *Internet on the Holocaust and Genocide* (Jerusalem), 8 (January 1987): 6.

15. International Commission of Jurists, *The Trial of Macias in Equatorial Guinea: The Story of a Dictatorship,* report submitted by Alejandro Artucio (Geneva: International Commission of Jurists, 1978); and International Commission of Jurists, "Bangladesh," *The Review* (Geneva) 11 (1973): 30–33.

16. "Sharpen the Consciousness of the Proletarian Class to Be as Keen and Strong as Possible," *Revolutionary Flags,* special issue (September–October 1976): 33–97, trans. Kem Sos and Timothy Carney, reprinted as Appendix B in Karl D. Jackson, ed., *Cambodia, 1975–1978: Rendezvous with Death* (Princeton, NJ: Princeton University Press, 1989), 278.

17. Kenneth M. Quinn, "The Pattern and Scope of Violence," in Jackson, *Rendezvous with Death,* 184–89.

18. "Sharpen the Consciousness of the Proletarian Class," Appendix B in Jackson, *Rendezvous with Death,* 282.

19. For earlier versions of this definition and explanations of its terms see Kurt Jonassohn and Frank Chalk, "A Typology of Genocide and Some Implications for the Human Rights Agenda," in *Genocide and the Modern Age,* ed. Isidor Wallimann and Michael Dobkowski (New York: Greenwood Press, 1987), 3–20; Frank Chalk and Kurt Jonassohn, "The History and Sociology of Genocidal Killings," in *Genocide: A Critical Bibliographic Review,* ed. Israel Charny (London: Mansell Publishing Ltd., 1988); and Chalk and Jonassohn, *The History and Sociology of Genocide.*

20. *Wall Street Journal,* 24 February 1986.

21. Political groups were included in the General Assembly's resolution on genocide, passed on 11 December 1946 (96-I), and in Article II of the Ad Hoc Committee's draft convention which stated: "In this Convention genocide means any of the following deliberate acts committed with the intent to destroy a national, racial, religious or *political group,* on grounds of the national or racial origin, religious belief, or *political opinion* of its members" (emphasis added).

22. Drost, *The Crime of State,* 2: 29–30, 60–63, 125.

23. As reported in International Commission of Jurists, *The Trial of Macias,* esp. 27–35, 44–47.

24. UN Economic and Social Council, Commission on Human Rights, *Revised and Updated Report on the Question of the Prevention and Punishment of the Crime of Genocide,* report submitted by Ben Whitaker, UN Doc E/CN.4/Sub.2/1985/6 (2 July 1985), 18–19.

25. For a contrary view, see Fein, "Genocide: A Sociological Perspective," 12–13. I return to the issue of killings by settlers at the end of this chapter.

26. Wallimann and Dobkowski, *Genocide and the Modern Age,* introduction, xvi.

27. Ibid.

28. Ibid., xvii.

29. Tony Barta, "Relations of Genocide: Land and Lives in the Colonization of Australia," in Wallimann and Dobkowski, *Genocide and the Modern Age,* 238.

30. Ibid.

31. Seamus Thompson, "Summary Statement," presented at the annual meeting of the International Studies Association, 29 March–2 April 1988, St. Louis, MO.

32. Ibid.

33. Wallimann and Dobkowski, *Genocide and the Modern Age,* introduction, xvii–xviii.

34. Barta, "Relations of Genocide," 238–39.

35. Ibid., 239–40.

36. Ibid.

37. On the Hereros, see Jon Bridgman, *The Revolt of the Hereros* (Berkeley: University of California Press, 1981); and Horst Drechsler, *"Let Us Die Fighting": The Struggle of the Herero and the Nama against German Imperialism (1884– 1915),* trans. Bernd Zollner (London: Zed Press, 1980; original German edition, Akademie-Verlag, 1966).

38. Thompson, "Summary."

39. See Norman Cohn, *The Pursuit of the Millennium,* revised and expanded ed. (New York: Oxford University Press, 1970; original ed. 1957); *Warrant for Genocide: The Myth of the Jewish World-Conspiracy and the "Protocols of the Elders of Zion,"* 3d ed. (Chico, CA: Scholars Press, 1981; original ed. 1967); and *Europe's Inner Demons: An Enquiry Inspired by the Great Witch-Hunt* (New York: Basic Books, 1975; reprint, New York: New American Library, Meridian Books, 1977).

40. Sir Isaiah Berlin, "On the Pursuit of the Ideal," *The New York Review of Books,* 17 March 1988, 11–18.

41. Ibid.

42. Ibid.

43. Jason Clay, director of research, Cultural Survival, "Genocide: An Activist's Views of Academic Research," a paper presented at the annual meeting of the International Studies Association, 29 March–2 April 1988, St. Louis, MO.

44. *The Gazette* (Montreal), 1 April 1988.

45. Clay, "Genocide."

46. See the useful discussion of this point in Kuper, *Genocide,* 37–38. Kuper also summarizes the arguments presented to the UN for including acts committed by nongovernmental perpetrators under the terms of the Genocide Convention.

47. *Revised and Updated Report on the Question of the Prevention and Punishment of the Crime of Genocide,* 20.

48. For a discussion of these removal operations and the difficulty of sustaining them, see James Brooke, "To Protect Amazon Indians, Brazil Ferries Out 3,000 Miners," *International Herald Tribune* (Paris), 9 March 1993, p. 8.

49. "Court Orders End to Bosnia Genocide," *International Herald Tribune,* 9 April 1993, p. 4.

Toward a Generic Definition of Genocide

Israel W. Charny

Introduction

The definition of genocide adopted in law and by professional social scientists must match the realities of life, so that there should be no situation in which thousands and even millions of defenseless victims of mass murder do not "qualify" as victims of genocide. Insofar as there is ever a major discrepancy between the reality of masses of dead people and our legal-scholarly definitions, it is the latter which must yield and change.

The definition of genocide must also be consistent with the everyday usage of the word by reasonable people when they stand and face a mass of murdered people and naturally apply to such an event the only word there is in the human language for such occurrences. Thus, the mass murders of twenty million Soviet citizens by Stalin,[1] the massacre of one hundred thousand or more of the communist opposition by Indonesia, the murders of one to two million Cambodians by the Khmer Rouge are all instances of clear-cut genocide. And instances of mass murders of a lesser magnitude by governments—five thousand Tamils in Sri Lanka and five thousand students in Tiananmen Square in China, for example—are also, in common sense and understanding, genocidal events, although there may be a consensus to characterize these numerically smaller events as *genocidal massacres,* as Leo Kuper,[2] the doyen of genocide scholars, has proposed.

This chapter proposes a generic definition of genocide, which at the same time is supplemented by a series of subcategories of different types of genocide. I shall also propose at least two new categories of genocide: first, accomplices to genocide, and second, genocide as a result of ecological destruction and abuse. I shall introduce these two proposed concepts first, and then we shall meet them once again in the context of their places in the schema of a generic definition of genocide.

Accomplices to Genocide

The concept of accomplices to murder is well established in criminal law; it refers to a person who, knowingly and willfully assists, prepares, or furnishes a murderer with the weapon with which he commits murder. But there has been no corresponding concept for those who assist, prepare, or furnish the mass murderers of the world with the means to exterminate huge numbers of people. Included in this definition are the scientists who research and design the mega-weapons, the engineers who plan and oversee their production, the businessmen who trade the murder-weapon systems, the barons of finance who profit from enabling the transactions to take place, the government bureaucrats who knowingly or tacitly license or allow the illegal shipments of materials needed to create mega-weapons, as well as the institutions, companies, and various governmental groups which make the mass murders possible. Needless to say, the events leading up to the Gulf War (1991) are being revealed to have included hundreds of major crimes of accomplices to genocide.[3]

Under the present proposal, international laws and laws adopted by national governments would provide a base not only for prosecuting accomplices for violating or conspiring to evade laws about trade licenses and illegal sales of weaponry, but for prosecuting them under laws of genocide as full-blown criminals who are to be held accountable for degrees of responsibility for the actual deaths of victims as a consequence of their actions.

Genocide as a Result of Ecological Destruction and Abuse

Destruction of any number of facets of the ecosystem in which man exists can cause the deaths of countless human beings: thus, nuclear radiation not only as a result of purposeful war but as a result of malevolent or haphazard indifference to safety requirements in nuclear installations has affected hundreds of thousands of people and can reach more calamitous proportions in the future. Poisoning the water supplies of soldiers has long been a strategy of war, but larger-scale poisoning of reservoirs and of waterways, seas and oceans, whether as a result of the haphazard handling of industrial pollutants or of the purposeful poisoning of the waters, can also wipe out innumerable lives. The list of chemical, biological, and physical hazards that can be unleashed on human beings unwittingly-carelessly or wittingly-malevolently is endless. As the human capacity to harness forces of nature increases enormously, the possibilities of man becoming Destroyer of Nature correspondingly increase.

Again it is clear that recent events in the Gulf include the demonstrated readiness of a brutal dictator-led government to destroy and poison major components of the ecosystem, and, although at this writing, the actual extent of the loss of life which has and will result from these measures is not clear, the fact that new vistas of ecocidal genocide increasingly loom before the human race cannot be minimized.

Under the present proposal, international laws and parallel laws adopted by national governments would provide a basis for prosecuting those who destroy and abuse the ecology not only for the destruction of natural resources and properties, but under laws of genocide as full-blown criminals who are to be held accountable for degrees of responsibility for the actual deaths of victims as a consequence of their actions.

Before we develop the classification of genocides further, I propose that we develop some perspective about the kinds of establishments that bring to bear political pressures in our field of study, each of which has an interest in establishing a given definition of genocide to suit its political purposes.

Political Interests in the Definition of Genocide

Unfortunately, the process of selecting and developing definitions that are more correct than incorrect is not only a function of the good sense and excellence of scholars, nor is it only a function of pure scientific inquiry, experimentation, and demonstration. Even in a society where the scientific method is the valued and prevailing mode, definitions are subject to enormous ideological and political pressures from the societal establishments within which thinkers do their work.

Throughout the history of ideas, there are endless illustrations of how certain definitions were ruled out from the outset because they were intolerable to the ruling establishment, while other definitions were forced upon the people of their times despite the damage they did to the accurate perception of reality. The legions of thinkers who have suffered at the hands of the censors, interdictors, and inquisitors throughout history is replete with the greatest and finest. Many thousands of lesser scholars and inquirers have also paid in excommunication, exile, and on guillotines and gallows for the ideas they advanced to their hostile societies.

In those societal contexts that are not quite so severe as to take the actual heads of the thinkers, there are nonetheless enormous political pressures that are brought to bear to disallow errant ideas. Even if the originators of the ideas are not subjected to grievous bodily harm, forced into exile, or personally barred, banned, and excommunicated, they are frequently unable to find proper settings for their work or outlets for their communication of ideas. The ideas themselves are subjected to outright censorship in totalitarian societies, but even in democratic societies, the power of ruling elites and the self-interest of conformists and sycophants lead de facto to a banning of full-scale inquiry and the development of ideas that are not acceptable to those in power in the culture. In the medical sciences and professions, for example, there are noxious surgical procedures, such as the unnecessary hysterectomies of millions of women that continue to this day in many areas of the United States, or the mind-destroying psychosurgeries, such as the lobotomies that were forced on an enormous number of psychiatric patients over the course of two decades if not more in the last half of this century. Many medical policies are linked to outright battles against any alternatives that are promoted by nonmedical practitioners, for example, the promotion of radical orthopedic surgery in lieu of chiropractic, osteopathy, and other nonmedical procedures including the Alexander Method and the Feldenkreis Method; wars of ophthamologists to banish optometrists and their nonsurgical corrective procedures; or the power tactics of psychiatrists against psychologists and social workers whose client interventions are generally less intrusive. In all the sciences, McCarthy-type loyalty rituals have plagued the lives and careers of many scientists in democracies as well as in dictator-run governments.

Our goal of correctly defining genocide in order to advance further research and legislation to prevent genocide and to punish its perpetrators is no less subject to the political and ideological self-interest groups that seek to define genocide according to their ideologies and their quest for power.[4]

Those familiar with the history of genocide hardly require an elaborate introduction to the many outright revisionists who seek to rule out the truth of the Holocaust in order to maintain their virulent anti-Semitic purposes; nor do they need to be instructed about the brutal use of political power by Turkey, a seemingly modern state (a NATO member in good standing and recently a welcome ally of the U.S. against Saddam Hussein) which has committed millions of dollars and first-line political resources to insisting that the Armenian Genocide be written out of the history books. These revisionist conceptions are grotesque to any normal thinking person, but they are sponsored by powerful people and groups and cannot simply be dismissed as irrelevant, despite the fact that they are so patently distorted as to be far out of line with the simplest requirements of scholarship.

Along with these dangerous if farcical denials of known realities, there are other insidious types of political pressures on the definition of genocide that issue from entirely respectable intellectual circles. The subject of genocide draws intense political fire over which events of mass murder are to be considered bona fide genocides. The following are four of the most frequent types of political pressures that are brought to bear on the act of defining genocide:

1. Pressures to define genocide so that certain events will be excluded and not generate legal responsibility to the perpetrator country or individual perpetrators who executed the event.
2. Pressures to exclude from the definition of genocide certain events for purposes of realpolitik, such as interests in maintaining diplomatic or economic ties with a genocidal government.
3. Pressures to define genocide so that a given event of mass murder emerges as more "important" than another, including especially pressures to claim for a given genocide the crown of "ultimate importance." A closely related argument has to do with the assignment of relative degrees of evil to different events of mass murder, so that a given event is taken to represent the greater, incarnate evil in comparison to other events of genocide, which are treated somewhat as more usual events of massacre and slaughter in human history.
4. Blatant denials and revisionism of known historical events of mass murder.

1. *Pressures to define genocide so that certain events will be excluded and not generate legal responsibility to the perpetrator country or individual perpetrators who executed the event.* The oldest tactic for resisting a full and open definition of murder is that he who commits a murder, or who plans to, or who is an accomplice to the commission of a murder by others, will seek to minimize, attenuate, and confound any definition that will put the murderer or the accomplice in a legally culpable position. It has always struck me as bizarre about justice systems in democracies that the goal of many attorneys is to play a game in which, irrespective of the truth, the attorney instructs even the guilty to deny responsibility totally, and if there is too much evidence to get away with that, the legal practitioner nonetheless seeks to reduce the severity of the definition of murder from first to second degree, to manslaughter, to whatever categories of lesser responsibility.

When it comes to perpetrators of genocide, the game, sadly, is no different. Fortunately, in most cases when the perpetrator takes as his defense the claim that he was only following orders of superiors, the courts have ruled that there can be no shirking of one's responsibility not to accept orders to commit war crimes and genocide.[5] Unfortunately, in practice, relatively few perpetrators of genocide are brought to justice. Moreover, even in the greatest democracies in the world, perpetrators have been known to receive preferential treatment even after conviction (as in the case of Lieutenant Calley, convicted for the massacre at My Lai, whose sentence was reduced thereafter by President Nixon), and have been strangely and secretly supported and rewarded with high and comfortable positions after release from jail (for example, several Israeli soldiers convicted for massacring innocent Arabs in 1956 are reported to have been assisted by no less an official than Prime Minister David Ben-Gurion following their release from relatively brief jail sentences).[6] As for nations, legal procedures and sanctions against perpetrator nations have never been taken. David Hawk and his associates at the Cambodia Documentation Commission made herculean efforts in recent years to bring legal charges under the UN Genocide Convention against Cambodia, but no government was found willing to bring the charges before the World Court.[7]

There are especially strong pressures by many countries to bar definitions of any military actions as genocide. The question of whether events of mass deaths of civilians, such as massive or nuclear bombing in the course of wars, are to qualify as genocide or are to be excluded from the universe of genocide, is understandably controversial. The heart that cries out for peace on earth must in principle oppose wars; and straightforward logic tells us that wars are a prime precondition of many genocides, hence we would want to do everything to avoid them. Realistically, however, wars are a fact of human society, and the status of the present development of human civilization may preclude an encompassing idealistic definition of all mass deaths caused by wars as genocide. Most scholars of genocide reluctantly back off from defining war and the massive killing that goes on during war within the universe of genocide. As a result, a number of forms of massive killings of civilians in wartime—such as the saturation bombings of Dresden in the course of what most of us have no doubt was a just war against evil incarnate, and the atomic bombings of Hiroshima and Nagasaki in a war against classic military imperialism and cruelty—are treated gingerly and suspiciously by many otherwise well-meaning scholars of genocide. Even those of us who are quite convinced that those mass deaths of civilians in unjust wars which are not objectively in the service of self-defense must be enjoined as criminal by the international system are aware that the problems of objectively defining self-defense are so great that it too will be a difficult task at this point in the history of ideas.[8]

2. *Pressures to exclude from the definition of genocide certain events for purposes of realpolitik.* Every definition of genocide carries with it policy implications at the levels of international law and international relations as well as for political and economic interests; such implications are even experienced at the level of those who write the historical and moral record of a given people and government. In an ideal universe, the definition of genocide should, in the view of many of us, justify interventions by international legal and political systems, certainly international relief and disaster operations on behalf of the victims, and also humanitarian-based military interventions on the part of neighboring countries and international peacekeeping forces which would employ military force to stop the genociding nation in its tracks.[9] Today's battles over the proper intellectual and political definition of genocide will someday have very real implications. The spokesmen of darkness in human affairs—and there are many—who openly espouse genocidal policies and also the many who more subtly seek to protect a nation's "right to commit genocide" will seek to limit definitions of genocide that encroach on their ability to conduct their affairs of state they wish.[10]

If we consider the present definition of genocide under the UN Convention, the most obvious exclusions from the universe of genocide are political mass killings. Kuper has described how in the original deliberations on the United Nations Convention on Genocide, the big powers conspired and supported one another in an effort to remove from the basic definition events in which governments take action against their political opponents. Even a case such as the U.S.S.R.'s murder of an estimated twenty million (see Note 1) of its own citizens remained unknown to the majority of the free world for the longest time and was not labeled as genocide. It remained for scholars to slowly raise questions about such events and to seek ways to prove that even under the present legal structure some of the victims constitute a definable ethnic minority group.[11] Therefore the events constitute genocide under the present UN Convention and should not be relegated to a government's conduct of its "internal affairs." So too, in connection with the Cambodian genocide (which a UN Commission labeled "auto-genocide"), scholars have resorted to the proof that there were at least two clearly defined target groups of the Khmer Rouge, the Buddhist priesthood and the Cham people, and that therefore a bona fide definition of genocide applied.[12]

One implication of such strained proofs remains that planned killing of even millions of one's political opponents would not constitute genocide if one were careful that they were all of different faiths or different ethnic backgrounds.[13] In other words, our human civilization has reached the point in its ethical evolution at which the murder of a single person is murder most foul, but there are conditions under which the murder of millions of people can still fall into a definitional void. We are reminded of Raphael Lemkin's impassioned protest: "Why is the killing of a million a lesser crime than the killing of a single individual?"[14] What Lemkin saw as bizarre in human society was the fact that collective murder of a single target people, the genocide he recognized most familiarly, went unacknowledged, while the murder of a single person generally aroused all the natural emotional concerns one would expect, as well as the proper reactions of the justice system. What we are now adding to Lemkin's cry is the concern that mass killings, on an enormous scale, can fail to qualify as genocide under the present definition if the victims are either a heterogeneous group or native citizens of the country that is destroying them. How absurd, and ugly. It is not surprising that, increasingly, voices are calling for the expansion of the definition of genocide to include all political killings and all mass murders of one's own people (see in particular the proposals by the authoritative Whitaker Commission of the United Nations in 1985).[15] Unfortunately, attempts to exclude cases of mass murder from the definition of genocide for purposes of protecting one's policy interests is, sadly and outrageously, a matter of operational government policy even on the part of the great democracies of our human civilization. Thus, until the summer of 1990 when there were increasing signs of a danger (that has still not passed) that the genocidal Khmer Rouge might again take control of Cambodia,[16] the United States had carefully sustained its political and also economic recognition of the Khmer Rouge as the ruling government of Cambodia in order to further its avowed opposition to the Vietnamese Communist government and its sponsored government in Cambodia, which has vied with the Khmer Rouge and others for control of the country.

Decent people around the world were not only concerned but outraged at the United States' initial failure to protect millions of Kurdish people in Iraq from mass deaths, either at the hands of Saddam Hussein or in the frenzied mass flight from Saddam Hussein's troops, a situation of genocide which the Bush administration unbelievably labeled an "internal affair" of the Iraqis.[17]

Similarly, one American administration after another has gone along to some extent with the exclusion of the Armenian Genocide from the universe of the definition of genocide, lest NATO-ally Turkey be offended. Every few years we are privy to ludicrous and obscene scenes of would-be and actual American presidential candidates promising their support to the Armenian community for its right to mark and remember the genocide of its people; but on assuming office, the newly elected president bows to prevailing State Department policy and its rhetoric, which refers to the murder of the Armenians as an "alleged genocide" and emphasizes that the historical record of the time is a matter of some "controversy."[18]

3. *Pressures to define genocide so that a given event of mass murder emerges as more "important" than another.* I never fault or argue with a survivor's claim that a given genocide was the ultimate evil of all, nor do I find fault with collective expressions of such demands for uniqueness of a given genocide when they spring from the same natural folk-outpouring of grief, disbelief, horror, and rage at the tragedy and infamy done to one's people. However, when possible, and certainly in scholarly forums, I do caution that the phenomenological belief that the genocide committed against one's people was the worst crime ever perpetrated in human history is a natural response, and that this legitimate, subjective reaction itself does not assign objective credence to the position.

I object very strongly to the efforts to name the genocide of any one people as the single, ultimate event, or as the most important event against which all other tragedies of genocidal mass deaths are to be tested and found wanting. Thus, with regard to the Holocaust of my own people, I do believe that the configuration of the events of the Holocaust, including the totality of the persecution, the unbearably long trail of dehumanization and unspeakable tortures suffered by the victims, the modern organization and scientific resources committed to the mass extermination, the active participation and complicity of every level of society, including the public institutions of an ostensibly civilized people, have afforded the Holocaust a timeless meaning and a deserved position as the archetypal event of mass murder in human history. Nonetheless, it is by no means the only event of organized mass murder, and the deadly outcomes for its victims are no more deadly and therefore no more tragic than the outcomes for the victims of other peoples' genocides. It is also by no means the last word on how human beings at this stage of evolution produce mass deaths on this planet. I strongly oppose any efforts to place the Holocaust beyond the ranges of meanings that attend the destruction of other peoples, and I object to any implications that we should be less sensitive or outraged at the murders of other peoples (see Kuper's criticism of "the alienation of the unique").[19]

4. *Blatant denials and revisionism of known historical events of mass murder.*
Finally, one must refer again to those outrageous but nonetheless
prevalent attempts by groups and governments to deny, censor, revise,
and destroy the records of human history about known genocides.
Anti-Semitic groups of all sorts, including political enemies of Israel
who are also entirely comfortable exploiting anti-Semitism in their
battles against Israel, claim that there was no Holocaust, that there
were no gas chambers, that the number of more than six million Jewish
victims is grossly exaggerated, that Hitler never gave an order to kill
the Jews, and that if something happened to the Jews on whatever
smaller scale, it was at the behest of low-level commanders.[20]

The most insidious revisionists are those who don't deny that people
were killed but who seek cleverly to deny that the given historical event
fulfills the demanding criteria that they ostensibly seek to ensure in
the definition of genocide. It is abominable to see pseudo-intellectual
products in ostensibly academic journals and books by bona fide, ten-
ured academicians of prestigious institutions of scholarship (for example, Arthur Butz[21]) who rewrite the facts and figures of known mass
deaths in order to disqualify an event of genocide.

Another insidious variant of revisionism is seen in recent publications by German historians, prominent among them Professor Ernest
Nolte, who seek to diminish the significance of the events of the Holocaust, and in effect to diminish the significance of the underlying
category to which it belongs, by advancing the observations that after
all such events of mass murder have always occurred in history, thus
the Holocaust should not be treated as being of unusual significance
and certainly not as a historically definitive event. To play a sophisticated game of revisionism properly, one must, of course, add a caveat
that one's intention is not at all to dismiss the significance of any
genocide, it is only to put it in a proper perspective; but the underlying
meaning of such arguments is that the event of genocide need not be
an object of civilization's great concerns. The real purpose of revisionism, in its various propagandist forms, is always to re-create a climate of
moral support and approval of genocide past, present, and future.

Even democratic governments such as the United States and Israel—which in addition to being a democracy is, on another level,
the representative of a victimized people who should certainly know
better—enter into full-blown conspiracies of denial and revisionism.
As previously mentioned, the U.S. State Department has made its
share of references to the Armenian Genocide as an "alleged genocide"
and has opposed even commemorative events about the Armenian
Genocide because of its ongoing political interest in relations with the

arch-revisionist Turks who to this day deny that there ever was an Armenian Genocide at their hands. It is a sad and obscene commentary on the cultural history of our times that the executive branch of the United States government has several times devoted its full energies to diverting the Congress from passing legislation that would have created a ceremonial day of remembrance for the victims of the Armenian Genocide (to join the literally hundreds of other days of commemoration that have been mandated by congressional legislation)—a day that was, as defined by its Armenian sponsors, also to have commemorated the victims of all genocides in history. It is by now well known that Israel, the land of Holocaust memorial—which protests, as it should, every vestige of revisionism of the Holocaust—conspires to suppress the story of the Armenian Genocide, whether in the massive government efforts to stop the International Conference on the Holocaust and Genocide in 1982 (which has become a cause célèbre in the history of academic freedom and a critical example of governmental suppression of information about genocide)[22] or more recently in assisting Turkish diplomats to lobby the American Congress against the Armenian Genocide bill.[23]

In all these instances, the battle is not only about history and the authenticity of the records of past events in our civilization, it is about the extent to which we today hold our governments responsible for their actions. For as long as there is normative support for the realpolitik of government revisionism, we will see the facts of current history erased within days after massacres by governments everywhere, in Tiananmen Square, Sri Lanka, Kurdish villages in Iraq, and elsewhere.

Toward a Generic Definition of Genocide

What is needed, I would argue, is a generic definition of genocide that does not exclude or commit to indifference any case of mass murder of any human beings, of whatever racial, national, ethnic, biological, cultural, religious, and political definitions, or of totally mixed groupings of any and all of the above.

I propose that whenever large numbers of unarmed human beings are put to death at the hands of their fellow human beings, we are talking about *genocide*. Shortly after the adoption of the UN Convention on Genocide, Dutch jurist Pieter Drost wrote:

A convention on genocide cannot effectively contribute to the protection of certain described minorities when it is limited to particular defined groups. . . . It serves no purpose to restrict international legal protection to some groups; firstly, because the protected members always belong at the same time to other unprotected groups.[24]

In 1985 the authoritative Whitaker Commission of the UN, referred to earlier, called for decisive amendment of the Convention to include all political mass murders. Some years ago, I proposed *a humanistic definition* of genocide, namely, "the wanton murder of a group of human beings on the basis of any identity whatsoever that they share—national, ethnic, religious, political, geographical, ideological."[25] Similarly, John Thompson has written, "There seems to be no adequate conceptual criteria for distinguishing between groups whose destruction constitutes genocide and groups whose destruction does not."[26]

With the regrettable but necessary exception of actual military combat, I call on fellow scholars to be faithful to the commonsense meanings of loss of human lives so that we do not exclude in arbitrary, cynical, or intellectual elitist ways the deaths of *any* group of our fellow human beings from our definitions of genocide. I believe there is no task of greater importance than that of committing ourselves to the protection of all human lives.[27]

In Table 2, I have assembled a proposed matrix for a new, encompassing definition of genocide.

I would argue that a *generic definition of genocide* be as follows:

Genocide in the generic sense is the mass killing of substantial numbers of human beings, when not in the course of military action against the military forces of an avowed enemy, under conditions of the essential defenselessness and helplessness of the victims.

Raphael Lemkin correctly underscored the overriding motivation of many mass killings to exterminate a given people, and therefore wisely called to our attention that the murder of a people's culture or elimination of their rights and abilities to maintain biological continuity are also forms of destruction of the species to which we dare not be indifferent. First and foremost, however, we must have a language that clearly defines as genocide any actual *biological* murder of masses of people, even if the people are not all of the same ethnicity, religion, or race.

At the same time, since there are also a great many important reasons to distinguish between different kinds of genocide, having defined genocide in its generic sense, we also need to create a series of definitions of categories of genocide. Each event of genocide is to be classified into the one or more subcategories for which it qualifies. It is to be expected that, over the course of time, there will always emerge new categories, as the complexity of life and reality unfold; for example, in our time we may witness the creation of a category to define accomplices to genocide who supply deadly weapons of mass destruction to those who commit genocide, and some day in the future perhaps of a

TABLE 2. A Proposed Definitional Matrix for Crimes of Genocide.

A. *Generic Definition of Genocide*
Genocide in the generic sense is the mass killing of substantial numbers of human beings, when not in the course of military action against the military forces of an avowed enemy, under conditions of the essential defenselessness and helplessness of the victims.

1. *Genocidal Massacre*
Mass killing as defined above in the generic definition of genocide but in which the mass murder is on a smaller scale, that is, smaller numbers of human beings are killed.

2. *Intentional Genocide*
Genocide on the basis of an explicit intention to destroy a specific targeted victim group (ethnic/religious/racial/national/political/biological/or other), in whole or in substantial part.

    a. *Specific Intentional Genocide* refers to intentional genocide against a specific victim group.

    b. *Multiple Intentional Genocide* refers to intentional genocide against more than one specific victim group at the same time or in closely related or contiguous actions.

    c. *Omnicide* refers to simultaneous intentional genocide against numerous races, nations, religions, etc.

3. *Genocide in the Course of Colonization or Consolidation of Power*
Genocide that is undertaken or even allowed in the course of or incidental to the purposes of achieving a goal of colonization or development of a territory belonging to an indigenous people, or any other consolidation of political or economic power through mass killing of those perceived to be standing in the way.

4. *Genocide in the Course of Aggressive ("Unjust") War*
Genocide that is undertaken or even allowed in the course of military actions by a known aggressive power, e.g., Germany and Japan in World War II, for the purpose of or incidental to a goal of aggressive war, such as massive destruction of civilian centers in order to vanquish an enemy in war.

5. *War Crimes Against Humanity*
Crimes committed in the course of military actions against military targets, or in treatment of war prisoners, or in occupation policies against civilian populations which involve overuse of force or cruel and inhuman treatment and which result in unnecessary mass suffering or death.

6. *Genocide as a Result of Ecological Destruction and Abuse*
Genocide that takes place as a result of criminal destruction or abuse of the environment, or negligent failure to protect against known ecological and environmental hazards, such as accidents involving radiation and waste from nuclear installations, uncontrolled smog, or poisonous air from industrial pollution, pollution of water supplies, etc.

TABLE 2. *Continued*

B. *Accomplices to Genocide*
   Persons, institutions, companies, or governments who knowingly or
   negligently assist individuals, organizations, or governments who are
   known murderers or potential murderers to gain access to mega-weapons
   of destruction, or otherwise to organize and execute a plan of mass
   murders, are to be held responsible as accomplices to the defined crimes
   of genocide or war crimes.

C. "Cultural Genocide"

   1. *Ethnocide*
      Intentional destruction of the culture of another people, not
      necessarily including destruction of actual lives (included in original
      UN definition of genocide but, in present proposed definitions,
      ethnocide is not subsumed under *genocide*).

      a. *Linguicide*
         Forbidding the use of or other intentional destruction of the
         language of another people—a specific dimension of *ethnocide*.

category for the destruction of planets (which I have elsewhere called
planeticide, partial planeticide, as well as *attempted planeticide*).[28]

Genocidal Massacre

Events of mass murder that are on a smaller scale than mass events may
be defined, as Leo Kuper[29] originally proposed, under a category of
"genocidal massacre." I would define *genocidal massacre* as follows:

Mass killing as defined above in the generic definition of genocide, but in which
the mass murder is on a smaller scale, that is, smaller numbers of human beings
are killed.

With this category we are now equipped to describe many pogroms,
mass executions, and mass murders that are, intrinsically, no less vicious and no less tragically final for the victims, but in which the
numbers of dead are small in comparison to the events of genocide and
of which even the well-meaning people who do not approve concep-
tually of "numbers games" have found it difficult to speak of as genocide. Thus, we would apply the specific concept of genocidal massacre
to the government of Sri Lanka's rounding up some five thousand
Tamils over a weekend and executing them;[30] and to the government
of China's mowing down an estimated similar number in Tiananmen
Square.[31]

Intentional Genocide

The category for which there is generally the greatest interest is that of genocides that are executed on the basis of an ideological and operational commitment to destroy a specific targeted people. In a sense, this has been the most "coveted" category, that is, the ultimate, pure form of genocide, in which the premeditated, malevolent intention and the totality of operational commitment to destroy a specific people generate a comprehensive evil plan.

If there were to be only one ultimate, seemingly pure form of genocide, this would be its definition; but this pure-form definition, sadly, has also set off competitions between different events of mass extermination, where the debate as to which would be admitted to the "royal club" of "true genocide" has taken precedence. In some cases, there developed claims that only the Holocaust qualified as a true genocide, to which no other mass murder could be compared. I refer once again to Leo Kuper's recent criticism of demands for exclusivity and a dubious categorization of "uniqueness" for the Holocaust at the expense of common sensitivity and respect for the plights of many other peoples who, although they were not led to slaughter in the Holocaust's terrifying scenarios of protracted persecution, torture, and organized factories of death, were no less wantonly slaughtered.

As noted earlier, the present proposal is for a definitional matrix that combines a generic definition of genocide and specific subcategories. Such a definitional matrix makes it possible, first, to recognize all events of mass murder as genocide, and second, to assign each event to a further definitional category in which the specific characteristics of each event are recognized and groups of phenomena that share common structural features can be subjected to analyses of their characteristic sequences and dynamics and to comparative analyses with other types of genocide.

I would define *intentional genocide* as follows:

Genocide on the basis of an explicit intention to destroy a specific targeted victim group (ethnic/religious/racial/national/political/biological/or other), in whole or in substantial part.

Under the category of intentional genocide, I would further define *specific intentional genocide* as intentional genocide against a specific victim group; *multiple intentional genocide* as intentional genocide against more than one specific victim group at the same time or in closely related or contiguous actions; and *omnicide* as simultaneous intentional genocide against numerous races, nations, religions, and so on.[32]

The heartbreaking events of the Armenian Genocide, the Holocaust of the Jews, the Holocaust of the Gypsies, the Holocaust of homosexuals, Sukarno's massacre of the Communists in Indonesia, the tragic gassing of the Kurds in recent years by Iraq, and many other events qualify in the category of intentional genocide. Note that within this communality, there are still many further distinctions to be made in the course of the analyses of the different incidents, involving, for example, numbers of victims, totality of intention, commitment to implementation, and many more; and there is every reason to establish the specific ways in which a given genocide was unique, but without in the process downplaying the recognition of other events as genocide.

Genocide in the Course of Colonization or Consolidation of Power

Genocides in the course of colonization have taken the lives of countless indigenous peoples. Such genocidal colonization of indigenous peoples continues throughout the world.[33]

Using this category in combination with the earlier category of genocidal massacre to describe, as has Richard Arens,[34] the mass killing of the Ache Indians, we will finally solve the difficult conceptual problems created by that admirable and electrifying report. Arens described the murder of perhaps a thousand people, and yet adopted the powerful term *genocide* without further subspecification or definition. An uncomfortable intellectual situation thus developed whereby the cruel killings of a quantitatively small indigenous people was being defined in liberal circles as *genocide,* while some years later the murder of millions of Cambodians was excluded from the field of inquiry of genocide on the grounds of its being an internal affair of the Cambodian government. The present proposed definitional system would confirm from the outset, without hesitation, that both events were indeed genocide under a generic definition of mass killings of defenseless human beings; the specific type of genocide then is assigned to further categories, both as to the type of genocide and as to its quantitative aspects.

There are also numerous situations in which governments seek to consolidate their power through genocidal campaigns against constituent minority ethnicities or against political opponents. At this point at least, I choose to combine these situations with events of genocide in the course of colonization in a single conceptual category. These too are first of all prima facie cases of genocide in the generic sense, since masses of helpless human beings are exterminated. Thus, it will no longer be necessary to struggle laboriously to justify including Stalin's record of murdering perhaps twenty million victims as genocide (again, see note 1, below). I believe one reason that, incredibly, the Western world for the longest time acted as if it did not know of this monstrous record was that as long as the crime had no name and did not qualify in the same category of genocide that included the Holocaust's six million Jewish victims, there was no convenient conceptual-experiential basis for people to organize the information. (I would note that the same is true for the other estimated six million non-Jewish victims of Nazi Germany,[35] including those whom we identified earlier as victims of specific intentional genocide [e.g., Gypsies and homosexuals] and including the many millions of civilians of all nationalities in the countries invaded by Nazi Germany, whom we will identify shortly in the next definitional category as victims of genocide in the course of war.) Under the existing limited definition of genocide, it was necessary for scholars, such as those previously referred to, to argue that because there were instances in which specific ethnicities were eliminated by Stalin, it was legitimate to call these events genocide, and it was necessary, also as noted earlier, to resort to the same intellectual tour de force to prove that the Pol Pot regime committed genocide in Cambodia. But it is absurd, as well as intellectually corrupt, for us to resort to such devices to allow us to justify calling clear cases of mass murder by the name genocide.

I propose the following definition of *genocide in the course of colonization or consolidation of power:*

Genocide that is undertaken or even allowed in the course of or incidental to the purposes of achieving a goal of colonization or development of a territory belonging to an indigenous people, or any other consolidation of political or economic power through mass killing of those perceived to be standing in the way.

Genocide in the Course of Aggressive ("Unjust") War

Above and beyond the fact that genocides of all categories take place frequently under conditions of war, there are mass murders of defenseless noncombatant civilians in the course of war that are an important definitional focus in their own right. The number of civilians who die in the course of wars increases with the growth of destructive mega-weapons. Anatol Rapoport observes that since 1945, "the proportion of civilian deaths in war has ranged from 65% to 90%," and that "these killings, being indiscriminate, could well be subsumed under genocide" unless "only deliberate selective extermination of identifiable groups is subsumed under genocides."[36]

There are two legal categories* for serious crimes against human life in the course of conduct of war: *war crimes* or crimes committed

---

*I am indebted to Professor Irwin Cutler for his reading of an earlier draft of this chapter and discussion of these legal concepts.

primarily against combatants but also against noncombatants, in the course of military actions, and *crimes against humanity* or crimes committed against civilians in particular.

Whether mass deaths of civilians in the course of war should also qualify as a form of genocide is a complex subject that necessarily raises many serious legal, political, and philosophical questions regarding uses of mega-weapons and the large-scale destruction of civilian populations during wartime. The issues are at their sharpest focus when one considers whether massive civilian deaths are to be understood as (1) tragically inadvertent and necessary in the course of intrinsically "just wars" of self-defense against an acknowledged mass murdering power, such as Nazi Germany, and against a war-initiating power intent on aggressive occupation of another people's lands, or (2) as mass killings of civilians in the course of "unjust wars." I therefore propose to take advantage of the distinction between "just" and "unjust" wars to suggest that the mass civilian deaths committed by aggressive powers in pursuit of "unjust" wars at the onset be defined decisively as genocidal. By first addressing genocide in the course of *aggressive ("unjust") war*, we postpone until later consideration of the issue of mass civilian deaths by intended victim peoples fighting "just wars" of self-defense. In the present category, the issue of mass civilian deaths is unambiguously genocide. The deaths issue from an identifiably aggressive war, and the attacks on civilians are made by rulers such as Hitler, Hirohito, and Saddam Hussein; there is no question that they are not at war in self-defense.

The following definition is proposed for *genocide in the course of aggressive ("unjust") war:*

Genocide that is undertaken or even allowed in the course of military actions by a known aggressive power, such as Germany and Japan in World War II, for the purpose of or incidental to a goal of aggressive war, such as massive destruction of civilian centers in order to vanquish an enemy in war.

War Crimes Against Humanity

In addition to massive killing of civilians who are specifically and purposely targeted for killing in the course of war, there are also many events where large numbers of soldiers, and perhaps also civilians, are killed as the result of overly cruel or lethal means employed to conduct the war or to manage the detention of captured enemy soldiers, and where large numbers of civilians are terrorized and killed by being taken hostage or under the brutal control of occupied territories. As indicated, mass deaths brought about by such extreme policies have been defined as *war crimes* and/or as *crimes against humanity*.

I propose a single combined category of *war crimes against humanity*, which is intended to define any use of overly cruel or lethal means of war in the course of military actions during the war, or after the war, in such acts as treatment of war prisoners or in the conduct of occupation of an enemy land and rule of its people. When mass deaths result from overuse of force by a warring country, even if it is morally justified by self-defense in its original conduct of the war, it retains no moral advantage with respect to genocidal policies of overkill in its military tactics or in its treatment of the enemy's war prisoners or occupied civilians. Note especially that this category defines genocidal crimes against soldiers and civilians *regardless* of whether the war being waged is aggressive or in self-defense.

Personally, I yield to the fact that, at least at this point in human evolution, there must be allowance for war and certainly for truly just wars of self-defense, and that under the circumstances of modern war there is a certainty and perhaps even inevitability of disasters to large numbers of noncombatant civilians. This has to be true at times when technologies of mass destruction are utilized purposefully against operational enemy centers in heavily populated civilian neighborhoods, such as the enemy's war ministry, communication headquarters, and so on. Nonetheless, caring people and history must be free to question whether the large number of dead, such as that which resulted from the Allied firebombing of Dresden and the nuclear bombing of Hiroshima and Nagasaki in World War II, should be defined as excessive and therefore criminal, and not be allowed to slip unnoticed into being simply another aspect of war. I acknowledge that this categorization of events is intellectually and emotionally extremely painful to many of us in the free world, but I prefer such distress over feigned ignorance or the denial of events where millions died, and over indifference to the issues.

Whatever one's personal opinions, the category of war crimes against humanity organizes these events for further analysis. We need the category to capture the many events in which millions of innocent people are killed because of extreme uses of power, so that we are forced into painful encounters with the moral dilemmas such events present. Defining events in this category does not preclude continuing political and moral analysis and debate as to what instances of mass killing of defenseless people in the course of just wars may be justified.

I propose the following definition of *war crimes against humanity:*

Crimes committed in the course of military actions against military targets, or in treatment of war prisoners, or in occupation policies against civilian populations which involve overuse of force, or cruel and inhuman treatment, and which result in unnecessary mass suffering or death.

Genocide as a Result of Ecological Destruction and Abuse

Increasingly, it becomes clear that many human lives are being lost to man-made ecological disasters that are a result of the criminal destruction or abuse of the environment, or of uncaring malevolent indifference to the inevitability of the disaster because of palpable ecological negligence. Direct military abuse of the environment as a weapon of genocidal destruction, such as the Germans' poisoning of the Herero people's water holes at the beginning of the century, are obvious genocidal instances. But there are also degrees of abuse of nature that are more negligent in origin, such as the development of an increasingly large hole in the ozone layer surrounding our planet, which is attributable to widespread use of aerosols and which is already seen as causing a dramatic increase in melanomas; the poisoning of frighteningly large numbers of bodies of water on Earth; the pollution of the air above cities; the radioactive contamination of a huge geographical area (smaller instances around nuclear installations in the U.S., and the largest instance at Chernobyl in the U.S.S.R.[37]) that require new policies of intergovernmental cooperation, even among long-standing military rivals, to forestall ecological mass disasters. It is now indisputable that as the instruments of man's power grow, the hazards of massive ecological destruction increase.

I propose the following definition of *genocide as a result of ecological destruction and abuse:*

Genocide that takes place as a result of criminal destruction or abuse of the environment, or negligent failure to protect against known ecological and environmental hazards, such as accidents involving radiation and waste from nuclear installations, uncontrolled smog, or poisonous air from industrial pollution, pollution of water supplies, and so on.

I would add that the subject of ecology also leads us to consider the tragic extent to which millions die each year of hunger, and that there is room to consider those actions that create the conditions of unnecessary starvation, which cause the deaths of millions, as genocidal.[38]

Accomplices to Genocide

It is now time to define a new category of accomplices to genocide. If in normal criminal law there are concepts pertaining to a party that supplies a known murderer or intended murderer with the murder weapon, I believe there needs to be clear legal definitions of the direct responsibility of those who supply the financial and technical means to mass murderers. We need legal criteria for defining the responsibility of the contractors, scientists, and others—individuals, companies, and governments—who, knowingly and maliciously, arm a mass murderer, and for assigning lesser criminal responsibility to those who were perhaps more innocent yet should not have been when they undertook to work for known and would-be killers who were heard to threaten the massacre or incineration of a people. Such perfidies require firm responses under international law.

I propose to define *accomplices to genocide* as follows:

Persons, institutions, companies, or governments who knowingly or negligently assist individuals, organizations, or governments who are known or potential murderers to gain access to mega-weapons of destruction, or otherwise to organize and execute a plan of mass murders, are to be held responsible as accomplices to the defined crimes of genocide or war crimes.

Cultural Genocide

As noted earlier, Raphael Lemkin was correctly concerned not only with the physical destruction of a people but also with the destruction of their cultural identity. However, Lemkin's definitional system inadvertently leads to situations in which destruction of a culture's continuity is labeled as committing genocide while others in which millions of people are actually murdered are not.

Ethnocide

I propose to utilize a specific category of *ethnocide* for major processes that prohibit or interfere with the natural cycles of reproduction and continuity of a culture or a nation, but not to include this type of murderous oppression directly under the generic concept of genocide. Note again, that as in the case of the other proposed classifications, so long as data of a given type of events are assembled into a clearly labeled definitional context, they are awaiting the emergence of new thinking and a new consensus as scholars continue to struggle with the enormous issues that are raised by virtually every definition. Note also that retaining this category of ethnocide adjacent to and in effect as part of the overall matrix of definitions of genocide (rather than removing it to a separate list of further human rights violations) retains a recognition of the closeness of the subjects, and also retains respect for the historical inclusion of ethnocide in the original definition of genocide that the world community first adopted. I strongly prefer, however, to reserve the concept of genocide for actual mass murders that end the lives of people. I propose to define *ethnocide* thus:

Intentional destruction of the culture of another people, not necessarily including destruction of actual lives (included in the original UN definition of genocide but, in the present proposed definitions, *ethnocide* is not subsumed under genocide).

Linguicide

Linguicide is a definitional subcategory of ethnocide which involves forbidding various uses of a people's language—printing of books, teaching the language, or everyday communication in the language.[39] I define *linguicide* thus:

Forbidding the use of or other intentional destruction of the language of another people—a specific dimension of *ethnocide*.

Degrees of Criminal Responsibility

Finally, I believe that the definitional system will gain if it is also possible to assign different weights or gradations to various crimes of genocide. One system for doing so that is immediately familiar for purposes of legal definition is to utilize known gradations of murder; thus, genocide in the first degree, second degree, and third degree. Just as definitions of individual murder vary in degree of premeditation, purposeful organization, cruelty, and more, so do programs of mass extermination.

I propose the following criteria by which to define degrees (first, second, third) of genocide, war crimes, and ethnocide:

- Premeditation
- Totality or singlemindedness of purpose
- Resoluteness to execute policy
- Efforts to overcome resistance
- Devotion to bar escape of victims
- Persecutory cruelty

Table 3 presents the overall proposed matrix of definitions that we saw previously with the addition of the option to further classify and assign degrees of criminal responsibility.

Although it has not been included in the table at the present time, I also suggest that the classification system lends itself to concepts of *attempted genocide*, in much the same way as "attempted murders" are categorized.

TABLE 3. A Proposed Definitional Matrix for Crimes of Genocide (Extended).

A. *Generic Definition of Genocide*
Genocide in the generic sense is
the mass killing of substantial
numbers of human beings, when
not in the course of military
action against the military forces
of an avowed enemy, under
conditions of the essential
defenselessness and helplessness
of the victims.

To establish first, second, or third
degree of genocide, evaluate extent
of:
• Premeditation
• Totality or singlemindedness of
  purpose
• Resoluteness to execute policy
• Efforts to overcome resistance
• Devotion to bar escape of victims
• Persecutory cruelty

1. *Genocidal Massacre*
   Mass killing as defined above
   in the generic definition of
   genocide but in which the
   mass murder is on a smaller
   scale, i.e., smaller numbers of
   human beings are killed.

To establish first, second, or third
degree genocidal massacres, evaluate
extent of:
• Premeditation
• Totality or singlemindedness of
  purpose
• Resoluteness to execute policy
• Efforts to overcome resistance
• Devotion to bar escape of victims
• Persecutory cruelty

2. *Intentional Genocide*
   Genocide on the basis of an
   explicit intention to destroy a
   specific targeted victim group
   (ethnic/religious/racial/
   national/political/biological/or
   other), in whole or in
   substantial part.

TABLE 3. *Continued*

<table>
<tr>
<td></td>
<td>To establish first, second, or third degree intentional genocide, evaluate extent of:
• Premeditation
• Totality or singlemindedness of purpose
• Resoluteness to execute policy
• Efforts to overcome resistance
• Devotion to bar escape of victims
• Persecutory cruelty</td>
</tr>
<tr>
<td>a. Specific Intentional Genocide refers to intentional genocide against a specific victim group.</td>
<td></td>
</tr>
<tr>
<td>b. Multiple Intentional Genocide refers to intentional genocide against more than one specific victim group at the same time or in closely related or contiguous actions.</td>
<td></td>
</tr>
<tr>
<td>c. Omnicide refers to simultaneous intentional genocide against numerous races, nations, religions, etc.</td>
<td></td>
</tr>
<tr>
<td>3. Genocide in the Course of Colonization or Consolidation of Power Genocide that is undertaken or even allowed in the course of or incidental to the purposes of achieving a goal of colonization or development of a territory belonging to an indigenous people, or any other consolidation of political or economic power through mass killing of those perceived to be standing in the way.</td>
<td></td>
</tr>
<tr>
<td></td>
<td>To establish first, second, or third degree genocide in the course of colonization or consolidation of power, evaluate extent of:
• Premeditation
• Totality or singlemindedness of purpose
• Resoluteness to execute policy
• Efforts to overcome resistance</td>
</tr>
</table>

TABLE 3. *Continued*

- Devotion to bar escape of victims
- Persecutory cruelty

4. *Genocide in the Course of Aggressive ("Unjust") War*
Genocide that is undertaken or even allowed in the course of military actions by a known aggressive power, e.g., Germany and Japan in World War II, for the purpose of or incidental to a goal of aggressive war, such as massive destruction of civilian centers in order to vanquish an enemy in war.

To establish first, second, or third degree genocide in the course of aggressive ("unjust") war, evaluate extent of:
- Premeditation
- Totality or singlemindedness of purpose
- Resoluteness to execute policy
- Efforts to overcome resistance
- Devotion to bar escape of victims
- Persecutory cruelty

5. *War Crimes Against Humanity*
Crimes committed in course of military actions against military targets, or in the treatment of war prisoners, or in occupation policies against civilian populations which involve overuse of force or cruel and inhuman treatment and which result in unnecessary mass suffering or death.

To establish first, second, or third degree war crimes against humanity, evaluate extent of:
- Premeditation
- Totality or singlemindedness of purpose
- Resoluteness to execute policy
- Efforts to overcome resistance
- Devotion to bar escape of victims
- Persecutory cruelty

TABLE 3. *Continued*

6. *Genocide as a Result of Ecological Destruction and Abuse*
   Genocide that takes place as a result of criminal destruction or abuse of the environment, or negligent failure to protect against known ecological and environmental hazards, such as accidents involving radiation and waste from nuclear installations, uncontrolled smog, or poisonous air owing to industrial pollution, pollution of water supplies, etc.

   To establish first, second, or third degree genocide as a result of ecological destruction and abuse, evaluate extent of:
   • Premeditation
   • Totality or singlemindedness of purpose
   • Resoluteness to execute policy
   • Efforts to overcome resistance
   • Devotion to bar escape of victims
   • Persecutory cruelty

B. *Accomplices to Genocide*
   Persons, institutions, companies, or governments who knowingly or negligently assist individuals, organizations, or governments who are known murderers or potential murderers to gain access to mega-weapons of destruction, or otherwise to organize and execute a plan of mass murders, are to be held responsible as accomplices to the defined crimes of genocide or war crimes.

   To establish first, second, or third degree complicity to genocide, evaluate extent of:
   • Premeditation
   • Totality or singlemindedness of purpose
   • Resoluteness to execute policy
   • Efforts to overcome resistance
   • Devotion to bar escape of victims
   • Persecutory cruelty

TABLE 3. *Continued*

C. "Cultural Genocide"

1. *Ethnocide*
   Intentional destruction of the
   culture of another people, not
   necessarily including
   destruction of actual lives
   (included in original UN
   definition of genocide but, in
   present proposed definitions,
   ethnocide is not subsumed
   under *genocide*).

   a. *Linguicide*
      Forbidding the use of or
      other intentional
      destruction of the language
      of another people—a
      specific dimension of
      ethnocide.

To establish first, second, or third
degree cultural genocide, evaluate
extent of:
- Premeditation
- Totality or singlemindedness of
  purpose
- Resoluteness to execute policy
- Efforts to overcome resistance
- Devotion to bar escape of victims
- Persecutory cruelty

On the Ills of "Definitionalism"

To conclude, the basic spirit and intention of the proposed definitional
matrix is that, almost without exception, most events of mass deaths of
innocent, helpless people qualify under the generic rubric of *genocide*.
At the same time, my intention is to develop a rational, systematic
series of differential classifications of subtypes of genocide. Both the
generic definition of genocide and the various subcategories should
stand up, first of all, to the test of natural logic and understanding;
there should be no instance in which masses of human beings lie murdered while our definitional categories do not encompass the event of
their deaths. The classification of different categories of genocide will
allow for effective further study of their different properties and the

development of proper legal definitions for assigning criminal responsibility in each case.

Most definitions of genocide have tended to be exclusive, that is, they sought to define what types of mass killings deserve to be called genocide, and hence also to define, directly or indirectly, what types of mass killings were to be excluded from the universe of genocide.[40] The present proposal is strongly inclusive; it seeks to create a wide conceptual base that includes all known types of mass murder and mass deaths that are brought about at the hands of man, and thus to insure that few tragic events of destruction of large numbers of human lives will fall by the theoretical wayside, as if they were of no legal, historical, or spiritual importance. The advantage of treating genocide first of all as a generic category is that one brings into the net virtually all instances of mass killings at the hands of man (other than bona fide wars of self-defense). At the same time, this conceptualization allows room to subclassify into more specific and stringent classificatory groups the different types of events of mass killing. Once the competition to decide which tragic events will and won't be accepted into the vaunted "genocide club" is ended, one can study the different types of genocide more honestly and come to understand their individual characteristics and differences from one another. It would be a moral absurdity and an insult to the value of human life to exclude from full historical recognition any instance of mass killing as if it were undeserving of inclusion in the record.

I would like to conclude with a serious criticism of what I shall call "definitionalism," which I define as a damaging style of intellectual inquiry based on a perverse, fetishistic involvement with definitions to the point at which the reality of the subject under discussion is "lost," that is, no longer experienced emotionally by the scholars conducting the inquiry, to the point that the real enormity of the subject no longer guides or impacts on the deliberations. The discussions about whether a given massacre or mass murder can be considered genocide are often emotionless, argumentative, and superrational, and one senses that the motivations and meta-meanings of the discussions often are based on intellectual competition and the claims to scholarly fame of the speakers rather than on genuine concern for the victims. The predominant intellectual goal of most participants in these definitional turf battles over what is and is not genocide is generally to exclude unfavored categories from the field.

For me, the passion to exclude this or that mass killing from the universe of genocide, as well as the intense competition to establish the exclusive "superiority" or unique form of any one genocide, ends up creating a fetishistic atmosphere in which the masses of bodies that are not to be qualified for the definition of genocide are dumped into a conceptual black hole, where they are forgotten.

I propose that, instead of expressing our dubious zeal for excluding categories of mass deaths from the realm of genocide, we put together the whole rotten record of all types of mass murder committed by man (an excellent collection of such events can be found in the scenarios created by Fein,[41] who uses fictitious names in order to highlight the various models of genocide), and thereby generate an even more powerful force that will protest, intervene, and seek to reduce and prevent any and all occurrences of mass destruction of human lives. In my opinion, that is the real purpose of genocide scholarship.

Notes

1. The figure of twenty million victims of Stalin's U.S.S.R. was generally accepted by scholars for many years. Most recently, political scientist R. J. Rummel of the University of Hawaii has marshaled systematic evidence that no less than "61,911,000 people, 54,769,000 of them citizens, [were] murdered by the Communist party—the government—of the Soviet Union from 1917 to 1987" (R. J. Rummel, "The Death Toll of Marxism in the Soviet Union," Special Section of *Internet on the Holocaust and Genocide,* double issue 30/31 [February, 1991]: 9–12). On the Soviet mass killings, see R. J. Rummel, *Lethal Politics: Soviet Genocide and Mass Murder since 1917* (New Brunswick, NJ: Transaction Press, 1990). For other cases of genocide, see R. J. Rummel, *China's Bloody Century: Genocide and Mass Murder since 1900* (New Brunswick, NJ: Transaction Press, 1991), and *Democide: Nazi Genocide and Mass Murder* (New Brunswick, NJ: Transaction Press, 1991).

2. See the following works by Leo Kuper: *Genocide: Its Political Use in the Twentieth Century* (New Haven, CT: Yale University Press, 1982); *International Action Against Genocide* (London: Minority Rights Group, 1984); and *The Prevention of Genocide* (New Haven, CT: Yale University Press, 1985).

3. "Germany Strongly Implicated in Build-up of Iraq Mega-Weapons," *Internet on the Holocaust and Genocide* 29 (November, 1990): 1.

4. Israel W. Charny, "The Psychology of Denial of Known Genocides," in *Genocide: A Critical Bibliographic Review, Volume 2,* ed. Israel W. Charny (London: Mansell Publishing Ltd.; New York: Facts on File, 1991); Richard G. Hovannisian, "Genocide and Denial: The Armenian Case," in *Toward the Understanding and Prevention of Genocide* (Proceedings of the International Conference on the Holocaust and Genocide), ed. Israel W. Charny (Boulder, CO: Westview Press; London: Bowker Publishing, 1984), 84–99.

5. Herbert C. Kelman and F. Lee Hamilton, *Crimes of Obedience: Toward a Social Psychology of Authority and Responsibility* (New Haven, CT, and London: Yale University Press, 1989).

6. Daliah Karpel, "What Happened to the Killers of Kfar Kassem?" *Ha'ir* (Hebrew weekly newspaper, Tel Aviv), 10 October 1986, p. 10.

7. "Campaign to Bring Khmer Rouge to Trial," *Internet on the Holocaust and*

Genocide 10 (June 1987): 1; "Legal Charges of Genocide Versus Lynch," *Internet on the Holocaust and Genocide* 24 (January 1990): 2.

8. Israel W. Charny, *How Can We Commit the Unthinkable?: Genocide, the Human Cancer* (Boulder, CO: Westview Press, 1982; paperback, with title change: *Genocide, the Human Cancer: How Can We Commit the Unthinkable?*, New York: Wm. Morrow Co. [Hearst Professional Books, 1983]); Charny, *Toward the Understanding and Prevention of Genocide;* Israel W. Charny, ed., *Genocide: A Critical Bibliographic Review, Volume 1* (London: Mansell Publishing Ltd.; New York: Facts on File, 1988).

9. See Barbara Harff, "Humanitarian Intervention," 146–53; David Kader, "Progress and Limitations in Basic Genocide Law," 141–45; and Barbara Harff and David Kader, "Bibliography of Law and Genocide," 154–72, all in Charny, *Genocide: A Critical Bibliographic Review, Volume 2.*

10. Irving Louis Horowitz, *Taking Lives: Genocide and State Power*, 3d ed. (New Brunswick, NJ: Transaction Books, 1980 [first edition, 1976]).

11. Lyman H. Letgers, "The Soviet Gulag: Is It Genocide?" in Charny, *Toward the Understanding and Prevention of Genocide*, 60–66; James E. Mace, "Genocide in the U.S.S.R.," in Charny, *Genocide: A Critical Bibliographic Review,* 116–36.

12. David Hawk, "Pol Pot's Cambodia: Was it Genocide?" in Charny, *Toward the Understanding and Prevention of Genocide*, 51–59; David Hawk, "The Cambodian Genocide," in Charny, *Genocide: A Critical Bibliographic Review,* 137–54.

13. Israel W. Charny, "How to Avoid (Legally) Conviction for Crimes of Genocide: A One-Act Reading," in *Genocide: Issues, Approaches, Resources,* ed. Samuel Totten, special issue of *Social Science Record* 24, no. 2 (1987): 89–93.

14. Raphael Lemkin, unpublished papers. With permission of the Rare Books and Manuscripts Division, the New York Public Library, Astor, Lenox, and Tilden Foundations.

15. Ben Whitaker, UN Economic and Social Council, Commission on Human Rights, *Revised and Updated Report on the Question of the Prevention and Punishment of the Crime of Genocide,* UN Doc. E/CN.4/Sub.2/1985/6 (1985).

16. "Fears of Khmer Rouge in Cambodia Mount," *Internet on the Holocaust and Genocide* 18 (December 1988): 1–2; "In Cambodia It Can Happen Again," *Internet on the Holocaust and Genocide* 23 (November 1989): 4.

17. "Special Section on the Genocide of the Kurds," *Internet on the Holocaust and Genocide* 32 (April 1991): 1–2, 11–12.

18. Richard G. Hovannisian, "The Armenian Genocide," in Charny, *Genocide: A Critical Bibliographic Review,* 89–115; Roger Smith, "Denial of the Armenian Genocide," in Charny, *Genocide: A Bibliographic Review, Volume 2,* 63–85.

19. Leo Kuper, "An Agonizing Issue: The Alienation of the Unique," *Internet on the Holocaust and Genocide* 27 (June 1990), special supplement, 2 pp.

20. Erich Kulka, "Denial of the Holocaust," in Charny, *Genocide: A Critical Bibliographic Review, Volume 2,* 38–62.

21. Arthur R. Butz, *The Hoax of the Twentieth Century* (Richmond, Surrey, England: Historical Review Press, 1975).

22. Israel W. Charny and Shamai Davidson, eds., *The Book of the International Conference on the Holocaust and Genocide: The Conference Program and Crisis* (Tel Aviv: Institute of the International Conference on the Holocaust and Genocide, 1983); Terrence Des Pres, "On Governing Narratives," *Yale Review* (Summer 1986).

23. "Government Opposition to Armenian Genocide Bill Provokes Widespread Protest in Israel," *Internet on the Holocaust and Genocide* 23 (November 1989): 2.

24. Pieter N. Drost, *The Crime of State*, vol. 2, *Genocide* (Leyden: A. W. Sythoff, 1959), 122–23.

25. Israel W. Charny, "Genocide: The Ultimate Human Rights Problem," *Social Education*, 49, no. 6 (1985): 448–52.

26. John L. P. Thompson, "Genocide as Boundary-Crossing Behavior," *Internet on the Holocaust and Genocide*, special issue, 21 (June 1989): 1–9.

27. Israel W. Charny, "To Commit or Not Commit to Human Life: Children of Victims and Victimizers—All," *Contemporary Family Therapy*, 12, no. 5 (1990): 407–26.

28. Israel W. Charny, "Fiction: Intergalactic Council for Protection of Ethnic and Planetary Human Rights and the Prevention of Genocide," *Internet on the Holocaust and Genocide*, 25–26 (April 1990): 13–14.

29. Leo Kuper, "Other Selected Cases of Genocide and Genocidal Massacres: Types of Genocide," in Charny, *Genocide: A Critical Bibliographic Review*, 155–71.

30. "Sri Lanka Soldiers Slaughter Tamil Villagers," *Haaretz* (Tel Aviv daily newspaper), 21 August 1984; see also "More Killing in Sri Lanka," *New York Times*, 19 August 1984.

31. "China Gives Contemporary Example of Government Denial of Genocidal Massacre," *Internet on the Holocaust and Genocide* 22 (September 1989): 1.

32. John Somerville, "Omnicide: The New Face of Genocide," in Charny and Davidson, *The Book of the International Conference on the Holocaust and Genocide*, 244.

33. Jason W. Clay, "Genocide in the Age of Enlightenment," *Cultural Survival Quarterly* 12, no. 3 (1989): 1.

34. Richard Arens, ed., *Genocide in Paraguay* (Philadelphia: Temple University Press, 1976).

35. Michael Berenbaum, ed., *A Mosaic of Victims: Non-Jews Persecuted and Murdered by the Nazis* (New York: New York University Press, 1990).

36. Anatol Rapoport, personal communication (1991); Rapoport, *The Origins of Violence* (New York: Paragon House, 1989) and "Preparation for Nuclear War: The Final Madness," *American Journal Orthopsychiatry* 54 (1984): 524–29.

37. Robert Peter Gale, *Final Warning: The Legacy of Chernobyl* (New York: Wayne Communications, 1988).

38. George Kent, "'The Children's Holocaust,'" a special report, *Internet on the Holocaust and Genocide*, 28 (September, 1990): 3–6.

39. J. B. Rudnyckyj, "Linguicide: Concept and Definition," in Charny, *Toward the Understanding and Prevention of Genocide*, 217–19.

40. Frank Chalk and Kurt Jonassohn, *The History and Sociology of Genocide: Analyses and Case Studies* (New Haven, CT: Yale University Press, 1990); Helen Fein, "Genocide: A Sociological Perspective," *Current Sociology* 38, no. 1 (Spring 1990). (Repr. Beverly Hills, CA: Sage Publications, 1993).

41. Helen Fein, "Scenarios of Genocide: Models of Genocide and Critical Responses," in Charny, *Toward the Understanding and Prevention of Genocide*, 3–31.

Genocide, Terror, Life Integrity, and War Crimes: The Case for Discrimination

Helen Fein

Since genocide is widely conceived of as the most reprehensible of crimes, many people use genocide-labeling both to vent outrage and to describe situations in which they perceive themselves as threatened, regardless of how these situations have come about, the source of threat, the truth of accusation against the putative perpetrator, and so on. Their reasoning seems to be: if this is awful, it must be genocide. Such labeling draws attention to causes of putative victims and stigmatizes opponents and social policies. Jack Nusan Porter observed in 1982 that

genocide has been applied to all of the following: "race mixing" (integration of blacks and non-blacks); drug distribution; methadone programs; and the practice of birth control and abortions among Third World people; sterilization and "Mississippi appendectomies" (tubal ligations and hysterectomies); medical treatment of Catholics; and the closing of synagogues in the Soviet Union.[1]

The wave of misuse and rhetorical abuse parallels the alphabet: abortion, bisexuality, cocaine addiction, and dieting have also been labeled as examples of genocide—as well as suburbanization. At times such labeling verges on the paranoid and incendiary, as when Westerners or Jews are accused of genocide by giving Africans or African-Americans AIDS.

Thus we study, work, and act in a public arena in which the term "genocide" has been so debased by semantic stretch that its use stirs suspicion. Virtually everything but genocide, as Raphael Lemkin first defined it—"the destruction of a nation or of an ethnic group"—is called genocide![2]

My aim is to retrieve genocide as a usable concept for social-scientific discourse in order (1) to understand genocides that have occurred, and (2) to anticipate and deter those that might occur. The latter goal replaces the more positivistic social-scientific formula of prediction and control, for we cannot "predict" future cases in which our action—and especially our inaction—is a critical factor. And we cannot "control" multi-actor situations in historical flux as we can experimental situations. Leo Kuper reminds us that human rights activists and non-governmental organizations start out as powerless in comparison to states that control the means of violence.[3]

In order to retrieve genocide as a usable concept, we need (1) a clear definition relating it to law and social theory, and (2) a conception of how genocide is related to other causes of mass deaths, such as gross violations of human rights and war crimes.

Definition and Discontent: Approaches and Critiques

The definition of genocide in international law is that of Article II of the United Nations Genocide Convention:

In the present Convention, genocide means any of the following acts committed with intent to destroy, in whole or in part, a national, ethical, racial or religious group, as such:
(a) Killing members of the group;
(b) Causing serious bodily or mental harm to members of the group;
(c) Deliberately inflicting on the group conditions of life calculated to bring about its physical destruction in whole or in part;
(d) Imposing measures intended to prevent births within the group;
(e) Forcibly transferring children of the group to another group.

Although the litany of acts specified include biological destruction (killing and causing conditions leading to physical destruction and preventing births coercively) and indirect sociobiological destruction ("forcibly transferring children of the group to another group"), most scholars of genocide use the presence of a significant part of the group or the number or percent killed as the sole operational index of genocide. Lemkin viewed (b), (c), and (d) as steps toward (a) in most instances of genocide.[4]

There are many problems with the Convention: the principal one, in my view, is its unenforceability, as the perpetrator of genocide, the state, is responsible for its prosecution. There has been much criticism of the Convention's definition because of (1) the exclusion of political groups and social classes as victims; and (2) the ambiguity of "intent to destroy [a] . . . group, as such."[5]

Taking account of the variety of human groups (sexual groups, social classes, political and other subcultures) and the universalistic aims of Lemkin, I have attempted to generalize sociologically from the UN definition, in order to embrace all nonviolent collectivities who have or may become victims. My definition (with corresponding terms of the Convention in brackets):

Genocide is sustained purposeful action by a perpetrator to physically destroy a collectivity directly [Article II (a–c)] or through interdiction of the biological [Article II (d)] and social reproduction of group members [Article 2e].[6]

Another major criticism of the Convention is the difficulty of demonstrating "intent to destroy [a] . . . group, as such." After thinking about this for many years and reviewing the legal charges made (which could have led to indictments had there been the political will) against the Soviet Union in Afghanistan and against the Khmer Rouge in Cambodia,[7] I am now convinced one can demonstrate intent by showing a pattern of purposeful action, constructing a plausible prima facie case for genocide in terms of the Convention.[8] The critics who dwell on the difficulty of establishing such intent often do not understand the difference between intent and motive. Intent, Reisman and Norchi argue, is demonstrated on prima facie grounds by deliberate or repeated (criminal) acts—acts violating laws of war and of peace—with foreseeable results, leading to the destruction of a significant part of the Afghan people, regardless of the political motives behind that intent.[9]

The sociological concept of purposeful action (used in my definition) is the bridge paralleling the legal concept of intent in the Genocide Convention: this lies between legal guilt (a judicial act) and the perpetrator's "motive" or rather, the perpetrator's social accounting for its action. To examine whether a purported series of events is a case of genocide or not, I proposed a paradigm to detect and trace genocide, including the following necessary conditions (explicated in detail in the paradigm):

1. There was a sustained attack or continuity of attacks by the perpetrator to physically destroy group members;
2. The perpetrator was a collective or organized actor [usually the state] or commander of organized actors;
3. The victims were selected because they were members of the collectivity;
4. The victims were defenseless or were killed regardless of whether they surrendered or resisted; and
5. The destruction of group members was undertaken with intent to kill and murder was sanctioned by the perpetrator.[10]

Genocide, Morton Winston noted,[11] is intrinsically a "fuzzy concept": its exact borders are unclear and there are both overlapping and marginal phenomena. The definitions we adapt imply different borders between genocide and state terror or repression (in legal terms, gross violations of human rights) and genocide, mass killing in war, and war crimes.

Just as the study of genocide has been ignored or marginal in sociology, the study of terror and repression has until recently been barely admitted in political science, which constructed an antiseptic, neutralized state based on "governance without blood."[12] The connection between genocide and terror is not just that they have been overlooked, but that (1) both have led to mass death, and (2) they often are produced by the same states since terrorist states are often genocidal states. The difference between the two is the victims: victims of terror are selected because they are believed to have committed "subversive" acts or they are chosen arbitrarily rather than as members of a group as are victims of genocide.

Unfortunately, many comparisons of state victimization are solely quantitative comparisons that ignore how and why victims were chosen and the percent of the population at risk victimized. When we compare victims of totalitarian states, the Soviet Union's "democide" from 1917 to 1987, estimated by Rummel at about 61,911,000 victims, exceeds that of Nazi Germany during this century.[13] However, Rummel devises this concept ("democide") because he does not discriminate victims of terror from victims of genocide: his total comprises people killed by execution, deportations, labor camps, and famine, some of whom were selected individually and some as members of a collectivity. Later work by Rummel shows that Nazi democide rates in occupied Europe and in Germany exceeded the rate of the Soviet Union on an annual basis; Nazi genocide rates for Jews, Gypsies, and Slavs are many times higher than democide rates, especially for Jews.[14] From 90 to almost 100 percent of Jews became victims in seven of eight states in the zone of complete SS domination.[15]

Genocide comparisons and comparisons of genocide and mass terror often have scarcely veiled political implications in the "real world." A debate among German historians erupted after Nolte misused such a comparison, relating the victims of Auschwitz to those of the Gulag, thereby clouding the question of the German origin of and guilt for Nazi Germany's "Final Solution of the Jewish Question," which led to the murder of five to six million European Jews.[16] The value of distinctions, Maier concludes, is not to rank state terrorists and those who commit genocide but to "save" the concepts:

Raymond Aron was able to preserve the difference without excusing either regime: "Of course, I do not ignore the fact that Stalin probably massacred more people as enemies of the revolution than Hitler did in the name of the purity of the race. . . . Hostility based on the class struggle has taken on no less extreme or monstrous forms than that based on the incompatibility of races. But if we wish to 'save the concepts' there is a difference between a philosophy whose logic is monstrous and one which can be given a monstrous interpretation." It is indeed crucial to "save the concepts."[17]

Some definitions of genocide, such as that of Chalk and Jonassohn, ignore the need for such distinctions by embracing all victims of the state: "*Genocide* is a form of one-sided mass killing in which a state or other authority intends to destroy a group, as that group and membership in it are defined by the perpetrator."[18]

Their "groups" include those constructed by the paranoid imagination of despots—Stalin's "wreckers." This makes genocide coextensive with mass terror; if the dictator labels a victim a member of an imaginary group or conspiracy, all enemies of the state become group members. By enlarging the concept, they may have lost the specific causes and consequences of destroying real collectivities as opposed to mass intimidation and atomization resulting from terror.

Although the borderlines between genocide and "democide" in the Soviet Union are unclear, we do have case studies of the destruction of nations that fit the Convention definition of genocide: the Ukrainians in 1932–33 decimated by man-made famine,[19] and the deportations of suspect people during and after World War II in conditions that caused almost half to die.[20]

Harff and Gurr have delineated another resolution to this problem, discriminating victims of "genocide" from those of "politicide": communal or group victims are distinguished from real and alleged political opponents, including those in rebellion.[21] Almost half their cases are mixed, indicating that these are not exclusive entities, that motives for genocide are often retributive, and that these are "fuzzy concepts."

Another focus of disagreement is the inclusion by some of civilian casualties of wartime bombardments as victims of genocide. Leo Kuper has never defined genocide, claiming that he is using the Convention definition, but has labeled as genocide such mass killings as occurred at Hiroshima and Nagasaki, Dresden and Vietnam.[22] Here, I believe, he has conflated the question of war crimes and genocide without examining the pattern of destruction and the selection of victims. The concept of "total war," the failure to regulate nuclear and other weapons of mass destruction, and the use of terror-bombing in World War II provoke serious problems of reconciling even just wars with intrinsically unjust means.[23] But putting such events in the same class as genocide risks merging phenomena with different causes, leading to body counts that ignore the cause of death. It is first the "intent to destroy . . . a . . . group, as such," leading to the purposeful collection of Jews throughout occupied Europe for gassing, which discriminates the victims of Auschwitz from the victims of the atomic blasts of Hiroshima and Nagasaki and the firebombing of Dresden. Charny goes beyond Kuper in omitting intent as a criterion in his definition, criticizing my (previously cited) definition as follows:

> Yet I am also uncomfortable that her definition is used to exclude a number of classes of mass murders. . . . I apply the word *genocide* to *all* situations where masses of human beings are led to their deaths at the willful hands of others for whatever intended and unintended reasons, and through whatever intentional or less intentional programs and means of destruction. . . . I do disagree and resent the painstaking efforts to exclude any number of categories of mass deaths at the hands of man from the universe of genocide, as if the most severe cases of intended mass destruction will suffer a loss of significance when we admit other types of events into the definitional frame. Ultimately, I trust that Helen Fein also feels and believes that all unnecessary human deaths are an abomination, but she does argue her way into assigning hierarchical value to different kinds of mass death.[24]

For Charny, genocide is not a concept but first and last a moral judgment. He uses genocide (as do many partisans) as a generic label for all kinds of deaths that should not have occurred—whether caused by war (adhering to the war convention) or war crimes, industrial or nuclear accident, environmental degradation, or demographic influx of settlers. Some may also put cigarette and auto manufacturers into the category of what Charny calls "genociders"—purveyors of mass death.

Charny argues that my distinction among crimes and between crimes, accidents, and defense strategies is amoral. Distinctions, he infers, imply exclusivity and hierarchical assignment of superior value to some groups of victims and indifference to others.

First, his last inference is completely unwarranted, for my distinctions are not based on any valuation of the victim. Second, I maintain that discrimination of crimes and events is necessary and both scientifically and morally justified. I regard social science in this area which does not lead to productive insights as not only time-wasting but morally unjustified. Without clear and delimited concepts, one cannot arrive at clear explanations. If we aggregated all cases of mass death—from war, genocide, migrations, and slavery—together, we would probably reach rather banal and very general conclusions.

Charny believes that what some call gross violations of human rights—"mass murders such as of sundry political opponents"—should be included under genocide. I consider these as life integrity violations: the right to life and to be free from bodily violation are primary life integrity rights. Examples of violations of these include mass killing and massacre, selective killings and extrajudicial executions, and torture and rape. Genocide is the maximal escalation of such violation, taking the lives of all or many members of groups who offer no threat. But not all life integrity violations result in genocide. This point demands some explication.

The Concept of Life Integrity and Its Violations

Life integrity is a concept identifying a class of rights not previously clearly delineated in controversies about human rights.[25] Understanding the prevalence of human rights and wrongs (or their violation) is often confounded by different presuppositions and divisions. Some question the basis and universality of the concept of rights. Many debate priorities among human rights, assuming there are but two classes: political and civil rights, aspects of freedom or democracy, and social and economic rights, aspects of equity or just distribution.

I begin from a different approach, without judgment on the underlying philosophic justifications for rights. Rights are regarded sociologically as expressions of human need—which means all humans can enjoy them—and as claims successfully wrested by peoples (rules with sanctions, norms governing expectations). These claims tend to expand as previously won rights are exercised.

However, both international law and common experience suggest that one needs to secure some claims before others: the right to life, to be free from violation of the body, and to the integrity of the person, family, and group. The right to life is basic in both domestic and international law—indeed "all other human rights become meaningless if the basic right to life is not duly protected."[26]

The right to life is not an absolute right in international law; neither capital punishment nor war is categorically outlawed by any international covenant.[27] But respect for the right to life is obligatory in times of war and peace. Both homicide and genocide are now general crimes in domestic and international law.

Linked to the right to be are other rights implying the claim to be let alone: the right to be not violated, to be free from arbitrary fear, to be the owner of one's body and labor, to be mobile, and to be part of a family. Foremost among these is the right to be free from invasion of one's body and mind through torture, rape and sexual abuse, and humiliating punishments. Freedom from fear of arbitrary arrest is also

TABLE 4. Life Integrity Rights and Their Violations.

Rights	Violations	International Law Against Violation/Date in Force
1. The right to life	Genocide*; mass killing; summary/extrajudicial executions; "disappearances"	UN Genocide Convention, 1951; UDHR** 3; ICPR** 6
2. The right to personal inviolability/not to be hurt	Torture; rape and sexual abuse; inhuman and degrading treatment and punishment	UN Torture Convention, 1987; UDHR 5; ICPR 7
3. The right to be free from fear of arbitrary seizure, detention, and punishment	No due process or any process; arbitrary detention; lack of fair trial	UDHR 3; ICPR 9
4. The right to own one's body and labor	Slavery; forced labor; debt slavery, and equivalent institutions	Slavery Convention, 1927; Supplementary Convention, 1957; Convention Concerning Abolition of Forced Labour, 1959
5. The right to free movement without discrimination	Group macro-segregation (apartheid); microsegregation; group detention; and forced resettlement	Convention on the Suppression and Punishment of the Crime of Apartheid, 1976; International Convention on the Elimination of All Forms of Racial Discrimination, 1969; ICPR 9, 13
6. The right to create and cohabit with family	No marriage or family formation permitted; kidnapping and adoption or involuntary transfer of children*	UDHR 3; ICPR 9

*Besides mass killing, genocide also may include (1) murder through starvation and poisoning of air, water, or food, and (2) the involuntary transfer of children when such practices are directed against a national, ethnic, religious, or racial group with intent to destroy the group.

**Reference is to articles of the following: UDHR—Universal Declaration of Human Rights (not a convention), 1948; ICPR—International Covenant on Civil and Political Rights, 1976.

basic to enjoying other rights. There is general agreement (see cove-nants in Table 4) among people as to the value of being free rather than being owned, of being able to move without discrimination, and of living as part of a family and community from which one derives identity and meaning.

Violations of many of these rights (noted in Table 4) are criminalized in international law and the domestic law of many states. Four of the six rights are subjects of special conventions; listed in the order of their passage, the outlawed practices are slavery, genocide, racial discrimina-tion and apartheid, and torture.

At times these practices have been labeled violations of physical or legal integrity or of the integrity of the person; at other times they have been termed gross violations of human rights, basic human rights, or non-derogable rights. In 1977, U.S. Secretary of State Vance discrimi-nated civil and political rights and "the right to the fulfillment of . . . vital needs" from "the right to be free from governmental violations of the integrity of the persons."[28] His examples included torture; cruel, inhuman, or degrading treatment or punishment; and arbitrary arrest or imprisonment.

I label the violations of the rights specified in Table 4 as *life integrity violations* because they imply an integrated set of claims defending the biological and social integration of persons and groups: of body and mind among all humans (denied by genocide, murder, and torture); of self-ownership, mobility, and social dignity (denied by slavery, segrega-tion, and apartheid); of self and family (denied by prohibiting mar-riage and family development); and of the reciprocal guarantees for protection of human groups (denied by genocide). How these rights are related to civil and political rights and to social and economic rights is a question that demands empirical inquiry; indexing life integrity rights separately will enable researchers to probe this.

This concept was operationalized to index violations in fifty states in 1987 and reported in *Lives at Risk*.[29] In this study, I developed indexes and a scale to assess the scope and victims of violation, differentiating B (BAD) states, which practice torture, from C (CALCULATED KILL-ING) states, which kill selected victims because of their imputed acts, from D (DISASTER/DANGER) states, which show a pattern of mass killing (usually of members of collectivities) and which might become states of E (EPIDEMIC GENOCIDE)—fortunately not found in 1987.

Calculated killing and organized state murders frequently precede genocide. Nazi Germany is a prime example of this. The categorical murders of defective Aryan children and elders in Germany in 1939, mistakenly called "euthanasia" by many writers, became a "prototype for future mass extermination" that was justified by the same ultimate goal as was "the final solution of the Jewish question"—creating a race "of pure blood."[30] Unlike genocide, these murders were intended to improve, not to destroy, the Aryan race. Murders they remain: murders authorized voluntarily by German doctors and psychiatrists— not self-selected Nazis. To understand how the later genocides occurred, one must understand these earlier state-sanctioned individual murders. This illustrates that we must and can relate crimes without conflating them.

Nuclear Weapons, Mass Destruction, and Genocide

Both Kuper and Charny argue that saturation bombing and nuclear, chemical, and biological weapons are intrinsically means of genocide because they kill part of another national group indiscriminately. This position cannot simply be rejected out of hand but needs to be critically assessed so as to clarify debate.

Genocide has been accomplished throughout history by all kinds of weapons, including Iron Age tools. Yet it is clear that some weapons pose a greater threat against civilians than others. Because of their indiscriminate nature, the use of chemical and biological weapons is already illegal, and the threat of their use is a criminal threat. However, my brief review of international law and historical examples of use persuade me that whether the use of a weapon is a war crime or a crime against humanity or is licit depends not only on the weapon but on the context of its use.

Characterizations of nuclear or atomic bombing as genocidal imply two contexts: future related or hypothetical uses and past use. If we are considering hypothetical uses of nuclear weapons, there has been extensive legal commentary on whether they are ever licit or whether their use is categorically illegal under international laws of war and a possible violation of the Genocide Convention.[31] It involves many questions, including the legitimacy of tactical use of nuclear weapons, the use of nuclear threat as a deterrent, and retaliation to first strikes. Many (including myself) view MAD (mutual assured destruction) strategy as collective suicide. Whether one regards nuclear weapons as means of genocide, omnicide, or suicide, one cannot evade judgment on the legitimacy of their use, of defense against their use, and of nuclear threats.

Boxing Victims and Denying Genocide

If the question is judgment on past uses of atomic arms, I disagree with the genocide-labelers. To equate Hiroshima with Auschwitz belies the distinctive ends and design of each plan and their distinctive effects. It ignores all evidence that the atomic bombings of World War II were considered means to end that war. Many now believe that this was a mistaken and unnecessary strategy; some (including me) view it as a war crime. But certainly it was not—like genocide—"sustained regardless of the surrender or lack of threat offered by the victim" (one of my criteria), unless we completely disassociate the Japanese state from Japanese society.

Further, such feckless comparison may have unintended malign implications which will undermine any future study of genocide, relativizing its victims into obscurity. By ignoring the context and intent of the carpet bombing and atomic bombing of World War II and equating both with genocide, we come dangerously close to accepting the argument of neo-Nazi apologists and right- and left-wing extremists that nothing (that is, no gas chambers) or nothing special happened in Auschwitz. And after all, they may argue, if both sides committed genocide (equating Dresden and Hiroshima with Treblinka and Auschwitz), why was just one perpetrator punished?

Confusing these events would reduce recognition that the causes of the genocides occurring during two world wars in this century, the Turkish genocide of the Armenians in World War I and the Nazi genocides in World War II, were distinct from that of civilian casualties of war. This would nicely complement the work of the apologists for the Turkish and German perpetrators who consistently try to confuse and conflate the number of victims of genocide with the number of war dead.[32]

A Concluding Note

Definition hones our critical faculties and focuses our attention on a set of cases; it need not obscure our attention to related events. Genocides, states of terror, and states of violation of life integrity often overlap in time in the same place, as they are usually products of the same perpetrators. My concern as a social scientist is what I can usefully do to track and scale the atrocities violating life integrity. These may result in genocide but also result in many other deaths, maiming, numbing, and degradation. Disappearance, arbitrary murders, and torture are pervasive around the globe and unacceptable—indeed an abomination. The research agenda I propose, integrating detection of potential genocide and other life integrity violations, implies a responsibility to all victims and makes a case for early intervention to stop such practices and deter escalation. We do not help victims of any of these violations by labeling them with a superblanket of generalized compassion as certified victims of "genocide."

Notes

1. Jack Nusan Porter, "Introduction," in *Genocide and Human Rights: A Global Anthology,* ed. Jack Nusan Porter (Washington, DC: University Press of America, 1982), 9–10.

2. Raphael Lemkin, *Axis Rule in Occupied Europe* (Washington, DC: Carnegie Endowment, 1944), 79.

3. Leo Kuper, "Reflections on the Prevention of Genocide," in *Genocide Watch,* ed. Helen Fein (New Haven, CT: Yale University Press, 1992).

4. Lemkin, *Axis Rule,* 81–88.

5. On this question, see Frank Chalk and Kurt Jonassohn, *The History and Sociology of Genocide: Analyses and Case Studies* (New Haven, CT: Yale University Press, 1990); Leo Kuper, *Genocide: Its Political Use in the Twentieth Century* (New Haven, CT: Yale University Press, 1981); Isidor Walliman and Michael Dobkowski, eds., *Genocide and the Modern Age* (New York: Greenwood Press, 1987); Henry Huttenbach, "Locating the Holocaust on the Genocide Spectrum," *Holocaust and Genocide Studies* 3, no. 3 (1988): 298–304; John L. Thompson and Gail A. Quets, "Genocide and Social Conflict: A Partial Theory and Comparison," in *Research in Social Movements, Conflict and Change,* ed. Louis Kriesberg (Greenwood, CT: JAI Press, 1990); and Ben Whitaker, UN Economic and Social Council, Commission on Human Rights, *Revised and Updated Report on the Question of the Prevention and Punishment of the Crime of Genocide,* UN Doc. E/CN.4/Sub.2/1985/6 (1985). These sources are reviewed and the controversy assessed in Helen Fein, *Genocide: A Sociological Perspective* (London: Sage Publications, 1993): 8–31.

6. Fein, *Genocide: A Sociological Perspective,* 24.

7. W. Michael Reisman and Charles H. Norchi, "Genocide and the Soviet Occupation of Afghanistan," *Institute for the Study of Genocide Newsletter,* 1 (Spring 1988), 4; and Hurst Hannum and David Hawk, *The Case Against the Standing Committee of the Communist Party of Kampuchea* (New York: Cambodia Documentation Commission, 1986).

8. Fein, *Genocide: A Sociological Perspective,* 19–20.

9. Reisman and Norchi, "Genocide and the Soviet Occupation of Afghanistan," 10.

10. Fein, *Genocide: A Sociological Perspective,* 25–30.

11. Comment made in a session on definition of genocide at the conference convened by the Institute for the Study of Genocide, Genocide Watch, John Jay College for Criminal Justice, New York City, 22–23 May 1989.

12. John F. McCamant, "Governance without Blood: Social Science's Antiseptic View of Rule," in *The State as Terrorist: The Dynamics of Government Violence and Repression,* ed. M. Stohl and G. Lopez (Westport, CT: Greenwood Press, 1984).

13. R. J. Rummel, *Lethal Politics: Soviet Genocide and Mass Murder Since 1917* (New Brunswick, NJ: Transaction Books, 1990).

14. R. J. Rummel, "Power Kills: Absolute Power Kills Absolutely," *Internet on the Holocaust and Genocide* 38 (June 1992): 4.

15. Helen Fein, *Accounting for Genocide: National Responses and Jewish Victimization During the Holocaust* (New York: Free Press, 1979), 52–53.

16. Ernest Nolte, "Between Myth and Revisionism? The Third Reich in the Perspective of the 1980s," in *Aspects of the Third Reich,* ed. H. W. Koch (New York: St. Martin's Press, 1985); and Charles S. Maier, *The Unmasterable Past:*

History, Holocaust and German National Identity (Cambridge, MA: Harvard University Press, 1988).

17. Raymond Aron, *Clausewitz* (New York: Simon and Schuster, 1986), 369, cited by Maier, *The Unmasterable Past*, 78.

18. Chalk and Jonassohn, *The History and Sociology of Genocide*, 23.

19. Commission on the Ukraine Famine, *Report to Congress* (Washington, DC: USGPO, 1988); and Robert Conquest, *The Harvest of Sorrow: Soviet Collectivization and the Terror-Famine* (New York: Oxford University Press, 1986).

20. Robert Conquest, *The Nation-Killers: The Soviet Deportation of Nationalities* (New York: Macmillan, 1970); and A. M. Nekrich, *The Punished Peoples: The Deportation and Fate of Soviet Minorities at the End of the Second World War* (New York: Norton, 1978).

21. Barbara Harff and Ted Gurr, "Toward Empirical Theory of Genocides and Politicides: Identification and Measurement of Cases since 1945," *International Studies Quarterly* 37, 3 (1988): 359–71.

22. Kuper, *Genocide: Its Political Use in the Twentieth Century*, 14, 17, 34–35, 45–46, 50, 55, 91–92, 102–39.

23. Michael Walzer, *Just and Unjust Wars* (New York: Basic Books, 1977).

24. See Israel Charny's review of Helen Fein's "Genocide: A Sociological Perspective" (which appeared in *Current Sociology*, 38, no. 1 [Spring 1990], repr. Sage Publications 1993), in *Internet on the Holocaust and Genocide*, nos. 30–31 (February 1991): 5–6.

25. Helen Fein, *Lives at Risk: A Study of Violations of Life-Integrity in 50 States in 1987 Based on the Amnesty International 1988 Report* (New York: Institute for the Study of Genocide, March 1990), 5–6.

26. C. Van Aggelen, "Review: The Right to Live in International Law," *American Journal of International Law* 80 (1986): 743.

27. Paul Sieghart, *The International Law of Human Rights* (Oxford: Clarendon Press, 1983), 130–31.

28. Cyrus Vance, "Law Day Speech on Human Rights and Foreign Policy [1977]" in *The Human Rights Reader*, ed. Walter Laquer and Barry Rubin (New York: New American Library, 1990), 344.

29. Fein, *Lives at Risk*, 7–27.

30. Fein, *Accounting for Genocide*, 26.

31. Nagendra Singh and Edward McWhinney, *Nuclear Weapons and Contemporary International Law*, 2d rev. ed. (Dordrecht: Martinus Nijhoff, 1989).

32. Helen Fein, "Political Functions of Genocide Comparisons," *Remembering for the Future*, vol. 3 (Oxford: Pergamon Press, 1982), 2427–41.

Part II
The Reality of Genocide

Etiology and Sequelae of the Armenian Genocide

Richard G. Hovannisian

The Armenian Genocide of 1915 was the supremely violent historical moment that removed a people from its homeland and wiped away most of the tangible evidence of its three thousand years of material and spiritual culture. The calamity, which was unprecedented in scope and effect, may be viewed as a part of the incessant Armenian struggle for survival and the culmination of the persecution and pogroms that began in the 1890s, or it may be placed in the context of the great upheavals that brought about the disintegration of the multiethnic and multireligious Ottoman Empire and the emergence of a Turkish nation-state founded on a monoethnic and monoreligious society. The Turkish government, dominated by the Committee of Union and Progress or the Young Turk party, came to regard the Armenians as alien and a major obstruction to the fulfillment of its political, ideological, and social goals. Its ferocious repudiation of plural society resulted in a single society, as the destruction of the Armenians was followed by the expulsion of the Greek population of Asia Minor and the suppression of the non-Turkish Muslim elements to effect their turkification and assimilation. The method adopted to transform Ottoman plural society to Turkish single society was genocide.[1]

Mass killings and "little wars" under the cover of major conflicts did not begin with the Armenian Genocide. Civilian populations have fallen victim to the brutality of invading armies, bombing raids, lethal substances, and other forms of indiscriminate killing. In the Armenian case, however, the Turkish government openly discarded the obligation to defend its citizenry and instead turned all its might against one segment of the population. In international law there were certain rules and customs of war that were intended to protect in some measure noncombatant, civilian populations, but these regulations did not cover domestic situations or a government's mistreatment of its own people. Only after the Holocaust during World War II was that aspect included in the United Nations Convention on the Prevention and Punishment of the Crime of Genocide. Nonetheless, at the time of the Armenian deportations and massacres, many governments termed the atrocities as crimes against humanity and made public their intent to hold the Turkish government individually and collectively accountable.[2]

There has been much political and scholarly debate on the precise definition of the term genocide and the compromise wording that was incorporated into the Genocide Convention.[3] Some have found the United Nations definition ambiguous and open to such broad interpretation as to allow for the inclusion of nearly all cases of persecution. There is a tendency on the part of groups that have been victimized, especially Jews and Armenians, to insist on a narrow definition in order to prevent the dilution or trivialization of their own suffering.[4] Many human rights activists, on the other hand, find the United Nations definition too restrictive, especially as it excludes political and social groups from the questionable protection afforded by the Genocide Convention.[5] According to that document, genocide means the "intent to destroy, in whole or in part, a national, ethnical, racial or religious group, as such" in any one of the following ways:

(a) Killing members of the group;
(b) Causing serious bodily or mental harm to members of the group;
(c) Deliberately inflicting on the group conditions of life calculated to bring about its physical destruction in whole or in part;
(d) Imposing measures intended to prevent births within the group;
(e) Forcibly transferring children of the group to another group.[6]

What is compelling in the Armenian case is that the victims were subjected to each and every one of the five categories. Such drastic and absolute methods underscore not only the premeditated intent of the violence, but also the single-minded determination of the perpetrators to expunge the Armenians from a new Turkish society.

Scholars have begun to categorize the characteristics of genocide and the circumstances under which it is more likely to occur. Applied to the Armenian experience, these include the existence of a plural society with clearly defined racial, religious, and cultural differences; a sense of deprivation or danger felt by the dominant, perpetrator group; the relative social and economic upward mobility of the victim group; the espousal and propagation by the perpetrators of an ideology or belief system emphasizing the nobility and righteousness of its own group as opposed to the alien, exploitative nature of the intended victims; the determination to establish a new regional order and in that process eliminate elements posing real, potential, or perceived threats to achieving that goal; the mobilization of the state machinery and the military establishment for measures against the victims; and the seizure and retention of the material wealth and resources of the dispossessed population. In the Ottoman Empire, government and party merged as the Young Turk dictatorship created the *Teshkilati Mahsusa* ("Special Organization") to supervise the extirpation of the Armenians. Killer battalions were organized, and in every significant town and city party functionaries were at work to ensure the execution of directives and to remove weakhearted and recalcitrant officials. Young Turk officers were assigned to critical command posts to assist in implementing the grand design. Moreover, even in a country as undeveloped as Turkey in 1915, the use of technological advances such as the telegraph allowed for unprecedented coordination in the genocidal process. The intended victims didn't stand a chance and were doomed from the start.[7]

The Ghost of the Past

The Armenian Genocide began in 1915 and culminated in the flight or expulsion in 1921–22 of the survivors who after the war had returned to the region of Cilicia. The Armenians had been violently and irreversibly separated from their lands and cultural-religious foundations of many centuries. The social, political, economic, cultural, and religious infrastructure was completely demolished, leaving the bewildered survivors scattered around the world in alien surroundings and without the means of rapid recovery. For the rest of the twentieth century, their collective energies were concentrated on the building of a new infrastructure in the countries of the Middle East and with less success in Europe and the Western Hemisphere, where the opportunities for social and economic mobility were counterbalanced by the processes of rapid acculturation and assimilation. A source of hope during these difficult decades was the existence of Soviet Armenia, the smallest of the constituent republics of the Soviet Union.

While most of the historic Armenian territories had fallen within the Ottoman Empire, the easternmost sector had been included in Persia and then in the nineteenth century in the Russian Empire. From this division had evolved the terms Russian (Eastern) Armenia and Turkish (Western) Armenia. The destruction of Turkish Armenia during World War I imperiled Russian Armenia, which also figured in the grand designs of the Young Turk dictators. Amid the turmoil created by the

Russian revolutions in 1917 and the Turkish invasion in 1918, the Russian Armenians tried to salvage whatever possible by declaring the independence of the Republic of Armenia around the city of Erevan. Thousands of Turkish Armenian refugees crammed into the small state, where subsequently a large percentage of them perished as the result of starvation, epidemics, and exposure. Nonetheless, the little state, which was confined to less than half of Russian Armenia, managed to endure until the end of the World War.[8]

Armenians the world over celebrated the defeat of the German and Ottoman empires in November 1918, believing that the time of reckoning had finally arrived, that the victorious Allied Powers would punish the perpetrators of the genocide, repatriate and rehabilitate the survivors, and establish and lend assistance to a united Armenia encompassing both the western and eastern sectors of historic Armenia. Although the Allied Powers finally created such a state on paper in the Treaty of Sèvres in August 1920, they were unwilling to commit the armed forces necessary to remove the Turkish divisions from Turkish Armenia. On the contrary, they stood by and watched helplessly as the revitalized Turkish Nationalist armies of Mustafa Kemal even invaded and put an end to the small Russian Armenian republic. Placed between an inescapable vise formed by the Turkish armies in the southwest and the Soviet Red Army in the northeast, the Armenian government had to cede half of Russian Armenia to Nationalist Turkey and save the rest of the country by relinquishing power and acquiescing in the proclamation of Soviet rule.[9] The strategies of the Turkish Nationalists furthered the Young Turk objective of creating a single, homogeneous society. The choice of Ankara as the Nationalist capital symbolized Mustafa Kemal's repudiation of the plural society represented by European, cosmopolitan Constantinople.

From 1921 onward, the only part of historic Armenia that still bore that name was the Soviet republic of about 12,000 square miles. With all its limitations and problems, that small state alone provided for the uninterrupted flow of Armenian life. National culture was allowed to develop within limits imposed by the Soviet system. Between 1920 and 1990, the population of Soviet Armenia grew from barely one million to three million, while the worldwide Armenian population increased to between six and seven million, at last replenishing itself and reaching its 1914 pregenocide level. It took the Armenians two generations simply to recover, while the rest of the world was experiencing a population explosion.[10]

In the aftermath of the genocide the survivors and succeeding generations suffered from the psychological and emotional trauma caused by the calamity, world indifference, and Turkish attempts to deny or rationalize the crime. Yet the event had passed, and there did not appear to be any real danger of renewed massacres, except perhaps in the minds of those who had been so severely affected that they suffered from paranoia or other disorders. However great the oppressive policies and shortcomings of the Soviet system, Armenia was protected by the armies and resources of the mighty Soviet Union, and the people could live without serious fear of Turkish invasion or interethnic violence in Soviet Georgia and Soviet Azerbaijan, each with approximately half a million Armenian inhabitants. Armenians were disgruntled that Armenian-populated Mountainous Karabagh, which was adjacent to Soviet Armenia, had been awarded to Azerbaijan, and they repeatedly petitioned for the return of that highland district, but these measures did not affect the Soviet control mechanism throughout Transcaucasia, and life remained relatively secure and predictable.[11]

The trade-off by which Armenia gave up much of its freedom, including the right to seek redress and world recognition of the Armenian Genocide in exchange for the protection afforded by the Soviet Union, changed abruptly in 1988. Genocide was no longer a haunting, terrible memory but a living reality. In the early part of that year, the Armenians of Mountainous Karabagh and of Soviet Armenia took General Secretary Mikhail Gorbachev's program of *glasnost* and *perestroika* seriously, as they did his declarations that the time had come to rectify past errors of the Stalin era. For the Armenians a cardinal crime of Stalin (and Lenin if he could have been named then) was the award of Karabagh to Azerbaijan. When the population and local government organs of the Mountainous Karabagh Autonomous Region petitioned for the right of self-determination and incorporation into Soviet Armenia, hundreds of thousands of people in Erevan and elsewhere in Armenia took to the streets in support of the Karabagh movement. The massive demonstrations were unprecedented in the Soviet Union and captured headlines in the broadcast and print media around the world. A wave of optimism engulfed the Armenians both inside the Soviet Union and in the diaspora. Dormant Armenian communities in Russia began to stir, and the Armenians abroad rallied to the cause. Spirits were high and the mood was festive, as it seemed that for once in the twentieth century the continuous process of dimunition of the living space of the Armenians might be reversed, since the proposed shift of boundaries could be affected as an internal Soviet affair.

Armenian optimism was dampened at the end of February 1988, by the outbreak of anti-Armenian violence in the Azerbaijani industrial city of Sumgait. The indiscriminate, brutal torture and killing, the mutilation and rape, the looting and burning sent shock waves into Armenian communities far and near. The terms "massacre," "po-

grom," and even "genocide" became current, and immediate, spontaneous associations with 1915 were made everywhere. The Azerbaijanis, related by race, language, and culture to the Turks, became in
Armenian minds the same vicious and heartless people who had perpetrated the genocide in 1915, and the victims of Sumgait were simply
the most recent martyrs exacted from the nation since antiquity and
especially since the Turanic domination of Armenia. Seventy years of
Soviet mythology about the resolution and elimination of nationality
problems and the friendship and brotherhood of all Soviet peoples
dissolved in a single instant, and the traumatized Armenians came face
to face with the ghost of the past.[12]

What was most disconcerting in the aftermath of the Sumgait po-
grom was the failure of the central authorities to take swift, decisive
action to apprehend and punish the perpetrators. Gorbachev may not
have wished to jeopardize his image as a reformer who had repudiated
the use of force, and there were those who accused the central government of resorting to the old imperial formula of divide and rule. It was
inconceivable that massacres could occur in the Soviet Union without
the complicity or tacit assent of the mechanisms of control. In any
event, the inaction of the center exacerbated Armenian-Azerbaijani
tensions, the raids and attacks along the frontier between the neighboring republics, and the Azerbaijani economic stranglehold on Armenia,
which received 80 percent of its food supplies and other goods over the
railroads that passed through Azerbaijan. Once again, the forced starvation of hundreds of thousands of Armenians in 1915 became a living
experience for the blockaded people of Mountainous Karabagh and
Armenia.[13]

The conflict intensified in the fall of 1988, as the Armenians of
Kirovabad and the surrounding countryside were driven from their
homes and forced to seek haven in Armenia, while the frightened
Azerbaijani minority in Armenia fled eastward into Azerbaijan. Still
greater violence erupted in Baku in January 1990, catching by surprise
the 200,000 Armenians of the cosmopolitan Azerbaijani capital, which
was believed to be relatively secure. The ferocity of the riot knew no
limits, as women were bound together and set ablaze, throats were slit,
and the worst forms of mutilation that often characterize interracial
and interreligious conflicts were fully manifested. Most of the Armenian minority in Azerbaijan abandoned home and business and fled
with only the clothes on their backs to Armenia and many other parts
of the Soviet Union. Even the forces of nature seemed to conspire with
the perpetrators, as a massive earthquake in December 1988 devastated a third of Armenia, leaving 500,000 people homeless and claim-

ing as many as 50,000 lives. Man and nature, it was said, had joined to deprive the Armenians of stability, prosperity, peace, and justice.[14]

The Karabagh crisis and subsequent developments in the Caucasus and the entire Soviet Union reveal much about the transgenerational psychological impact of genocide. In the best of circumstances, the trauma persists for decades, even for generations, and manifests itself in unexpected ways. The trauma is clearly compounded when the perpetrators are left unpunished, when there are no acts of contrition or indemnification, and when external society or governments find it inexpedient to join in remembrance. With the interethnic strife, the pronounced anti-Semitism, and the increasing sense of deprivation in the former Soviet Union, the Armenian experience must give us pause. Historical memory forcefully shapes contemporary outlook. The past is present.

A Plural Society

The Armenians are an ancient people who inhabited the highland region between the Black, Caspian, and Mediterranean seas for several millennia. They are noted in Greek and Persian sources as early as the sixth century B.C., and they existed as a people and coalescing state long before that time. On a strategic crossroad between East and West, Armenia was sometimes independent under its native dynasties, sometimes autonomous under princes who paid tribute to external powers, and sometimes subjected to direct foreign rule. The Armenians were among the first nations to adopt Christianity, and they developed a distinct national-religious culture that kept them apart from their more powerful neighbors.[15]

Most of the territories that had formed the ancient and medieval Armenian kingdoms were incorporated into the Ottoman Empire in the sixteenth century. The Armenians were thus drawn into a multi-ethnic and multireligious society, but as a Christian minority in a Turkish-dominated Muslim realm they had to endure second-class citizenship, including the imposition of special taxes and levies, the inadmissibility of their testimony against true believers, and the prohibition against bearing arms. The Ottoman administrative structure was founded on unequal relationships sanctioned by Islamic legal and judicial precepts and customs. The Christians, as tolerated nonbelievers (*dhimmis*), were permitted to practice their religion in return for special obligations and acceptance of their inferior status. The structural inequalities in the Ottoman administrative system were institutionalized through the formal separation of Ottoman society into confessional-based Muslim, Jewish, Greek Orthodox, and Armenian *millets*. All Armenian Christians were born into and remained within the Armenian millet unless an individual opted to convert to Islam. The Armenian patriarch of Constantinople, as the head of the Armenian millet, had jurisdiction over the religious and civil affairs of his flock and, as a part of the sultan's administrative apparatus, was responsible for his people, the fulfillment of all their duties, and their behavior in a manner befitting *dhimmis*.[16]

The millet system allowed the Armenians to retain their cultural-religious identity in a plural society, but it rendered them powerless politically and militarily. Over the centuries, ruler and ruled—Muslim, Christian, and Jew—became accustomed to their stations in life and the accepted norms of behavior that allowed for a modus vivendi rooted in legal inequality. Some Armenians converted to Islam to find relief from the disabilities and sporadic persecution, but most held tenaciously to their faith and fulfilled the obligations of second-class citizenship. Many Armenians sought security and prosperity in the coastal cities or in Constantinople (Istanbul), where they became merchants, traders, artisans, interpreters, and professionals. The great majority, however, never left their homes on the great Armenian plateau, there descending into the status of tenant farmers and sharecroppers under a dominant Turkish and Kurdish Muslim feudal class.

So long as the Armenians fit into the mold of a plural, unequal society, so long as they performed their duties and endured the harshness of life, they posed no threat and were allowed to exist in something of a symbiotic relationship with the dominant Muslim millet. But in the eighteenth and nineteenth centuries the framework of the Ottoman Empire was seriously undermined by external challenges and internal unrest. Unable any longer to compete economically or militarily with the West, the sultans lost province after province and became hopelessly mired in debt. The resulting corruption and breakdown of law and order produced widespread revolts in the Balkan provinces and cracked the foundations of traditional Ottoman plural society.

The decline and decay of the Ottoman Empire were paralleled by cultural revival and emancipatory movements among several subject nationalities. The egalitarian principles inspired by the French Revolution ran counter to the institutionalized inequality of the Ottoman administrative system and culminated in violent upheavals in the Balkan peninsula. By the end of the nineteenth century, the Greeks, Romanians, Serbians, and Montenegrins, supported by one or more European power, had secured their independence from Turkish dominion, whereas Bulgaria had gained autonomy and would assert its complete independence in 1908.

The increasing threats to the continued existence of the Ottoman Empire forced the sultans to attempt reform measures to halt the process of deterioration. Encouraged and coerced by Great Britain and other powers, the sultans entered a period of restructuring that marked a radical departure from the traditional sociopolitical hierarchy. In the decrees of the so-called *tanzimat* period (1839–76), the sultans declared the theoretical equality of all Ottoman subjects. For traditionalists, these reforms constituted an attack upon their privileged status and on the interrelationship between true believers and infidels. In fact, however, the reforms did not bring equality to the distant Armenian provinces but only accelerated the breakdown of law and order by weakening the system of minimal protection that characterized feudal or semifeudal societies. Moreover, while the *tanzimat* reforms proclaimed the equality of Ottoman subjects before the law, they did not eliminate the confessional millet structure and the implicit inequality therein.[17]

Unlike the Balkan Christians, the Armenians were concentrated on the great plateau in eastern Asia Minor and no longer constituted a majority in many parts of their historic homeland. Many thousands of Armenian merchants, craftsmen, artisans, and professionals lived in Constantinople, Smyrna, and all the major towns and cities along the seacoasts and in Asia Minor proper (Anatolia). Under these circumstances the Armenian cultural and political revival of the nineteenth century did not develop into a program for independence or separation from the empire. Instead, it focused on reforms to guarantee the security of life and property and on the concept of Ottomanism, by which the obligations and privileges of citizenship were common and shared by all. There were Turkish intellectuals, too, who held the view that the Ottoman Empire could escape doom only through egalitarianism and constitutionalism, the underpinnings of Europe's strength and success. It was such sincere reformers who framed the Ottoman constitution which Sultan Abdul-Hamid promulgated for all the wrong reasons in 1876.[18]

Abdul-Hamid II (1876–1909) proclaimed the liberal constitution to ward off renewed European intervention on behalf of the Balkan Christians. Then, shortly after declaring war on Russia in 1877, the sultan suspended the constitution and prorogued the parliament that had just convened. His military and diplomatic defeat in the war led to the loss of most of the Balkan provinces and drew the European powers collectively into the "Armenian Question." During the war, Russian armies had occupied a part of the Armenian plateau and were prepared to remain there until reforms had been implemented to safeguard Armenian life and property from Kurdish tribesmen and other predators. As Great Britain and the other European powers were instrumental in forcing the Russian armies to withdraw from the region, they agreed to act collectively to ensure that the sultan honored his pledge to institute effective reforms that would eliminate Armenian grievances.[19]

The diplomatic intercession of the European powers in the absence of any real show of force only compounded Armenian troubles. Nor were the attempts of some Armenians to resist tyranny by organizing guerrilla bands and revolutionary societies effective in matching the power and control mechanisms of the state. Nonetheless, in their quest for security and equality, the Armenians posed one more challenge to the customary relationships of traditional society and as such came to be regarded as disloyal and dangerous.[20] Abdul-Hamid armed Kurdish brigands and gave them a semiofficial status in his determination to crush the incipient Armenian movement. The brutal suppression of an Armenian uprising in Sassun against Kurdish irregulars and Turkish tax collectors in 1894 led to renewed European pressure for reforms. Although Abdul-Hamid was coerced into issuing a compromise edict in the fall of 1895, his real response to external meddling was to unleash pogroms in nearly every province inhabited by Armenians. Within a year more than 100,000 Armenians lay dead, thousands more had fled into exile, and hundreds of towns and villages had been looted and burned or forced to convert to Islam.[21]

Lord Kinross, who has studied and written extensively about Turkey, describes the systematic nature of the pogroms:

Each operation, between the bugle calls, followed a similar pattern. First into a town there came the Turkish troops, for the purpose of massacre; then came the Kurdish irregulars and tribesmen for the purpose of plunder. Finally came the holocaust, by fire and destruction, which spread, with the pursuit of the fugitives and mopping-up operations, throughout the lands and villages of the surrounding provinces. This murderous winter of 1895 thus saw the decimation of much of the Armenian population and the devastation of their property in some twenty districts of eastern Turkey. Often the massacres were timed for a Friday, when the Moslems were in their mosques and the myth was spread by the authorities that the Armenians conspired to slaughter them at prayer. Instead they themselves were slaughtered, when the Moslems emerged to forestall their design.[22]

Upon analysis, it may be concluded that Abdul-Hamid's use of looting and massacre was a desperate attempt to preserve the status quo and his crumbling autocratic regime. His agents had little difficulty arousing the elements that were threatened by the Armenian demands for equality, self-government, and even the right to bear arms. Looting, burning, and murder, it was believed, were justified by the sedition and economic exploitation of the Armenians. Popular participation in the carnage was enhanced by the knowledge that no one would be held to account.

Abdul-Hamid differed radically from his Young Turk successors. He still needed the dues and services of the Armenians, and, although wishing to teach them a good lesson to stay in their place and turn away from Europe, the sultan did not conceive of their total eradication. What the Young Turks had in common with Abdul-Hamid was their reliance on violent methods, only on a much greater scale. The strategy of the Young Turks, however, was not to maintain the status quo but rather to bring about fundamental and far-reaching changes and to create an entirely new frame of reference in which the Armenians did not figure at all. Pogroms in the first instance were intended to preserve the old order, whereas genocide in the second instance was perpetrated to destroy the old order and its plural society and to replace it with a single, homogeneous society made up of and for the benefit of Turkey and the Turks.

The Young Turk Dictatorship

The Armenians were deeply disillusioned after the calamities of 1894–96, yet there seemed to be a glimmer of hope in the fact that various other groups, including liberal Turks committed to the concept of Ottomanism, were organizing against Abdul-Hamid's tyranny. Armenian intellectuals and political leaders were particularly attracted to the program of administrative decentralization and federalism as advocated by one of the sultan's alienated nephews. The Young Turks or Committee of Union and Progress did not hold a single view of how to resolve the monumental problems of the Ottoman Empire, but they were by and large European-educated and firm advocates of the constitutional system of government. In an unexpected series of events in 1908, Young Turk officers and sympathizers, in danger of imminent exposure and arrest, brought about a near bloodless coup, compelling Abdul-Hamid to reinstate the constitution of 1876 and relinquish most of his powers to serve as a figurative constitutional monarch. The Armenians hailed the Young Turk victory and collaborated enthusiastically with the new leaders of the Ottoman Empire. They participated in the parliamentary elections, engaged in legalized political activities, and for the first time gave their sons to serve in defense of the common Ottoman homeland.[23]

One of the most unexpected and, for the Armenians, most tragic developments was the transformation of the seemingly liberal, egalitarian Young Turks into xenophobic chauvinists bent on creating a new order and eliminating the Armenian presence. European exploitation of Turkish weaknesses after the 1908 revolution and the loss of more Ottoman territory in the Balkans contributed to the ascendancy of the radical, centralizing wing of the Young Turk movement. Already in 1909 some 20,000 to 30,000 Armenians were massacred in Adana and throughout the region of Cilicia. The Young Turk leaders blamed the reactionary forces loyal to Abdul-Hamid and deposed the sultan, but there were strong indications that supporters of the Young Turks had themselves participated in the bloodshed and looting.[24]

The Cilician massacres should have been an object lesson to the Armenians. Some of their leaders had taken the constitutional liberties at face value and immediately began to organize public rallies, demonstrations, and processions. They gave free flight to their fantasies in print and proclaimed without circumspection the end of the traditional relationships imposed by the *ancien régime*. In reality, as experienced by blacks in the United States and other minorities in reforming states, the promulgation of egalitarian legislation did not guarantee immediate implementation. Theory and practice are very different, and in the case of the Armenians and others enforcement of the law lagged far behind its issuance.

The crisis created by the attempted countercoup of Abdul-Hamid's traditionalist supporters in 1909 prompted the Young Turk government to declare a state of siege and suspend constitutional rights for several years. It was during this period that the concepts of "Turkism" and exclusive nationalism completely captivated the Young Turk extremists, who began to envisage a new, homogeneous state expanding as far as the Turkic homelands in Central Asia in place of the existing discredited, enervated, and exploited multiethnic conglomeration and its malfunctioning plural society.[25] In another coup at the beginning of 1913, the ultranationalists seized control from the liberals and from then until the end of World War I in 1918 dominated the Ottoman government under the leadership of a triumvirate composed of Minister of War Enver, Minister of Interior Talaat, and Minister of the Marine, and subsequently military governor of Syria, Jemal. They all espoused the ideology of Turkism and the goals of Pan-Turkism as expounded by Zia Gökalp and other ideologues. Dedication to God and sultan was replaced by devotion to the collective entity of Turkism. As reflected in the words of Gökalp, the nation was supreme:

I am a soldier; it is my commander
I obey without question all its orders
With closed eyes I carry out my duty.[26]

The victory of the Pan-Turkists eliminated the possibility of continued coexistence on the platform of Ottoman liberalism. The centralized dictatorship now possessed an ideology that made any and all actions acceptable for the sake of the amorphous nation of Turan. It sought the means and awaited the time to transform multinational Ottomanism into exclusive Turkism. Drawing upon the German military model as the blueprint for success, the Young Turks resolved to eliminate those elements that would not fit into the Turanic program.[27] Not only were the Armenians alien by culture and religion, but their historic lands lay in the middle of the projected Turkic realm. Their upward mobility and their avid absorption of Western education and ideas made them all the more dangerous. The Young Turk strategy was to bring the Ottoman Empire into the European war as an ally of Imperial Germany against Russia in exchange for the right to invade Transcaucasia and Central Asia and liberate the Turanic heartland.

The outbreak of World War I in the summer of 1914 deeply alarmed the Armenians. If the Ottoman Empire entered the conflict on the side of Germany, the Armenian plateau would become the inevitable theater of another Russo-Turkish war. Since the Armenian homelands lay on both sides of the frontier, the Armenians would suffer severely no matter who might eventually win the war. For these reasons, Armenian spokesmen implored the Young Turk leaders to maintain neutrality and spare the empire from certain disaster. What the Armenians did not know was that Enver and his cohorts had already sealed a secret military alliance with Imperial Germany and were preparing for the invasion of the Caucasus.[28] The Ottoman Empire's entry into the world conflict as a member of the Central Powers voided the last chance to solve the Armenian Question through administrative reforms. The time had come for Turkism to supplant Ottomanism and to give justifiable purpose to the unlimited violence necessary to create a homogeneous state and society. In *Accounting for Genocide,* Helen Fein has concluded:

The victims of twentieth-century premeditated genocide—the Jews, the Gypsies, the Armenians—were murdered in order to fulfill the state's design for a new order. . . . War was used in both cases . . . to transform the nation to correspond to the ruling elite's formula by eliminating the groups conceived of as alien, enemies by definition.[29]

The Genocidal Process

If there still was any hope for the Armenians, that vanished with the humiliating failure of Enver Pasha to conquer Transcaucasia at the

beginning of 1915. His one hundred thousand-man army was decimated by blizzards raging over the Armenian plateau, and his optimis-
tic confidence that his forces would soon join with the indigenous
Muslim population of the Caucasus and Central Asia against Russia
was buried with the mounds in the snow that marked where his men
had frozen. Such a staggering blow required an explanation—a scapegoat: the Armenians. And when the Allies tried to knock Turkey out of
the war by landing an expeditionary force at Gallipoli in the ill-fated
strategy to capture the Straits and Constantinople, the threat of internal subversion seemed to loom even greater.[30]

On the night of 23–24 April 1915, Armenian political, religious,
educational, and intellectual leaders in Constantinople were arrested,
deported to Anatolia, and put to death. Then in May, after mass
deportations had already begun, Minister of Interior Talaat, claiming
that the Armenians were disloyal, could offer aid and comfort to the
enemy, and were in a state of imminent rebellion, ordered ex post facto
their deportation from the war zones to relocation centers—actually
the deserts of Syria and Mesopotamia. The Armenians were driven
out, not only from areas near war zones but from the length and
breadth of the empire, except Constantinople and Smyrna, where
numerous foreign diplomats and merchants were located. Sometimes
Armenian Catholics and Protestants were exempted from the deportation decrees, only to follow once the majority belonging to the Armenian Apostolic Church had been dispatched. Secrecy, surprise, and
deception were all a part of the process.[31]

The whole of Asia Minor was put in motion. Armenians serving in
the Ottoman armies had already been segregated into unarmed labor
battalions and were now taken out in batches and murdered. Of the
remaining population, the adult and teenage males were, in most
instances, swiftly separated from the deportation caravans and killed
outright under the direction of Young Turk agents, the gendarmerie,
and bandit and tribal groups prepared for the operation. The greatest
torment was reserved for the women and children, who were driven
for months over mountains and deserts, often dehumanized by being
stripped naked and repeatedly preyed upon and abused. Intentionally
deprived of food and water, they fell by the thousands and the hundreds of thousands along the routes to the desert. In this manner an
entire nation was swept away, and the Armenian people were effectively eliminated from their homeland of several millennia. Of the
refugee survivors scattered throughout the Arab provinces and the
Caucasus, thousands more were to die of starvation, epidemics, and
exposure, and even the memory of the nation was intended for obliteration, as churches and cultural monuments were desecrated and

small children, snatched from their parents, were renamed and given out to be raised as non-Armenians and non-Christians.[32]

One paragraph from a report of the Italian consul general at Trebizond typifies the hundreds of chilling accounts by foreign officials and eyewitnesses:

The passing of the gangs of Armenian exiles beneath the windows and before the door of the Consulate; their prayers for help, when neither I nor any other could do anything to answer them; the city in a state of siege, guarded at every point by 15,000 troops in complete war equipment, by thousands of police agents, by bands of volunteers and by the members of the "Committee of Union and Progress"; the lamentations, the tears, the abandonments, the imprecations, the many suicides, the instantaneous deaths from sheer terror, the sudden unhinging of men's reason, the conflagrations, the shooting of victims in the city, the ruthless searches through the houses and in the countryside; the hundreds of corpses found every day along the exile road; the young women converted by force to Islam or exiled like the rest; the children torn away from their families or from the Christian schools, and handed over by force to Moslem families, or else placed by hundreds on board ship in nothing but their shirts, and then capsized and drowned in the Black Sea and the River Deyirmen Dere—these are my last ineffaceable memories of Trebizond, memories which still, at a month's distance, torment my soul and almost drive me frantic.[33]

Estimates of the Armenian dead vary from 600,000 to 2,000,000. A United Nations Human Rights subcommission report in 1985 gives the figure of "at least one million."[34] The important point in understanding a tragedy of such magnitude is not the exact and precise count of the number who died—that will never be known—but the fact that more than half the Armenian population perished and the rest were forcibly driven from their ancestral homeland. Another important point is that what befell the Armenians was by the will of the government. While a large segment of the general population participated in the looting and massacres, many Muslim leaders were shocked by what was happening, and thousands of Armenian women and children were rescued and sheltered by compassionate individual Turks, Kurds, and Arabs.[35]

The decimation of the Armenian people and the destruction of millions of persons in Central and Eastern Europe during the Nazi regime a quarter of a century later had particular and unique features. However, historians and sociologists who have pioneered the field of victimology have drawn some striking parallels. The similarities include the perpetration of genocide under the cover of a major international conflict, thus minimizing the possibility of external intervention; conception of the plan by a monolithic and xenophobic clique; espousal of an ideology giving purpose and justification to racism, exclusivism, and intolerance toward elements resisting or deemed unworthy of assimilation; imposition of strict party discipline and secrecy during the period of preparation; formation of extralegal special armed forces to ensure the rigorous execution of the operation; provocation of public hostility toward the victim group and ascribing to it the very excesses to which it would be subjected; certainty of the vulnerability of the targeted group (demonstrated in the Armenian case by the previous massacres of 1894–96 and 1909); exploitation of advances in mechanization and communication to achieve unprecedented means for control, coordination, and thoroughness; and the use of sanctions such as promotions and the incentive to loot or, conversely, the dismissal and punishment of reluctant officials and the intimidation of persons who might consider harboring members of the victim group.[36]

The Sequelae

The defeat of the Ottoman Empire and its allies at the end of 1918 raised the possibility of enacting the numerous pledges concerning the punishment of the perpetrators and the rehabilitation of the Armenian survivors. After the Young Turk dictators had fled the country, the new Turkish grand vizier admitted that they had committed such misdeeds "as to make the conscience of mankind shudder forever."[37] United States General James G. Harbord, following an inspection tour of the former Armenian population centers in 1919, reported on the organized nature of the massacres and concluded: "Mutilation, violation, torture and death have left their haunting memories in a hundred beautiful Armenian valleys, and the traveler in that region is seldom free from the evidence of this most colossal crime of all the ages."[38] The Paris Peace Conference declared that the lands of Armenia would never be returned to Turkish rule, and a Turkish military court-martial tried and sentenced to death *in absentia* Enver, Talaat, Jemal, and Nazim, notorious organizers of the genocide. No attempt was made to carry out the sentence, however, and thousands of other culprits were neither tried nor even removed from office. Within a few months the judicial proceedings were suspended, and even accused and imprisoned war criminals were freed and sent home.[39]

The release of the perpetrators of genocide signaled a major shift in the political winds. The former Allied Powers, having become bitter rivals over the spoils of war, failed to act in unison in the imposition of peace or in dealing with the stiff resistance of a Turkish nationalist movement. They concurred that the Armenians should be freed and rehabilitated but took no effective measures to achieve that objective.

They hoped that the United States would extend a protectorate over the devastated Armenian regions, but the United States was recoiling from its involvement in the World War and turning its back on the League of Nations. Unable to quell the Turkish nationalist movement, which rejected the award of any territory for an Armenian state or even unrestricted return of the Armenian refugees, the Allied Powers agreed to a drastic revision of the unratified Treaty of Sèvres and made their peace with the new Turkey. The Treaty of Lausanne in 1923 made no provision for the rehabilitation, restitution, or compensation of the Armenian survivors. Western abandonment of the Armenians was so complete that the revised peace treaty included no mention whatsoever of "Armenians" or "Armenia." It was as if the Armenians had never existed in the Ottoman Empire.[40] In Turkey, Armenian place-names were changed, and Armenian cultural monuments were obliterated or allowed to fall into disrepair. Attempts to eliminate the memory of Armenia included change of the geographical expression "Armenian plateau" to "Eastern Anatolia." The plural society of the Ottoman Empire had given way to the single society of the Republic of Turkey.

The dispersed Armenian survivors concentrated their collective energies on refugee and relief resettlement and the creation of a new diaspora infrastructure of cultural, educational, and religious institutions. They knew little of and often intentionally remained aloof from the governmental processes of their host countries, some because they continued to cling to the dream of someday returning to the homeland and others because they deemed it safer for the community not to become involved in local politics and instead to maintain proper relations with whatever group was in power. Embittered by world indifference to the plight of the exiled Armenians, the diaspora communities tended to internalize their frustrations, hostility, suffering, and even creative and constructive talents.

During the two decades between World War I and World War II, the Armenians commemorated the genocide with requiem services and programs in which they read sympathetic messages from government officials and foreign religious dignitaries. Yet on substantive issues, the Armenians could not make their voice heard. A dispersed people whose only remaining land was locked within Stalin's fortress, it had neither the political nor economic means to counter the growing appreciation and admiration in the West for Mustafa Kemal and his modernizing and secularizing Republic of Turkey. The strategy of Kemal and his successors was to encourage the propagation of the new image of Turkey and to avoid public discussion of the period of the

Armenian Genocide. The strategy was aimed at biding time until the Armenian survivors had passed from the scene and their children had acculturated in their host societies.

The Turkish government used the diplomatic and economic channels available to it to prevent activities that might keep alive international memory of the Armenian tragedy. When in 1934 the movie studios of Metro-Goldwyn-Mayer bought the film rights to Franz Werfel's celebrated novel, *The Forty Days of Musa Dagh*, depicting the desperate struggle for survival of several Armenian villages near the Mediterranean Sea, the Turkish government immediately interceded with the Department of State, which in turn interceded with MGM and the Motion Picture Association of America. All efforts of the studio to compromise and satisfy Turkish objections were rejected by the Ankara government, which let it be known that production of the film would not only have a detrimental effect on Turkish-American political relations but would also force Turkey to ban the showing of American films and engage in other forms of economic retaliation. The quiet diplomatic pressure was sufficient to force MGM to shelve the project.[41]

By World War II, the Armenian Genocide had virtually become the "forgotten genocide," and it was to become even more remote as millions of new victims were claimed in the conflagration of war and the Holocaust. The Armenians continued to remember their dead, but they were alone.

It was not until 1965 that the politically fragmented Armenian diaspora drew together sufficiently for a united commemoration of the fiftieth anniversary of the Armenian Genocide. This was paralleled by the first major demonstrations in Soviet Armenia, where discussion, let alone commemoration, of the genocide had been banned by the Soviet regime since the 1920s. The Armenian world, as if spontaneously, burst into frenzied activities aimed at national and international recognition of the genocide and various forms of restitution. Native-born generations of Armenians were able to write and speak as citizens of their host countries and to begin to work the political system in order to secure commemorative resolutions, messages from high-ranking officials, participation of government officials and politicians, and erection of monuments in memory of the victims of the genocide. In Montebello, California, for example, the community drew Governor Ronald Reagan, senators, congressmen, and numerous public officials, together with the United States Marine Band and military honor guards, to the dedication of a martyrs memorial. This was a scene mirrored in other communities and countries as well.

In 1973, the unexpected occurred. An elderly survivor of the genocide assassinated two Turkish consular officers in California, setting off a series of similar acts in various countries for several years. The political violence surprised everyone, most particularly the Armenians who had played the role of exemplary citizen as they strove for acceptance. But the press coverage of the assassinations invariably included reference and description of the Armenian Genocide. This gave the Armenians the opportunity to draw attention to the unrequited wrongs of the past while at the same time distancing themselves from the violence. For the Turkish government, however, the renewed attention given the Armenian case was unwelcome. Denouncing Armenian terrorism, the Turks had to engage in a new round of denials.[42]

The consolidation of Armenian legal and political action and the manifestation of illegal political violence ripped the Turkish veil of silence and undermined the strategy of avoiding discussion of the Armenian case while enjoying the benefits of the Armenian goods and properties for which no compensation had ever been offered. During the 1970s, therefore, the Ankara government decided to face the lingering stereotypes of the Turks by engaging in a worldwide propaganda campaign not only to denounce the Armenian violence in the present but also to explain Turkish measures against the Armenians in the past in terms of protective measures against Armenian terrorism. On the one hand playing up the strategic geopolitical position of Turkey and its role in the security and defense of the West, the propagandists, on the other hand, sought to demonstrate that there had been no organized persecution of Armenians.

In this effort, the Ankara government and its agencies reprinted or translated the anti-Armenian propaganda from the period of World War I and produced crude, illogical, and transparent polemics that could be easily exposed and refuted. From these shoddy beginnings, the new wave of Turkish denial literature became increasingly sophisticated during the decade of the 1980s. This was attributable largely to the input and assistance of sympathetic or professionally hired Americans and Europeans who could write and translate with native-language fluency and who understood the accepted form and style of scholarly treatises in the West and the effect of placing the Armenian issue in a relativist and rationalizing context rather than the hitherto unsuccessful approach of absolute denial. By the end of the decade the publications had become slick and polished, inclusive of archival references, notations, and bibliographies. Western scholars and major public relations firms were incorporated into the process.[43]

At the same time, however, the Armenian diaspora continued to organize and learn the use of political processes. In the 1980s, second- and third-generation French and American Armenians took the lead in efforts to gain reaffirmation and recognition of the Armenian Genocide and to seek legal remedies to heal the festering wound. They established channels of communication with the governments and legislatures of Europe and America and interacted with human rights associations. While the Armenians were articulating their primary points of concern and making significant headway in Europe, the political environment in the United States became increasingly charged and even hostile. This was a result of the heightened activity and pressure of the Turkish government and its agencies, the emergence of Turkish associations closely aligned with the Ankara government, and successive American administrations that placed perceived security considerations above respect for the historical record.

The Narrative of Power

That mere commemorative resolutions to honor the memory of the victims of the Armenian Genocide have created crises affecting United States foreign policy in itself points to the narrative of power. The erstwhile participation of army and marine bands and honor guards has been withdrawn in order to appease the Turkish government. During a national gathering in Washington, DC, on the occasion of the seventieth anniversary of the Armenian Genocide in 1985, the organizers were allowed to hold a memorial service in Arlington National Cemetery only under the guise of a tribute to American war dead. The program was censored and closely monitored by federal authorities. As Armenian-Turkish relations became more confrontational and tense during the 1970s and especially 1980s, the United States government began to equivocate and to take precautions not to allow pro-Armenian expressions to strain Turkish-American relations to a dangerous point. The American retreat went so far that by 1982 the *Bulletin* of the Department of State wrote: "Because the historical record of the 1915 events in Asia Minor is ambiguous, the Department of State does not endorse allegations that the Turkish Government committed genocide against the Armenian people."[44] The announcement drew a sustained response from the Armenian community and from influential voices in Congress, including that of Speaker of the House Tip O'Neill, until the State Department backed down somewhat by declaring that the article in its *Bulletin* did not necessarily represent the official view of the Department.[45] Nonetheless, the damage had been done. No previous American administration had expressed doubt about the truth of the Armenian Genocide.

In the same year that the narrative of power allowed the State Department to question the Armenian Genocide, the Turkish government exerted extraordinary pressure on the Israeli government to prevent discussion of the Armenian Genocide in an international conference on the Holocaust and other genocides, to be held in Tel Aviv. The Turkish blackmail, which has been documented in detail, led to withdrawal of official sponsorship of the conference by the Israeli government, Yad Vashem Institute, and Tel Aviv University, and crippled but did not cancel the proceedings.[46] It was clear that the Turkish government had determined to go to great lengths to prevent discussion of the Armenian Genocide at any level. The scenario has since been repeated often, and sometimes the power of intimidation has been sufficient to achieve results.

In a thoughtful essay, Terrence Des Pres has written: "Governments have always required short-term memory, but never more than now. The historical record either enhances or it hinders the ongoing process of propaganda, and the Free World doesn't need ugly events to question its virtue." He adds that in the narrative of power words such as "state security" and "national interest" take on exaggerated meanings given them by the military complex and that truth becomes subordinate to a state which claims for itself the power to lead human destiny. "Truth is at best a reckless element, a sort of wild card in a deck that otherwise is tightly stacked."[47]

During the Reagan administration, commemorative resolutions were introduced in the House of Representatives in 1985 and again in 1987. The resolutions recognized 24 April as a day of man's inhumanity to man with particular reference to the Armenian Genocide. Although half of the House was supportive of the resolutions, the acts went down to defeat on procedural motions after intense debates in which several themes emerged. On the one hand, most opponents rose to speak about the NATO connection, the military connection, and the business connection, but there were also those who contested the truth of the Armenian Genocide, emphasized that there were two sides to every story, and insisted that Congress was not a place to pass judgment on historical debates and that adoption of the resolution would encourage Armenian terrorism and contribute to the destabilization of a vital ally.[48]

What was new about these arguments was their coming straight out of materials produced by the Turkish embassy, the Institute of Turkish Studies, and the Turkish-American Associations, all linked closely with Ankara. The director of the Institute of Turkish Studies in Washington was instrumental in securing the signatures of sixty-nine scholars of Turkic studies in the United States on an open letter to the House of Representatives questioning the propriety of the Congress to act on such matters, asserting that rather than a genocide it seemed that the Armenians had been the victims of "communal warfare," that history should be left to scholars, and that hopefully the Turkish archives would soon be opened to shed light on this sad period during which Armenians and Turks suffered alike.[49] Arguments not used before except by the most active of deniers were now recited in the halls of Congress. It seemed to make little difference that the sixty-nine scholars were made up overwhelmingly of individuals who had no expertise whatsoever on the subject. Des Pres has noted that the efface-ment of memory is more the achievement of an all-too-wakeful con-sciousness than it is the result of its weakness and that the fury of the deniers comes from the fact that they must talk themselves out of what everyone else knows to be true before they can try to talk others out of it. And in the narrative of power the United States Executive, with its State Department, Defense Department, and National Security Coun-cil, joined collectively to relieve an allied nation of the responsibility of facing up to its past.

After 1987 many Armenians felt that no more effort should be wasted on commemorative resolutions in Congress. This sentiment increased as the democratic movement in Soviet Armenia began to go sour and a reactive Azerbaijani nationalism drove thousands of Arme-nians out of the country and as Soviet Azerbaijan imposed an economic blockade on Armenia. Nonetheless, the Armenian Assembly of Amer-ica and the Armenian National Committee took the lead in reviving the issue through the Senate. This was preceded by a number of questions made to the two candidates for president. After the intractability of the Reagan administration, the responses of both candidates Dukakis and Bush were encouraging. With several influential Republican Armenian-Americans giving encouragement, future President George Bush responded to the questionnaire as follows:

The United States must acknowledge the attempted genocide of the Armenian people in the last years of the Ottoman Empire, based on the testimony of survivors, scholars, and indeed our own representatives at the time, if we are to insure that such horrors are not repeated. The American people, our govern-ment, and certainly the Bush Administration will never allow political pres-sures to prevent our denunciation of crimes against humanity, and I would join Congress in commemorating the victims of that period.[50]

The declaration came back to haunt the president many times in 1989–90, after Senator Robert Dole introduced a joint resolution to commemorate 24 April 1990 as the seventy-fifth anniversary of the Armenian Genocide. The wording of the resolution was chosen care-fully to note that the Armenian Genocide had taken place before the establishment of the Republic of Turkey and that the present Turkish government was therefore in no way responsible. It was perhaps significant that Senator Dole sponsored the resolution shortly after he returned from a visit with Secretary of Labor Elizabeth Dole to Soviet Armenia, where they witnessed the ravages of the massive earthquake of December 1988.

Introduction of Senate Resolution 212 in September 1989 elicited an immediate reaction from the Turkish government, which by that time had considerable experience in marshaling support in the Departments of State and Defense, the National Security Council, the business community, and certain academic circles. Scores of American businesses were warned that passage of the resolution would affect future contracts with and opportunities in Turkey, and the full weight of the aerospace industries and many other major corporations was brought to bear on the Senate.

When the Judiciary Committee voted to forward the resolution to the floor of the Senate, the Turkish reaction was swift. American aerial operations in Turkey were curtailed, and the Ankara government threatened to take more drastic action if the Senate adopted the resolution. The State Department made a show of how serious the situation was by recalling Ambassador Morton Abramowitz from Ankara for consultations. The Turkish lobbyists and their influential public relations firms intensified efforts to pressure cosponsors of the resolution to withdraw their names to avoid responsibility for results that would seriously jeopardize the security interests of the United States. These forces also got to every major corporation doing business with Turkey to make it known that the significant trade relationship between the two countries would be adversely affected.[51]

While the agencies of the executive branch and Turkish lobby worked to defeat the resolution as if it were a serious threat to Turkey's territorial and political integrity, the proponents of the resolution read a large corpus of materials into the *Congressional Record*. These included statements of Ambassador Henry Morgenthau and other American diplomatic personnel in the Ottoman Empire at the time of the genocide; the testimony of American and foreign eyewitnesses to the systematic destruction of the Armenian population; descriptions of relevant archival holdings in the United States, Great Britain, France, Italy, the Vatican, Germany, Austria, and other countries; a résumé of past resolutions and presidential statements acknowledging the Armenian Genocide; an analysis of the arguments of the deniers; an exposé of the sixty-nine scholars whose advertisement questioning the genocide was repeatedly recited by opponents of the resolution; previous statements from the Senate floor; quotations from Adolf Hitler and Mustafa Kemal regarding the genocide; the postwar trials of the chief Turkish perpetrators; excerpts of the contemporary world press during the genocide; and an analysis of arguments that minimize the number of Armenians who perished, point to the Armenian "troubles" as actually being insurrection or civil war, and equate Turkish war dead with massacres of Armenians.

The resolution was debated on the floor of the Senate between 20 and 27 February 1990.[52] Senator Robert Byrd of West Virginia gave notice that he would filibuster against the resolution and throughout the proceedings organized and led the opposition. Fearing that consideration of the resolution would in fact end with a majority in favor, the opponents chose the filibuster strategy, since a motion for cloture would require three-fifths of the Senate. Nonetheless, during the debate, pages of materials relating to the Armenian Genocide were read into the official record and supporters of the resolution struck hard on the actuality of the genocide, the moral and ethical considerations involved, and the anomaly of the United States being subjected to blackmail by an allied government. They took care not to implicate the current government of Turkey, but they pointed to its moral obligation to cease and desist from efforts to distort and deny the historical record.

The opponents led by Byrd reiterated time and again geopolitical and military considerations, the impact on business and commerce, and the impropriety of using the word "genocide" to describe the "human tragedy" that affected not only Armenians but all the unfortunate peoples caught up in the strife of World War I. The great majority of opponents professed sympathy for the Armenian suffering but insisted on the primacy of United States security and economic interests. Only Byrd and Senator Malcolm Wallop of Wyoming directly repeated the Turkish arguments of denial, rationalization, and trivialization. Several senators nonetheless did take cover behind the argument that the Ottoman archives had not yet been studied and that it was too early to determine whether or not a genocide had occurred. The White House looked for a way out of the dilemma by indicating that it would not oppose a nonbinding concurrent resolution, which would not require presidential action, but Senator Byrd rejected the compromise. Two votes on cloture of the filibuster failed to muster the required three-fifths majority, and after several days of intense debate, the matter rested. The Senate, which passes judgment every day on issues of much greater importance, tried to persuade itself that it was not competent to determine whether the Armenian people had been victimized and whether the Senate should join with the descendants of the survivors in commemorating the seventy-fifth anniversary.

In a subsequent development in April 1990, the impact of continued Armenian pressure and of his own conscience was apparently sufficient to prompt President Bush to issue a formal statement on the occasion of the seventy-fifth anniversary of the Armenian calamity. Drawing attention to the long, enduring relationship between the United States and the Armenian people, the president noted that their faith, strength, and resilience had withstood the tragic earthquake of 1988 and "most prominently, the terrible massacres suffered in 1915–23 at the hands of the rulers of the Ottoman Empire." While Bush avoided use of the term genocide, he judged the "terrible massacres" to be a "crime against humanity," and he called on all peoples to observe the seventy-fifth anniversary on 24 April as a day of remembrance "for the more than a million Armenian people who were victims."[53] It was a forceful statement that afforded solace to the Armenians and caused grave misgivings to the deniers. Had the statement been issued before or during the Senate debate, the outcome on the commemorative resolution might well have been different. Nonetheless, the Armenians expressed their gratitude to the president, urging him to take the final step by acknowledging that the "terrible massacres" and "crime against humanity" were in fact "genocide."

It is fitting to conclude with the insightful summons of Terrence Des Pres:

Milan Kundera, the exiled Czech novelist, has written that "the struggle of man against power is the struggle of memory against forgetting." This single remark, in my view, sums up the human predicament today and put the burden of responsibility exactly where it falls—on writers, and now more than ever, on scholars. . . . National catastrophes can be survived if (and perhaps only if) those to whom disaster happens can recover themselves through knowing the truth of their suffering. Great powers, on the other hand, would vanquish not only the peoples they subjugate but also the cultural mechanisms that would sustain vital memory of historical crimes. . . . When modern states make way for geopolitical power plays, they are not above removing everything—nations, cultures, homelands—in their path. Great powers regularly demolish other peoples' claims to dignity and place, and sometimes, as we know, the outcome is genocide. In a very real sense, therefore, Kundera is right; against historical crimes we fight as best we can, and a cardinal part of this engagement is "the struggle of memory against forgetting."[54]

Notes

1. For bibliographies on the Armenian Genocide, see Richard G. Hovannisian, *The Armenian Holocaust: A Bibliography Relating to the Deportations, Massacres, and Dispersion of the Armenian People, 1915–1923* (Cambridge, MA: Armenian Heritage Press, 1980). See also Richard G. Hovannisian, "The Armenian Genocide," and Vahakn N. Dadrian, "Documentation of the Armenian Genocide in Turkish Sources," in *Genocide: A Critical Bibliographic Review*, ed. Israel W. Charny, 2 vols. (London: Mansell Publishing Ltd., 1988, and New

York: Facts on File, 1988–1991), 1:89–115 [Hovannisian], 2:86–138 [Dadrian]; Hamo Vassilian, ed., *The Armenian Genocide: A Comprehensive Bibliography and Library Resource Guide* (Glendale, CA: Armenian Reference Books Co., 1992).

2. See Richard G. Hovannisian, "The Allies and Armenia, 1915–18," *Journal of Contemporary History* 3 (January 1968): 145–55.

3. See, for example, Frank Chalk and Kurt Jonassohn, *The History and Sociology of Genocide: Analyses and Case Studies* (New Haven, CT: Yale University Press, 1990), 3–53; Leo Kuper, *Genocide: Its Political Use in the Twentieth Century* (New Haven, CT: Yale University Press, 1982), 19–39; Robert F. Melson, *Revolution and Genocide: On the Origins of the Armenian Genocide and the Holocaust* (Chicago: University of Chicago Press, 1992), 22–30.

4. Melson, *Revolution and Genocide,* 33–39; Vahakn N. Dadrian, "The Convergent Aspects of the Armenian and Jewish Cases of Genocide: A Reinterpretation of the Concept of Holocaust," *Holocaust and Genocide Studies* 3, no. 2 (1988): 151–70; Pierre Papazian, "A 'Unique Uniqueness'?" *Midstream* 39, no. 4 (April 1984), 14–25; Gregory F. Goekjian, "Genocide and Historical Desire," *Semiotica* 83, no. 3/4 (1991): 211–25; Yehuda Bauer, "Is the Holocaust Explicable?" in *Remembering for the Future,* vol. 2 (Oxford: Pergamon Press, 1988), 1167–75; Michael R. Marrus, "Recent Trends in the Historicity of the Holocaust," *Holocaust and Genocide Studies* 3, no. 3 (1988): 257–65; see also Lucy S. Dawidowicz, *The Holocaust and the Historians* (Cambridge, MA: Harvard University Press, 1981).

5. See, for example, Kuper, *Genocide: Its Political Use in the Twentieth Century,* 22–39; and Chalk and Jonassohn, *The History and Sociology of Genocide,* 12–23.

6. See Appendix I. The entire text of the Convention on the Prevention and Punishment of the Crime of Genocide is also included in Kuper, *Genocide: Its Political Use in the Twentieth Century,* 210–14, and Chalk and Jonassohn, *The History and Sociology of Genocide,* 44–49.

7. See Robert Melson, "Revolutionary Genocide: On the Causes of the Armenian Genocide of 1915 and the Holocaust," *Holocaust and Genocide Studies* 4, no. 2 (1989): 161–74; Vahakn N. Dadrian, "Genocide as a Problem of National and International Law: The World War I Armenian Case and Its Contemporary Legal Ramifications," *Yale Journal of International Law* 14, no. 2 (1989): 221–334, and by the same author, "Some Determinants of Genocidal Violence in Intergroup Conflicts—With Particular Reference to the Armenian and Jewish Cases, *Sociologus* 12, no. 2 (1976): 129–49.

8. For this period, see Richard G. Hovannisian, *Armenia on the Road to Independence, 1918* (Berkeley and Los Angeles: University of California Press, 1967).

9. See Richard G. Hovannisian, *The Republic of Armenia,* vols. 1–2 (Berkeley, Los Angeles, London: University of California Press, 1971, 1982), and "Caucasian Armenia between Imperial and Soviet Rule: The Interlude of National Independence," in *Transcaucasia: Nationalism and Social Change,* ed. Ronald G. Suny (Ann Arbor, MI: Michigan Slavic Publications, 1983), 259–92.

10. See Mary Kilbourne Matossian, *The Impact of Soviet Policies in Armenia* (Leiden: E. J. Brill, 1962); Ronald Grigor Suny, *Armenia in the Twentieth Century* (Chico, CA: Scholars Press, 1983), 35–83; Claire Mouradian, *De Staline à Gorbatchev: Histoire d'une république soviétique: l'Arménie* (Paris: Editions Ramsay, 1990).

11. Christopher J. Walker, *Armenia and Karabagh* (London: Minority Rights

Publication, 1991); Gerard J. Libaridian, ed., *The Karabagh File* (Cambridge, MA: Zoryan Institute, 1988); Richard G. Hovannisian, "Nationalist Ferment in Armenia," *Freedom at Issue*, no. 105 (November–December 1988): 29–35.

12. Mouradian, *L'Arménie*, 405–64; Nora Dudwick, "The Karabagh Movement: An Old Scenario Gets Rewritten," *Armenian Review* 42, no. 3 (1989): 63–70; Samvel Shahmuratian, ed., *The Karabagh Tragedy: Pogroms against Armenians in Soviet Azerbaijan* (New Rochelle, NY: Aristide D. Caratzas, 1990).

13. See, for example, Aleksandr Miasnikian State Library, *Blokada: Khronika*, ed. H. Ts. Liloyan and others, 2 vols. (Erevan: "Luis," 1990).

14. See, for example, Yuri Rost, *Armenian Tragedy* (New York: St. Martin's Press, 1990).

15. See, for example, Sirarpie Der Nersessian, *The Armenians* (New York and Washington: Praeger, 1970); Ara Baliozian, *The Armenians: Their History & Culture* (New York: Ararat Press, 1980).

16. See Kevork B. Bardakjian, "The Rise of the Armenian Patriarchate of Constantinople," in *Christians and Jews in the Ottoman Society*, ed. Benjamin Braude and Bernard Lewis, vol. 1 (New York: Holmes and Meier Publishers, 1982), 89–100; Christopher J. Walker, *Armenia: Survival of a Nation* (New York: St. Martin's Press, 1980), 85–89.

17. Roderic H. Davison, *Reform in the Ottoman Empire, 1856–1876* (Princeton, NJ: Princeton University Press, 1963); Edouard Engelhardt, *La Turquie et le tanzimat: Ou, Histoire des réformes dans l'empire Ottoman depuis 1826 jusqu'à nos jours* (Paris: Cotillon, 1882–84), 2 vols.; Bernard Lewis, *The Emergence of Modern Turkey* (London: Oxford University Press, 1968), 73–126.

18. See A. O. Sarkissian, *History of the Armenian Question to 1885* (Urbana: University of Illinois Press, 1938); Walker, *Armenia: Survival of a Nation*, 85–108.

19. Walker, *Armenia: Survival of a Nation*, 108–25; Great Britain, Parliament, House of Commons, Sessional Papers, *Correspondence Respecting the Conference at Constantinople and the Affairs of Turkey, 1876–1877*, vol. 91, Turkey no. 2, C. 1641 (1876–77); Sessional Papers, *Further Correspondence Respecting the Affairs of Turkey*, vol. 91, Turkey no. 15, C. 1738 (1877), and vol. 92, Turkey no. 25, C. 1806 (1877). See also Sir Edwin Pears, *Life of Abdul Hamid* (London: Constable & Co., 1917), 17–123.

20. Louise Nalbandian, *The Armenian Revolutionary Movement: The Development of Armenian Political Parties through the Nineteenth Century* (Berkeley and Los Angeles: University of California Press, 1963).

21. Johannes Lepsius, *Armenia and Europe: An Indictment* (London: Hodder & Stoughton, 1897); Great Britain, Sessional Papers, vol. 109, Turkey no. 1, C. 7894, (1895); vol. 95, Turkey no. 1, C. 7923, Turkey no. 2, C. 7927, vol. 96, Turkey no. 6, C. 8108, Turkey no. 8, C. 8273 (1896); vol. 101, Turkey no. 3, C. 8305 (1897); France, Ministère des Affaires Etrangères, *Documents diplomatiques: Affaires arméniennes: Projets de réformes dans l'empire Ottoman, 1893–1897*, and *Supplément, 1895–1896* (Paris: Imprimerie Nationale, 1897); Melson, *Revolution and Genocide*, 41–69; Walker, *Armenia: Survival of a Nation*, 133–74; Pears, *Abdul Hamid*, 214–68.

22. Lord [John Patrick Douglas Balfour] Kinross, *The Ottoman Centuries: The Rise and Fall of the Turkish Empire* (New York: William Morrow, 1977), 559–60.

23. Ernest E. Ramsaur, Jr., *The Young Turks* (Princeton, NJ: Princeton University Press, 1957), 124–39; Feroz Ahmad, *The Young Turks* (Oxford: Clarendon Press, 1969), 1–13; Charles R. Buxton, *Turkey in Revolution* (London: T. F. Unwin, 1909), 55–73.

24. Walker, *Armenia: Survival of a Nation*, 182–89; Duckett Z. Ferriman, *The Young Turks and the Truth about the Holocaust at Adana in Asia Minor, during April, 1919* (London, 1913); M. Seropian, *Les Vêpres ciliciennes: Les responsabilités, faits et documents* (Alexandria: Della Roca, 1909); Georges Brèzol, *Les Turcs ont passé là: Recueil de documents sur les massacres d'Adana en 1909* (Paris: L'Auteur, 1911).

25. Ahmad, *Young Turks*, 92–120; Wilhelm Feldmann, *Kriegstage in Konstantinopel* (Strassburg: K. J. Trübner, 1913), 106–71.

26. Uriel Heyd, *Foundations of Turkish Nationalism: The Life and Teachings of Ziya Gokalp* (London: Luzac, 1950), 124. See also Robert Melson, "A Critical Inquiry into the Armenian Genocide of 1915," in *The Armenian Genocide in Perspective*, ed. Richard G. Hovannisian (New Brunswick, NJ, and Oxford: Transaction Books, 1986), 75–78.

27. See James J. Reid, "Total War, the Annihilation Ethic, and the Armenian Genocide, 1870–1918," in *The Armenian Genocide: History, Politics, Ethics*, ed. Richard G. Hovannisian (London: Macmillan; and New York: St. Martin's Press, 1992), 21–52. For the German-Turkish alliance and the question of Germany's complicity in the Armenian Genocide, see Christoph Dinkel, "German Officers and the Armenian Genocide," *Armenian Review* 44, no. 1 (1991): 77–133; Ulrich Trumpener, *Germany and the Ottoman Empire, 1914–1918* (Princeton, NJ: Princeton University Press, 1968), esp. 167–270.

28. Trumpener, *Germany and the Ottoman Empire*, 15–61; Carl Mühlmann, *Das deutsch-türkische Waffenbündnis im Weltkrieg* (Leipzig: Koehler and Amelang, 1940), 15–16; Hovannisian, *Armenia on the Road to Independence*, 40–42.

29. Helen Fein, *Accounting for Genocide* (New York: Free Press, 1979), 29–30.

30. Hovannisian, *Armenia on the Road to Independence*, 45–46; Walker, *Armenia: Survival of a Nation*, 198–200; W. E. D. Allen and Paul Muratoff, *Caucasian Battlefields* (Cambridge: Cambridge University Press, 1953), 240–84; Trumbull Higgins, *Winston Churchill and the Dardanelles* (New York: Macmillan, 1963).

31. See, for example, Great Britain, Parliament, *The Treatment of the Armenians in the Ottoman Empire: Documents Presented to Viscount Grey of Fallodon, Secretary of State for Foreign Affairs*, pref. Viscount James Bryce (London: Sir Joseph Causton and Sons, 1916); Leo Kuper, "The Turkish Genocide of Armenians, 1915–1917," in Hovannisian, *The Armenian Genocide in Perspective*, 43–59; Walker, *Armenia: Survival of a Nation*, 200–240.

32. For firsthand accounts relating to the women and children, see Donald E. Miller and Lorna Touryan Miller, "Women and Children of the Armenian Genocide," in Hovannisian, *The Armenian Genocide: History, Politics, Ethics*, 152–72, and for the reports of American missionaries, see, in the same volume, Suzanne Elizabeth Moranian, "Bearing Witness: The Missionary Archives as Evidence of the Armenian Genocide," 103–28.

33. *Treatment of the Armenians in the Ottoman Empire*, 291–92.

34. United Nations, ECOSOC, Commission on Human Rights, Sub-Commission on Prevention of Discrimination and Protection of Minorities (38th sess.), UN Doc. E/CN.4/sub.2/1985/SR.36 (1985) (Item 57) at 7.

35. See Richard G. Hovannisian, "The Question of Altruism during the Armenian Genocide of 1915," in *Embracing the Other: Philosophical, Psychological, and Historical Perspectives on Altruism*, ed. Pearl M. Oliner, Samuel P. Oliner, and others (New York: New York University Press, 1992), 282–305.

36. Vahakn N. Dadrian, "The Structural-Functional Components of Genocide," in *Victimology*, ed. I. Drakpin and E. Viano, 3 (Lexington, MA: D. C. Heath, 1974): 123–35, and "The Common Features of the Armenian and

Jewish Cases of Genocide," 4 (1975): 99–120; Chalk and Jonassohn, *The History and Sociology of Genocide*, 27–32. See also Kuper, *Genocide: Its Political Use in the Twentieth Century*, 40–100 passim.

37. U.S. Department of State, *Papers Relating to the Foreign Relations of the United States, 1919: The Paris Peace Conference*, 4 (Washington, DC: Government Printing Office, 1943), 509.

38. U.S. Congress, *Conditions in the Near East: Report of the American Military Mission to Armenia*, prepared by General James G. Harbord, 66th Cong., 2d sess., Senate Doc. 266 (Washington, DC: Government Printing Office, 1920), 7.

39. Melson, *Revolution and Genocide*, 148–52; and the following studies of Vahakn N. Dadrian: "The Documentation of the World War I Armenian Massacres in the Proceedings of the Turkish Military Tribunal," *International Journal of Middle East Studies* 23, no. 4 (1991): 549–76; "A Textual Analysis of the Key Indictment of the Turkish Military Tribunal Investigating the Armenian Genocide," *Armenian Review* 44, no. 1 (1991): 1–36; "Genocide as a Problem of National and International Law," 281–310. The transcripts of the trials were printed in supplements of the Istanbul journal *Tekvim-i Vekayi*, relevant portions of which have been translated into Armenian by A. H. Papazian, *Hayeri tseghaspanutiune est Erit-Turkeri datavarutian pastatghteri* (The genocide of the Armenians according to the documents from the trials of the Young Turks) (Erevan: Armenian Academy of Sciences, 1988).

40. France, Ministère des Affaires Etrangères, *Recueil des actes de la Conférence de Lausanne*, 6 vols. (Paris: Imprimerie Nationale, 1923); Great Britain, Parliament, Sessional Papers, *Lausanne Conference on Near Eastern Affairs: Records of Proceedings and Draft Terms of Peace*, Turkey no. 1, Cmd. 1814 (1923), and *British and Foreign State Papers*, vol. 117 (London: His Majesty's Stationery Office, 1926), 543–639; Laurence Evans, *United States Policy and the Partition of Turkey, 1914–1924* (Baltimore, MD: Johns Hopkins Press, 1965), 323–417.

41. Department of State General Records, Record Group 59, 811.4061 *Musa Dagh*, National Archives, Washington, DC. See also Roger R. Trask, *The United States Response to Turkish Nationalism and Reform, 1914–1939* (Minneapolis: University of Minnesota Press, 1971), 90–91.

42. See, for example, *International Terrorism and the Drug Connection*, pub. of the Press, Information and Public Relations Office, Ankara University (Ankara: Ankara University Press, 1984). See also Gerard Chaliand and Yves Ternon, *The Armenians: From Genocide to Resistance* (London: Zed Press, 1983), 1–11; Anat Kurz and Ariel Merari, *ASALA: Irrational Terror or Political Tool* (Jerusalem: Jerusalem Post Press; and Boulder, CO: Westview Press, 1985); Khachig Tololyan, "Terrorism in Modern Armenian Political Culture," *Terrorism and Political Violence* 4, no. 2 (1992): 8–22.

43. For studies on the denial, rationalization, and trivialization of the Armenian Genocide, see the following contributions in Hovannisian, *The Armenian Genocide in Perspective:* Marjorie Housepian Dobkin, "What Genocide? What Holocaust? News from Turkey, 1915–1923: A Case Study," 97–101; Richard G. Hovannisian, "The Armenian Genocide and Patterns of Denial," 111–33; Vigen Guroian, "Collective Responsibility and Official Excuse Making: The Case of the Turkish Genocide of the Armenians," 135–52. See also Roger W. Smith, "Genocide and Denial: The Armenian Case and Its Implications," *Armenian Review* 42, no. 1 (1989): 1–38.

44. See Andrew Corsun, "Armenian Terrorism: A Profile," *Department of State Bulletin* 82 (August 1982): 31–35.

45. *Department of State Bulletin* 82 (September 1982): contents page.

46. See Israel W. Charny, "The Conference Crisis: The Turks, Armenians and the Jews," *International Conference on the Holocaust and Genocide*, Book 1, *The Conference Program and Crisis* (Tel Aviv: Institute of the International Conference on the Holocaust and Genocide, 1983), 269–330.

47. See Terrence Des Pres, "On Governing Narratives: The Turkish-Armenian Case," *Yale Review* 75, no. 4 (1986): 517–32.

48. Vigen Guroian, "Post-Holocaust Political Morality: The Litmus of Bitburg and the Armenian Genocide Resolution," *Holocaust and Genocide Studies* 3, no. 3 (1988): 305–22. See also *Congressional Record*, vol. 131, 99th Cong., 1st sess., 11921–47, and vol. 133, 100th Cong., 1st sess., 7315–35.

49. *New York Times* and *Washington Post*, 19 May 1985.

50. *Congressional Report Card, 100th Congress (1987–1988)* and *Presidential Candidate Questionnaire* (Washington, DC: Armenian Assembly of America, 1988).

51. See Vigen Guroian, "The Politics and Morality of Genocide," in Hovannisian, *The Armenian Genocide: History, Politics, Ethics*, 311–39.

52. See *Congressional Record*, vol. 136, 101st Cong., 2d sess., 1208–36, 1312–57, 1416–88, 1692–1716, 1731–32.

53. The White House, Presidential Statement, 21 April 1990.

54. Terrence Des Pres, "Introduction: Remembering Armenia," in Hovannisian, *The Armenian Genocide in Perspective*, 10–11.

Genocide in Kurdistan?: The Suppression of the Dersim Rebellion in Turkey (1937–38) and the Chemical War Against the Iraqi Kurds (1988)

Martin van Bruinessen

—*For Ismail Beşikçi*

Even as these lines are being written, Kurdish leaders in Iraq are appealing to the United Nations to prevent the genocide of their people at the hands of Saddam Hussein's army. In the aftermath of the Iraqi defeat in the Gulf War ("Operation Desert Storm"), the Kurdish population of northern Iraq had risen in rebellion against Saddam Hussein's government, as had the Arab Shiite population of the south. The rebellion appears to have been a largely spontaneous reaction to the rout of the army and to George Bush's call upon the people of Iraq to overthrow their dictator. It even surprised the Kurdish political organizations, which were relatively late in attempting to provide leadership for the rebellion. The scope of the rising was unprecedented; the Kurds took control of all towns and cities in the north, and the central government infrastructure collapsed. The successes of the Kurds, and their hopes of helping establish another regime in Iraq, lasted only a few weeks. Although the army had been severely beaten in the battle for Kuwait, enough destructive power remained to suppress all internal unrest. After putting down rebellions in the south, troops and helicopter gunships moved in on Kurdistan. The lightly armed and ill-organized Kurds were no match for the well-equipped elite troops, who proceeded with the utmost brutality. The cities were reoccupied at the cost of enormous destruction and untold numbers of civilian casualties. Most of the population fled into the mountains further north and east, where there is no infrastructure to support them. They are being mercilessly pursued by the army and pounded by gunships. Hundreds of thousands are massed along the borders of Turkey and Iran, hoping to be let in, as yet in vain. If aid is not forthcoming immediately, large numbers of Kurds will die of exposure and hunger, if they are not killed by Saddam's troops.

The question whether the present atrocities against the Iraqi Shiites and the Kurds warrant the term "genocide" is painfully irrelevant to them; what difference does it make whether they are massacred "as such" or simply massacred?[1] Genocide or not, the international community has shown itself unwilling to actively intervene and stop the killing; the best that may be hoped for is an international relief effort on behalf of the survivors. We cannot evade the embarrassing question whether these massacres could have been prevented or stopped before they assumed these massive dimensions. The perpetrators, obviously, are Saddam Hussein and his regime, but responsibility lies also with the anti-Saddam alliance, which called for rebellion and then looked on passively while Saddam took his revenge. But even in the absence of direct involvement, does not the international community have a moral responsibility to prevent such wholesale slaughter? Can this responsibility possibly hinge on the legal nuance of a definition of genocide? As long as nonintervention in any country's "internal affairs" remains a sacrosanct principle without further qualification, attempts to revise the definition of the term genocide are, I am afraid, bound to remain a futile intellectual exercise.

It is too early now to give a balanced account of the catastrophe brought upon the Kurdish people in these recent days, the worst in its sorrowful history. In this chapter I shall discuss two earlier massacres in Kurdistan that have by some been called genocide. Both took place in the course of the suppression of Kurdish rebellions, the first in Turkey, more than half a century ago, the other more recently in Iraq, where Saddam Hussein bombed his disobedient Kurdish subjects with chemical warheads.

Both massacres are borderline cases. While there are those who argue that they constitute genocide by the terms of the 1948 Convention, others (including, hesitantly, myself) are reluctant to use that term. It will be hard, on the one hand, to prove that in these two cases the state intended "to destroy, in whole or in part, [the Kurds] as such." On the other hand, these were not simply punitive actions carried out against armed insurgents. In fact, these massacres were only the tip of the iceberg and have to be understood within the context of the two regimes' overall policies toward the Kurds. These policies amount to variant forms of *ethnocide*—in the case of Turkey, deliberate destruction of Kurdish ethnic identity by forced assimilation, and in Iraq destruction of Kurdish social structure and its socioeconomic base. Both regimes presented these policies as fundamentally benevolent forms of engineered modernization, in the Turkish case even as a civilizing mission.

The Kurds: Geographical and Political Situation

After the Arabs, Turks, and Persians, the Kurds are the fourth most numerous people of the Middle East, numbering at present around twenty million. When after the First World War the map of the Middle East was redrawn, the Kurds ended up divided over four or five countries. About half of them now live in Turkey, some four million in Iraq, five million in Iran, and almost a million in Syria, while there are smaller Kurdish enclaves in the Soviet Union. Kurdistan, "the land of the Kurds," is not the name of a state but of the mountainous region where the Kurds have for centuries lived. It had long been a natural buffer zone between the two great Middle Eastern empires, the Persian and the Ottoman; after the collapse of the latter it was divided up among the successor states. Nationalism developed relatively late among the Kurds, which is one reason why they failed to establish a state of their own.[2] Islamic sentiment prevailed in and after the Great War, leading many of the Kurds to ally themselves with the Turks against the Christian powers, and resulting in the incorporation of a large part of Kurdistan into the new Turkey. Southern Kurdistan, occupied by the British, was added by them to newly created Iraq, while Iran consolidated its control of the eastern part.

In each of these states, the Kurds were soon in conflict with the central governments. From the 1920s on, there were numerous Kurdish rebellions in Iran, Iraq, and Turkey, all of limited geographical scope. In many cases these were primarily reactions to the imposition of central government control or to concrete government policies, but the rebellions had clear Kurdish nationalist overtones. The governments, in turn, had recourse to increasingly repressive policies vis-à-vis the Kurds, aimed at destroying their potential for separatism. The conflicts were most serious in Turkey and in Republican Iraq, which were based on Turkish and Arab nationalism, respectively.

A general survey of the Kurdish movement and of the treatment of the Kurds by the governments of these countries is beyond the scope of this chapter.[3] I shall restrict myself below to a discussion of only two cases of severe repression possibly constituting genocide. In both cases

I shall begin with a description of the physical violence first, and then analyze the context of government policy and Kurdish activities in which it took place. This will, I hope, allow me to throw light on the complex nexus of motivation and intent to destroy.

An Almost Forgotten Massacre: Dersim, 1937–38

In 1990 a book was published in Turkey that by its very title accused Turkey's one-party regime of the 1930s of having committed genocide in the Kurdish district of Dersim.[4] The book was immediately banned and did not generate the debate its author, the sociologist Ismail Be-şikçi, had hoped for. Beşikçi was the first, and for a long time the only, Turkish intellectual to publicly criticize Turkey's official ideology and policies regarding the Kurds, beginning with his 1969 study of the socioeconomic conditions of eastern Turkey through a whole series of increasingly polemical works. He paid a heavy price for his moral and intellectual courage; all his books were banned, and he spent more than ten years in prison for writing them. Although my conclusions may be slightly different from his, I wish to acknowledge my indebtedness to his committed scholarship, and dedicate this chapter to him.

The massacres with which Beşikçi's book deals occurred in the course of Turkey's pacification of the rebellious Kurdish district of Dersim (presently called Tunceli) in 1937 and 1938. The events represent one of the blackest pages in the history of Republican Turkey, gracefully passed over in silence or deliberately misrepresented by most historians, foreign as well as Turkish.[5] As the campaign against Dersim went on, the authorities made sure that little information about it reached the outside world. Diplomatic observers in Ankara were aware that large military operations were taking place, but had little idea of what was actually going on. After the events, however, the British consul at Trebizond, the diplomatic post closest to Dersim, spoke of brutal and indiscriminate violence and made an explicit comparison with the Armenian massacres of 1915. "Thousands of Kurds," he wrote, "including women and children, were slain; others, mostly children, were thrown into the Euphrates; while thousands of others in less hostile areas, who had first been deprived of their cattle and other belongings, were deported to vilayets (provinces) in Central Anatolia. It is now stated that the Kurdish question no longer exists in Turkey."[6]

I shall first, using the few available sources, attempt to give an impression of the situation in Dersim prior to the pacification campaign and sketch the events of 1937 and 1938. Then I shall attempt to show that what we are dealing with was not merely the brutal suppression of an internal rebellion but part of a wider policy directed against the Kurds as such.

Dersim is an inaccessible district of high, snowcapped mountains, narrow valleys, and deep ravines in central Eastern Turkey. It was inhabited by a large number of small tribes, eking out a marginal existence by animal husbandry, horticulture, and gathering forest products. Their total numbers were, by the mid-1930s, estimated at 65,000 to 70,000.[7] Dersim was a culturally distinct part of Kurdistan, partly due to ecological-geographical factors, partly to a combination of linguistic and religious peculiarities. Some of the tribes spoke Kurdish proper, but most spoke another, related language known as Zaza. All adhered to the heterodox Alevi sect, which separated them socially from the Sunni Kurds living to the east and south (among whom there were both Zaza and Kurdish speakers). Although there are Alevis in many other parts of Turkey, those of Dersim constitute a distinct group, with different beliefs and practices.[8]

Dersim was, by the mid-1930s, the last part of Turkey that had not been effectively brought under central government control. The tribes of Dersim had never been subdued by any previous government; the only law they recognized was traditional tribal law. Tribal chieftains and religious leaders wielded great authority over the commoners, whom they often exploited economically. They were not opposed to government as such, as long as it did not interfere too much in their affairs. Many chieftains, in fact, strengthened their position by establishing close relations with the military and police officers appointed to the region. There was a tradition of refusing to pay taxes—but then there was little that could be taxed, as the district was desperately poor. Young men evaded military service when they could, but by 1935 a considerable proportion of them did in fact serve in the Turkish army.

There were perpetual conflicts between the tribes, often taking the form of protracted feuds. Many of the tribesmen carried arms, and raids against neighboring tribes were not uncommon. The local military officials were often drawn into the tribal conflicts too, as some chieftains accused their enemies of conspiring against the state. At the same time there was Kurdish nationalist agitation among the tribes, carried out by the educated sons of leading families.[9] In 1936 Dersim was placed under military government, with the express aim of pacifying and "civilizing" it. The tribes' response to the modernization brought by the state, consisting of roads, bridges, and police posts, was ambiguous. Some chieftains sought accommodation with the military authorities, others resented this interference in their former independence. By early 1937, the authorities believed, or had been led to believe, that a major rebellion was at hand, a show of resistance against the pacification program, instigated by nationalists. The person said to be the chief conspirator was a religious leader, Seyyit Riza. Five tribes (out of around one hundred) were said to be involved in the conspiracy.

The military campaign against Dersim was mounted in response to a relatively minor incident, and it would seem that the army had been waiting for a direct reason to punish the tribes. One day in March 1937, a strategic wooden bridge was burned down and telephone lines cut. Seyyit Riza and the tribes associated with him were suspected. The army may have believed this to be the beginning of the expected rebellion. One Turkish source mentions that there was around the same time another minor incident elsewhere in Kurdistan and suggests coordination by Kurdish nationalists.[10] The official history of the military campaign, however, considers the incident as of a local nature only.[11] It is hard, in retrospect, to separate intertribal violence from deliberate rebellion against the state. One pro-Turkish source in fact suggests that the suspicions against Seyyit Riza were based on denunciations by his local enemies.[12] In any case, the army had its warrant for intervention. The first troops, sent in to arrest the suspects, were stopped by armed tribesmen. The confrontations soon escalated. When the tribes kept refusing to surrender their leaders, a large campaign was mounted. Military operations to subdue the region lasted throughout the summer of 1937. In September, Seyyit Riza and his closest associates surrendered, but the next spring the operations were resumed with even greater force. They must have been of unprecedented violence and brutality.

The few existing accounts of the events are necessarily partisan. One important book was written by a local man, the veterinarian and nationalist activist Nuri Dersimi, who was involved in the early stages of the rebellion, and who lost many relatives in the military reprisals. The book he published fourteen years later in Syrian exile is obviously colored by his nationalist views and may contain certain cosmetic corrections, but seems on the whole reliable.[13] The best I can do is to quote verbatim some passages.

When the Turkish troops began hunting down the rebellious tribes, the men gave battle, while the women and children hid in deep caves. "Thousands of these women and children perished," Dersimi writes, "because the army bricked up the entrances of the caves. These caves are marked with numbers on the military maps of the area. At the entrances of other caves, the military lit fires to cause those inside to suffocate. Those who tried to escape from the caves were finished off with bayonets. A large proportion of the women and girls of the Kureyshan and Bakhtiyar [two rebel tribes] threw themselves from high cliffs into the Munzur and Parchik ravines, in order not to fall into the Turks' hands."[14]

The Kirgan, a tribe that had opted for submission to the Turkish army and broken with the rebels, was not treated with greater clemency: "Because the Kirgan trusted the Turks they remained in their villages, while the rebel Bakhtiyar withdrew. As a result, they were destroyed. Their chieftains were tortured and then shot dead. All who tried to escape or sought refuge with the army were rounded up. The men were shot on the spot, the women and children were locked into haysheds, that were set fire to."[15]

When winter approached, and the army could not continue its operations, it offered a cease-fire and a peaceful settlement with the rebels, while promising to leave the other tribes in peace and to give compensation for the damage done.[16] These promises served to lure the chief rebel leader, Seyyit Riza, into the town of Erzincan (whose governor he knew and trusted). He was arrested, together with his retinue of some fifty men. They were summarily tried and eleven of them, including Seyyit Riza, were immediately executed.[17]

In the spring of 1938 military operations resumed on an even larger scale.

The Karabal, Ferhad and Pilvank tribes, which surrendered, were annihilated. Women and children of these tribes were locked into haysheds and burnt alive. Men and women of the Pilvank and Ashaghi Abbas tribes, that had always remained loyal to the government, were lined up in the In and Inciga valleys and shot. The women and girls in Irgan village were rounded up, sprinkled with kerosine and set alight. Khech, the chief village of the Sheykh Mehmedan tribe, which had already surrendered, was attacked at night and all inhabitants were killed by machine gun and artillery fire. The inhabitants of Hozat town and the Karaca tribe, men, women and children, were brought near the military camp outside Hozat and killed by machine gun. . . . Thousands of women and girls threw themselves into the Munzur river. . . . The entire area was covered by a thick mist caused by the artillery fire and air bombardments with poisonous gas. . . . Even young men from Dersim who were doing their military service in the Turkish army were taken from their regiments and shot.[18]

Another Dersim-born Kurdish nationalist, Sait Kirmizitoprak, published in 1970 under the pseudonym of Dr. Şivan a history of the Kurdish movement, in which he devotes a few pages to the Dersim massacres.[19] Though clearly indebted to Dersimi's book, he adds some information from oral sources. On the 1938 campaign he writes (in free translation):

In the spring of 1938, the government offered amnesty to all who would surrender their arms. The Karabal, Ferhad, Pilvank, Sheykh Mehmedan and

Karaca tribes, who responded to this call, were entirely annihilated. In a later stage, they also killed most of the Kureyshan tribe of Mazgirt district, the Yusufan and the Bakhtiyar tribes, not sparing women, old men and children. They were killed en masse, in many cases by the bayonet. Towards the end of summer, the Hormekan, Kureyshan and Alan of Nazimiye district, and part of the Bamasuran of Mazgirt were also annihilated, by poison gas bombs as well as by bayonets. Their corpses were doused with kerosine and set alight.[20]

Improbable though it may seem, these accounts are to a large extent confirmed by the documents published in the official military history of the campaign.[21] Only the claim that the army used poison gas in the 1938 offensive, made by both Dersimi and Şivan, cannot be substantiated. At several instances the reports mention the arrest of women and children, but elsewhere we read of indiscriminate killing of humans and animals. With professional pride, reports list how many "bandits" and dependents were "annihilated," and how many villages and fields were burned. Groups who were hiding in caves were entirely wiped out. The body count in these reports (in some engagements a seemingly exact number like 76, in others "the entire band of Haydaran tribesmen and part of the Demenan") adds up to something between three and seven thousand, while tens of villages are reported destroyed. In seventeen days of the 1938 offensive alone, 7,954 persons were reported killed or caught alive;[22] the latter were definitely a minority. According to these official reports, then, almost 10 percent of the entire population of Tunceli was killed. The Kurds claim that their losses were even higher.

Genocide or Ethnocide?

The killing in Dersim was undoubtedly massive, indiscriminate, and excessively brutal, but was it genocide? Was the killing done "with intent to destroy, in whole or in part" the Kurds (or only the people of Dersim) "as such"? Or was it only the suppression of an armed rebellion, with considerable overkill? I shall try to show that it was neither. There was never a policy of physically destroying the Kurds or part of them as such. There was, however, in the Dersim campaign, a deliberate intent to destroy rebels and potential rebels, and this was part of a general policy directed toward the Kurds as such. But this policy is more appropriately termed ethnocide, the destruction of Kurdish ethnic identity.

Intent to destroy may be inferred from the wording of the Secret Decision of the Council of Ministers on the Punitive Expedition to Dersim of 4 May 1937.[23] The decision envisages a final solution to the perpetual rebellions in Dersim. "This time," it reads, "the people in the rebellious districts will be rounded up and deported." But then it orders the army to "render those who have used arms or are still using them once and for all harmless on the spot, to completely destroy their villages and to remove their families." Given the fact that almost every man in Dersim was known to carry arms, this reads like a brief to kill all men in the area.

It is not immediately obvious from official sources that the Dersim campaign was directed against the Kurds as such. There are no explicit references to Kurds, because the Kurds by that time had already been defined out of existence. The military reports call all people of Dersim indiscriminately "bandits" (*haydut*). Interior Minister Şükrü Kaya, however, had found it necessary to inform the National Assembly that the people of Dersim were "authentic Turks," thereby implicitly mentioning the unmentionable ethnic dimension of the Dersim question.[24] The problem was, of course, that most people in Dersim were not yet aware of their Turkishness. Many did not know any Turkish at all, and the authorities had to communicate with them through interpreters;[25] airplanes dropped leaflets "in the local language."[26]

Dersimi and Şivan, both local men, are at pains to show that the Dersim rebellion was in fact a Kurdish nationalist rebellion, and that this was the reason for the brutality of the campaign. But they appear to project too much of their own sentiments on the rebels, who acted out of narrower interests and loyalties than lofty national ideals. The rebellion seems to have been primarily a response to government interference in the tribes' affairs, resistance to what the government saw as its "civilizing mission."

The regime presented this mission—begun well before the rebellion—as a determined struggle against backwardness and the oppression of the people by feudal lords, tribal chieftains, and reactionary religious leaders. One observer close to government circles enthused, soon after the Dersim campaign, on its civilizing effects: "the tribal chieftains, the mischievous religious leaders and their accomplices have been caught and deported to the west. The successful military operations have once and for all uprooted any possibility for a future bandit movement in Tunceli. Dersim is from now on liberated and saved. There remains no place in Dersim now where the army has not set foot, where the officers and commanders have not applied their intelligence and energies. Once again the army has, in performing this great task, earned the eternal gratitude of the Turkish nation."[27]

In practice, however, the thrust of the government effort, including the operations in Dersim, was not so much directed against "feudalism" and backwardness as against Kurdish ethnic identity. The brutal Dersim campaign was but the culmination of a series of measures taken in order to forcibly assimilate the Kurds, as I shall presently show.

The Kurdish Policies of Republican Turkey

The Republic of Turkey, proclaimed in 1923, owes its existence to the War of Independence fought by Mustafa Kemal and his associates against the various other nations claiming parts of the former Ottoman territories in the wake of the First World War—notably Greeks, Armenians, French, and Italians. A "National Pact" defined the extent of territory for which the independence movement fought as the former Ottoman lands inhabited by non-Arab Muslims—in other words, by Turks and Kurds, for these were the major non-Arab Muslim groups in the Empire. Kurds took part in this struggle along with the Turks, and the movement's leaders in fact often spoke of a Turkish-Kurdish brotherhood, and of the new state as being made up of Turks and Kurds. In January 1923, Mustafa Kemal still suggested there might be local autonomy for Kurdish-inhabited areas,[28] but his policies soon changed drastically. The very fact that the new republic was called "Turkey" (a borrowing from European languages) already indicated that some citizens were going to be more equal than others.[29]

The new republican elite, careful to preserve their hard-won victory, were obsessed with threats to territorial integrity and with imperialist ploys to sow division. In this regard, the Kurds were perceived to be a serious risk. There was a Kurdish independence movement, albeit a weak one, which had initially received some encouragement from the British. The call for Muslim unity, sounded during the War of Independence, had been more effective among the Kurds than Kurdish nationalist agitation, but when Turkey set on a course of secularization the very basis of this unity disappeared. The Kemalists attempted to replace Islam as the unifying factor by a Turkey-based nationalism. In so doing, they provoked the Kurdish nationalist response that they feared.

Some policies caused grievances among much wider circles than those of committed Kurdish nationalists alone. In the World War, numerous Kurds had fled to the west when Russian armies occupied eastern Anatolia. As early as 1919, the government decided to disperse them over the western provinces, in groups not larger than three hundred each, so that they would not constitute more than 5 percent of the population in any one locality. Some Kurds who wished to return to Kurdistan were prevented from doing so.[30] In the new Turkey, all modern education was henceforth to be in Turkish; moreover, traditional Islamic schools (*medrese*) were closed down in 1924. These two radical changes effectively denied the Kurds access to education. Other secularizing measures (abolition of the caliphate, the office of *shaikh al-islam,* and the religious courts, all in 1924) caused much resentment in traditional Muslim circles. Kurdish nationalist intellectuals and army officers then joined forces with disaffected religious leaders, resulting in the first great Kurdish rebellion, led by Shaikh Said in 1925.[31]

The rebellion was put down with a great show of military force. The leaders were caught and hanged, and severe reprisals were taken in those districts which had participated in the uprising. According to a Kurdish nationalist source, the military operations resulted in the pillaging of more than two hundred villages, the destruction of well over eight thousand houses, and fifteen thousand deaths.[32] Shaikh Said's rebellion did not pose a serious military threat to Turkey, but it constitutes a watershed in the history of the republic. It accelerated the trend toward authoritarian government and ushered in policies which deliberately aimed at destroying Kurdish ethnicity. Immediately after the outbreak of the rebellion, the relatively liberal prime minister Fethi Okyar was deposed and replaced with the grim Ismet Inönü. By way of defining his position on the Kurds, Inönü publicly stated, "We are openly nationalist. Nationalism is the only cause that keeps us together. Besides the Turkish majority, none of the other [ethnic] elements shall have any impact. We shall, at any price, turkicize those who live in our country, and destroy those who rise up against the Turks and Turkdom."[33]

Several other local rebellions followed, the largest of which took place in 1928–30 in the area around Mount Ararat. This was the most purely nationalist of all rebellions, organized and coordinated by a Kurdish political party in exile. In all these rebellions, however, tribes played the major part, acting under their own *aghas* (chieftains) and sometimes coordinated by *shaikhs,* religious leaders of wide-ranging authority. (Hence the emphasis, in Turkish public discourse, on the need to abolish "feudalism," tribalism, and religious reaction.) The government, perceiving this, responded by executing some shaikhs and aghas and separating the others from their tribes by deporting them to other parts of the country. Some entire tribes (notably those that had taken part in the Ararat rebellion) were deported and dispersed over western Turkey.

The first deportations were simply reprisals against rebellious tribes. In later years, deportations became part of the concerted effort to assimilate the Kurds. The turkification program announced by Inönü was embarked upon with characteristic vigor. The Kurdish language, Kurdish dress, Kurdish folklore, even the very word "Kurd" were banned. Scholars provided "proof" that the "tribes of the East" were of pure Turkish stock, and that their language was Turkish, though somewhat corrupted due to their close proximity to Iran. Henceforth they were to be called "Mountain Turks." It goes without saying that there was no place for dissenting views in academic or public life. Another historical theory developed under government sponsorship in those days held that all great civilizations—Chinese, Indian, Muslim, even ancient Egyptian and Etruscan—were of Turkish origin. Turkification, even when by force, was therefore by definition a civilizing process. The embarrassing question why it was necessary to turkify people who were said to be Turks already was never addressed.

Massive population resettlement was one measure by which the authorities hoped to strengthen the territorial integrity of the country and speed up the process of assimilation. Kurds were to be deported to western Turkey and widely dispersed, while Turks were to be settled in their place. The most important policy document, the Law on Resettlement of 1934, shows quite explicitly that turkification was the primary objective of resettlement. The law defined three categories of (re)settlement zones: one consisting of those districts "whose evacuation is desirable for health, economic, cultural, political and security reasons and where settlement has been forbidden," the second of districts "designated for transfer and resettlement of the population whose assimilation to Turkish culture is desired," and the third of "places where an increase of the population of Turkish culture is desired."[34] In other words, certain Kurdish districts (to be designated later) were to be depopulated completely, while in the other Kurdish districts the Kurdish element was to be diluted by the resettlement there of Turks (and possibly deportations of local Kurds). The deportees were to be resettled in Turkish districts, where they could be assimilated.

The intent of breaking up Kurdish society so as to assimilate it more rapidly is also evident from several other passages in the law. Article 11, for instance, precludes attempts by non-Turkish people to preserve their cultures by sticking together in ethnically homogeneous villages or trade guilds. "Those whose mother tongue is not Turkish will not be allowed to establish as a group new villages or wards, workers' or artisans' associations, nor will such persons be allowed to reserve an existing village, ward, enterprise or workshop for members of the same race."[35] This is clearly more than just legal discrimination; the Law on Resettlement provides the legal framework for a policy of ethnocide.

It is against the background of this law that the pacification of Dersim has to be considered. Dersim was one of the first regions where it was to be applied. A year after the Law on Resettlement, in December 1935, the Grand National Assembly passed a special law on Dersim.

The district was constituted into a separate province and placed under a military governor, who was given extraordinary powers to arrest and deport individuals and families. The Minister of the Interior of the day, Şükrü Kaya, explained the need for this law with references to its backwardness and the unruliness of the tribes. The district was in a state of lawlessness, caused by ignorance and poverty. The tribes settled all legal affairs, civil as well as criminal, according to their own primitive tribal law, with complete disregard of the state. The minister termed the situation a disease, and added that eleven earlier military campaigns, under the *ancien régime*, had failed to cure it. A radical treatment was needed, he said, and the law was part of a reform program (with "civilized methods," he insisted) that would make these people also share in the blessings of the republic.[36]

The minister's metaphor of disease and treatment appears to be borrowed from a report on Dersim that was prepared ten years earlier for the same ministry. This document was reproduced in the official history of the military campaign, as a guideline for military policy. The author, Hamdi Bey, called Dersim "an abscess [that] the Republican government . . . would have to operate upon in order to prevent worse pain." He was more explicit than Şükrü Kaya about the nature of Dersim's malady: it was the growing Kurdish ethnic awareness.[37]

The treatment began with the construction of roads and bridges, and of police posts and government mansions in every large village. The unrest resulting from this imposition of government control provided the direct reason for the pacification campaign of 1937–38, which at the same time served to carry out the first large-scale deportations under the 1934 law.[38] After the Dersim rebellion had been suppressed, other Kurdish regions being "civilized" from above knew better than to resist.

The Kemalist enterprise was a grandiose attempt to create a new world. Mustafa Kemal and his associates had created a vigorous new state out of the ruins of the Ottoman Empire, the Sick Man of Europe. By banning the Arabic script they destroyed all memory of the past and were free to rewrite history as they felt it should have been. The Kemalists set out to create a modern, progressive, unitary nation out of what was once a patchwork of distinct ethnic communities. Whatever appeared to undermine national unity, be it ethnic or class divisions, was at once denied and brutally suppressed. In the Kemalists' eyes, this was a process of liberation, an assertion of human dignity and equality. "The people of Ankara, Diyarbakir, Trabzon and Macedonia," Mustafa Kemal proclaimed, "are all children of the same race, jewels cut out of the same precious stone." Reality often turned out to be less equalitarian. Even today, a person whose identity card shows that he was born in Tunceli will be treated with suspicion and antipathy by officials and will not easily find employment, even if he is quite turkicized.[39] Another famous saying of Mustafa Kemal, inscribed on official buildings and statues throughout the country, is subtly ambiguous: "how fortunate is he who calls himself a Turk!"—implying little good for those who don't. Justice Minister Mahmut Esat was less subtle but robustly straightforward when he proclaimed in 1930, "The Turks are the only lords of this country, its only owners. Those who are not of pure Turkish stock have in this country only one right, that of being servants, of being slaves. Let friend and foe, and even the mountains know this truth!"[40]

The ambivalence, or internal contradiction, inherent in the Kemalist position on the Kurds has persisted for over half a century. The Kemalist concept of Turkishness is not based on a biological definition of race. Everyone in Turkey (apart from, perhaps, the Christian minorities) is a Turk, and many are the Kurds who have made brilliant political careers once they adopted Turkish identity. Both President Turgut Özal and opposition leader Erdal Inönü are of (partially) Kurdish descent. But there is also a sense of Turkish racial superiority that occasionally comes to the surface. Mutually contradictory though these attitudes are, they have reinforced one another in the suppression of Kurdish ethnicity.

The democratization of Turkey, which began after World War II, brought a resurgence of Kurdish ethnic awareness, along with an upsurge of left- and right-wing radicalism. Military coups in 1960, 1971, and 1980 sought to restore Kemalist purity, and resulted in renewed efforts at forced assimilation of the Kurds. Tunceli, the old Dersim, has come in for more than its share of repression. No longer a "den of ignorance and primitive tribalism," it has for the past few decades been considered a hotbed of communism, besides remaining ineradicably Kurdish. A few years ago, new plans were made to evacuate large parts of Tunceli and to resettle the inhabitants in the west, ostensibly for the sake of reforestation.[41] The majority of the people of Dersim now live in the diaspora, either in western Turkey or abroad. Not much is left of Dersim's distinctive culture.

The Chemical War Against the Iraqi Kurds

The other case of alleged genocide in Kurdistan that I wish to discuss took place in Iraq, fifty years after the Dersim massacres. Iraq had become a one-party state, ruled by the Arab nationalist Baath party; the regime was modernization-oriented, authoritarian, and increasingly totalitarian. The country had been at war with Iran since 1980. A guerrilla war fought by Kurdish nationalists against the central government had been going on for much longer but had received a new impetus during the Iran-Iraq War. The Kurdish parties of Iraq had contracted a tactical alliance with the Iranian regime, based on perceived common interests.

In mid-March 1988, Iraqi planes dropped chemical warheads on the Kurdish town of Halabja, close to the Iranian border, which had recently been conquered by the Iranian army with essential support from Iraqi Kurdish guerrilla fighters. The number of casualties given by different sources varies, but a figure of around five thousand dead has become widely accepted. Iran invited foreign journalists to witness the carnage and show the world some gruesome pictures. It was obvious that many of the victims were nonbelligerents. Photos of parents lying dead with babies still clenched in their arms are among the most moving images that the Iran-Iraq War has burned into our visual memory.

Even then, there were initially doubts as to whether Iraq had actually used chemical arms; the Iraqi government routinely denied it. The use of chemical agents, however, was established beyond doubt by a Belgian toxicological expert who visited Halabja a few weeks after the event. He interviewed surviving victims and took blood, urine, and hair samples. His conclusion was that at least three different types of poison gases had been used in combination: mustard gas, cyanide or derivatives, and tabun or similar nerve gases.[42] This was the first widely publicized case of chemical warfare against the Kurds, but by then Iraq had been using gas in Kurdistan for almost a year.

The first chemical attacks on the Kurds reportedly took place in April 1987, when areas controlled by Kurdish guerrilla fighters (*peshmergas*) were bombed. The targets were a *peshmerga* base and a number of villages. In one attack, on the Balisan Valley northeast of Arbil, more than a hundred casualties were reported, half of them civilians. The Patriotic Union of Kurdistan (PUK), against which these attacks had been mainly directed, attempted to draw world attention to them but met with great skepticism. Very few news media ever reported on them.[43] Immediately after the bombing of Balisan Valley, ground troops attacked and captured several dozen wounded. These were allegedly taken to a military hospital near Arbil, where they were filmed and photographed as being victims of an Iranian attack. Thereupon they were allegedly all executed.[44]

The most dramatic gas attacks, however, took place in August 1988 in northernmost Iraq. Valleys controlled by the Kurdistan Democratic Party (KDP, the other major Kurdish organization in Iraq), which had been under attack with conventional arms for some time, were bombed with a variety of chemical agents. Tens of thousands, civilians and *peshmergas,* fled in panic across the Turkish border.[45] The KDP later published a list of seventy-seven villages that had been hit; it estimates that some three thousand were killed in these attacks.

Genocide by the Iraqi Regime?

I am reluctant to use the term genocide for the Iraqi regime's chemical warfare against the Kurds, although it has been argued that this case appears to fit the definition of the 1948 Convention.[46] The final verdict will probably hinge on the question of intent. There are no indications that the Iraqi regime intended, by its use of chemical arms, to physically destroy the Kurds as such. The ultimate aim was the elimination of the Kurdish movement as a political problem; the gas killings were purely instrumental to that purpose. The Halabja bombing was apparently meant as both reprisal and warning, a deterrent against further rebellion. This is also apparent from later Iraqi references to it.[47] The August offensive apparently served a more ambitious dual aim: to break the Kurdish armed resistance and to enforce a massive resettlement program by frightening the civilian population into leaving their villages. This resettlement program was itself meant to impede future Kurdish guerrilla movements.

The horrors of chemical warfare are spectacular, especially when there are cameras to record them. It is not surprising that Iraq's use of chemical arms against the Kurds has drawn more international attention than other aspects of its Kurdish policies. It would be a mistake, however, to assume that these gas attacks represent the pinnacle of violent repression of the Kurds in Iraq. In terms of sheer numbers of casualties, the everyday disappearances and summary executions have demanded a much higher toll, not to mention conventional counterinsurgency operations. All this violence should be seen in the context of Iraq's overall Kurdish policies. The gas attacks are only the tip of the iceberg and are part of a more horrible strategy of overall destruction of Kurdish society.

Let me quote just one example that has, in spite of Kurdish efforts, received much less attention than the gas attacks but is in my eyes more unambiguously a case of genocide. I mean the disappearance without trace of eight thousand Barzani Kurds—about the same number as were killed in the gas attacks. In August 1983, Iraqi security troops rounded up the men of the Barzani tribe from four resettlement camps near Arbil. These people were not engaged in any antigovernment activities. The name of the tribe, of course, is associated with the legendary Kurdish leader Mulla Mustafa Barzani (around whose family this tribe had initially come into existence). Two of Barzani's sons at that time led the Kurdistan Democratic Party and were engaged in guerrilla activities against the Baghdad government, but only a part of the tribe was with them. The entire area of Barzan had, along with many other parts of Kurdistan, been evacuated by the government, and the Barzanis who had opted no longer to oppose the government had been moved to resettlement camps. All eight thousand men of this group, then, were taken from their families and transported to southern Iraq. Thereafter they disappeared. All efforts to find out what happened to them or where they had gone, including diplomatic inquiries by several European countries, failed. It is feared that they are dead. The KDP has received consistent reports from sources within the military that at least part of this group has been used as guinea pigs to test the effects of various chemical agents.[48] Insofar as the Barzanis constitute a very distinct group among the Kurds, the obliteration of a significant part of them (if this is true, as I fear) is an act of genocide by anyone's definition. They were killed because they were Barzanis.

Iraq's Kurdish Policies

The most striking aspect of Iraq's Kurdish policies, apart from the bloody violence generally characteristic of Baath politics, has been the deliberate transformation of Kurdish society by the destruction of villages and massive deportations. This is reminiscent of Turkey's policies of the 1930s, although Iraq's deportations are if anything more radical and more brutal. A major difference with Turkey, however, is that the Kurds are not only recognized as a separate ethnic group but that they enjoy more cultural rights in Iraq than in any neighbor country. Iraq has not sought to obliterate Kurdish language, folklore, music, and an awareness of Kurdish history, as Turkey has, but it has deliberately destroyed Kurdish culture in another sense, by annihilating almost all traditional villages and the way of life associated with them. The chief motive for this policy of destruction was to deprive the Kurdish guerrilla movement of its social support. At times, the government has sought to present it as a policy of modernization from above.

When the Baath party came to power in 1968, its initial attitude toward the Kurds was one of accommodation. In 1970 the government concluded a peace treaty with Barzani's KDP, granting the Kurds both autonomy and a share in the central government. A new constitution promulgated the same year also promised equal rights: "[t]he people of Iraq is formed of two principal nationalities, the Arab nationality and the Kurdish nationality. This Constitution shall recognize the national rights of the Kurdish people and the legitimate rights of all minorities within the unity of Iraq."[49] One perceives a certain tension, however, between this statement and the one immediately preceding it, which affirms that "Iraq is part of the Arab nation." This tension was never resolved; it became more serious as the Baath party came to consider itself the sole embodiment of the Arab nation, and as Saddam Hussein emerged as the sole leader of the Baath party.

The first problems emerged over the delimitation of the autonomous region, which, according to the agreement, was to include all districts with a Kurdish population majority. The government was, however, unwilling to relinquish control of the oil-producing districts of Kerkuk and Khaniqin, and of the strategically important Sinjar district near the Syrian border. It therefore embarked upon a policy of "Arabization": large numbers of Kurds were deported from these districts to southern Iraq, and Arabs settled in their stead. These and other districts were excluded from the region that was in 1974 proclaimed autonomous by the government.[50] There were more deportations in those years: Some forty thousand Shiite Kurds (known as Faylis), most of whom lived in Baghdad, were expelled to Iran because of their alleged Iranian descent.[51] Smaller numbers of the Kurdish Goyan tribe, which had members living on both sides of the Turkish border, were similarly expelled to Turkey.

These deportations and a number of other serious grievances severely disaffected the Kurds. Barzani and his KDP demanded a full implementation of the 1970 agreement and rejected the government's limited autonomy. This led to a resumption of guerrilla warfare on an unprecedented scale in March 1974. The Kurds received very important financial and military support from Iran, which was then establishing itself as the major regional power. The Shah had moreover secured the Kurds covert CIA support, while there were apparently also some Israeli advisers assisting the Kurds. In the view of the Baath regime, therefore, the Kurds committed high treason by collaborating with its worst enemies. It is probably true that the Kurds would not have rejected the limited autonomy if Iran had not assured them of all the support they would need in a war. In March 1975, Iran and Iraq concluded an important agreement, significantly signed at the OPEC conference in Algiers. Iraq made concessions to Iran in a long-standing border conflict, in exchange for which the Shah gave up his support of the Kurds. The guerrilla movement then soon collapsed, and perhaps as many as a hundred thousands Kurds, civilians and *peshmergas*, fled to Iran.

In the wake of the 1974–75 war, several new waves of deportations followed. Iraq proclaimed an amnesty for the Kurds who had taken part in the war, and invited the refugees in Iran to return. Tens of thousands did return to Iraq, while comparable numbers, not trusting the Iraqi regime, stayed behind in Iran. Many of the returnees were not allowed to go back to their original villages and towns but were sent to southern Iraq. Some of the rebels who had preferred to surrender to the Iraqi army rather than flee into Iran, too, were allegedly banished to southern Iraq. Many of these exiles, but by no means all of them, appear to have been able to return to northern Iraq in later years. It is, however, impossible to collate even vaguely approximative statistics.

Deportations of Kurds to the south, to which over the years several hundred thousand were subjected, served a number of related purposes. In the first place, of course, they were intended to reduce the proportion of Kurds in the northern districts. This was most clearly the chief motive of the deportations from Kerkuk and Khaniqin. Secondly, they served to remove potentially insurgent elements from the rest of the Kurdish population, thereby also working as a deterrent for those staying behind. Thirdly, it appears that one of the results hoped for was the gradual assimilation of the deportees. In the second half of the 1970s, the Iraqi regime had recourse to various methods of assimilation, while officially continuing to tolerate and even patronize Kurdish culture. The government offered, for instance, a financial bonus to every Arab man who married a Kurdish woman. The aim was apparently not an all-out assimilation as in Turkey but a gradual weakening of Kurdish ethnicity and reduction of the numbers of Kurds. Another consequence of the deportations to the south, which may not have been intended but did not cause the authorities great concern, was a significant increase in mortality. The desert climate demanded a high toll among the Kurds, who were used to the much cooler mountains.

Another wave of deportations, not all to the south, began as early as 1976 and continued until the late 1980s. A strip along the Iranian and Turkish borders, some fifteen to twenty kilometers wide, was entirely evacuated in order to prevent future penetrations of guerrilla fighters from across the border. The villages were destroyed, fruit trees burned or cut, and wells filled up to prevent people returning. The inhabitants were taken to resettlement camps in various parts of the country. People's resistance to these evacuations gave rise to a new guerrilla movement, which however remained limited in scale until the Iran-Iraq War began. With the onset of the war, Iran resumed support to the Iraqi Kurds, at first only the KDP, but eventually the PUK as well. Operating precisely from the evacuated zones along the borders, *peshmergas* gradually brought some of the inhabited parts of Kurdistan under their control too. The KDP did this in the northernmost part, the PUK further south, in the area around Sulaimaniya.[52]

During the war with Iran, Iraq gradually extended the scope of its deportations from Kurdistan—along with numerous other reprisals against the civilian population. If anything, the deportations and resettlements became even grimmer than before. In the 1970s, the resettlements were still accompanied by large-scale investments in agricultural infrastructure. New model villages were built, with modern amenities and facilities that were lacking in most of the traditional villages.[53] The entire program was presented as one of state-led modernization, with the best interests of the village population in mind. Some of those who were forced to vacate their villages appear to have ended up in such new agricultural settlements. Many others, however, possibly the vast majority, came to live in resettlement camps whose location was determined by security rather than agricultural considerations—in the plains of Kurdistan or in the ecologically alien and inhospitable south of Iraq. The large numbers that were deported during and immediately after the war were all relocated in strategic villages or deported to unknown destinations, without economic resources.

The 1988 Offensives

In retrospect, an important turning point in Iraq's Kurdish policies appears to have been the appointment, sometime in early 1987, of Saddam Hussein's cousin, Ali Hasan al-Majid, as the chief of the Baath party's Bureau for Northern Affairs. He was given absolute powers and could overrule all other civilian or military authorities. It was after his appointment that chemical arms began to be used against the Kurds. Al-Majid extended the zone along the borders that was to be emptied of all habitation to thirty kilometers. But villages that were located much further from the border were also destroyed and their inhabitants resettled. In 1987, parts of the "forbidden zone" were actually controlled by *peshmergas* of the various Kurdish organizations, so that the drive for deportation and struggle against the *peshmergas* had to go hand in hand. The dual aim was pursued in three violent military offensives ominously named *al-Anfal,* "Spoils." This is the title of the eighth chapter of the Koran, in which Muhammad and his followers are urged to fight courageously against the unbelievers until final victory is achieved or the enemies have accepted the faith. These offensives were not directly connected with the Iran-Iraq War.

The first *al-Anfal* offensive began in February 1988 and was completed before the Halabja massacre. It was directed against the Kurdish-controlled parts of the Sulaimaniya district, large parts of which were laid waste. The second offensive, directed against the mountainous parts of Kerkuk and southern Sulaimaniya, took place in spring 1988. All villages in the "liberated areas" were destroyed and people's possessions looted. According to Kurdish claims, chemical arms were again used during this campaign. Even valleys where there was no habitation were saturated with mustard gas to make sure no one hiding there could survive. Almost fifteen thousand people were reportedly taken to desert camps, where many of them perished.[54] The third offensive began after the cease-fire with Iran, and was directed against northernmost Iraq, the area controlled by the KDP. When conventional arms failed to secure the Iraqi troops a quick conquest, the notorious chemical attacks of 25 August took place, driving the surviving *peshmergas* and much of the village population across the Turkish border.

Both aims of the *al-Anfal* offensives were achieved: the Kurdish guerrilla forces were effectively destroyed and the civilian population was removed from the mountain villages. Those remaining in Iraq were either resettled in closely watched new towns in the plains, or deported to camps in the south. Altogether almost five thousand villages have been destroyed and their inhabitants deported.[55] Members of a medical relief organization who visited the area in November 1989 reported that little of the old society remained.[56] The town of Halabja had been razed to the ground, and instead some twenty kilometers further west a new town of concrete blocks had been erected, appropriately named "New Saddam City Halabja." Similarly, the old town of Qale Dize, some sixteen kilometers from the Iranian border, had been razed in mid-1989, and the resisting inhabitants carried off by force to resettlement camps. Fifteen "New Towns," housing between twenty thousand and forty thousand people each, had been established in 1989 alone. The "New Towns" are of the well-known "strategic village" type, and are surrounded by a ring of guard posts. Most of the people resettled here used to be farmers and have now no regular work or other sources of income.

The Iraqi regime has obliterated much of traditional Kurdish society, destroying its habitat and preventing the Kurdish villagers from pursuing their traditional agricultural and pastoral activities. The chief motivation was security-related; the deportations were either reprisals or preventive measures taken in connection with the Kurdish political and military struggle for autonomy. These measures were combined with a policy of economic modernization, violent military repression of the Kurdish guerrilla, attempts at co-optation of the urban Kurds and at assimilation. There were no attempts at extermination, but numerous individual Kurds were killed in the process, not just during military operations or in police custody, but also indirectly, as a result of the deportations. The chemical attacks of 1988 do not stand alone, but represent one phase in that ongoing process.

Conclusion

The recent destructive offensive mounted by the Iraqi army against the Kurds (as well as the other ethnic groups in the north, and the Shiite Arabs in the south) is so atrocious that all else mentioned in this chapter pales in comparison. One can only guess what the intentions of the regime are in mustering such brutal violence. Is it revenge against a population that has shown its unanimous rejection of a detested leadership that has ruined the country? Is it an attempt at wholesale destruction of the Kurds (and Shiites) or at their forced transfer to neighboring countries? Is the aim to destroy all opposition, or perhaps to change the demographic balance in favor of the Arab Sunnis, the only ethnic group among whom the regime has some roots?[57] The element of revenge for disloyalty is certainly a recurrent feature in Baathist politics, nor do I have any doubt that the regime would welcome demographic changes in favor of the Sunni Arabs. But the most likely explanation is that the regime, just as it has in the past, is using violence instrumentally, for the purpose of maintaining or, in the present case, reasserting its control of the population.

The question whether the present massacres in Iraq constitute genocide against the Kurds is not, I think, a very useful one, and it is bound to lead to a sterile debate as to whether there is "intent to destroy" and whether this intent is directed at the Kurds "as such." It would almost seem as if the present killings and other outrages were less terrible if they do not to fit the definition. Not being a legal scholar, I gladly leave final judgment to the experts in this field. Whatever their verdict, however, the moral question whether the world community can afford to tolerate such massive slaughter, and the practical one of how future occurrences can be prevented, seem much more urgent.

To return to the two cases discussed in this article, there too it is not immediately obvious whether it is appropriate to speak of genocide of the Kurds. I hope I have sufficiently brought out the complexity of both cases. The massacres took place in the course of the suppression of Kurdish insurgencies—which, however, were themselves at least in part reactions to the governments' *ethnocidal* policies. Neither for Turkey nor for Iraq was the physical destruction of significant numbers of Kurds an end in itself, but this does not make the overkill any less deliberate. The killings were intentional, even if they were only intended as means to the pacification and, in Turkey, the assimilation of the Kurds. The question whether the violence was directed against the Kurds as such invites ambivalent answers. There is little doubt that the victims were killed, among other reasons, because they were Kurds. On the other hand, however, many Kurds who were willing to be co-opted and to disassociate themselves from the nationalists suffered no persecution and at most mild discrimination.

Neither Turkey nor Iraq have officially sponsored the sort of racial theories that constitute a warrant for genocide. One does find racial discrimination and claims of racial superiority in both Turkish and Arab nationalist circles. Apart from a lunatic fringe, however, no one ever proposed a policy of extermination of the Kurds or of drastically reducing their numbers,[58] and there are no indications that mass killing of Kurds as such was ever part of a hidden agenda (until, perhaps, Iraq's recent offensive).

The massacres described above are not, however, isolated unfortunate incidents, excesses such as may occur in any repression of rebellion. They were part of a policy that transcended the suppression of individual rebellions and that aimed at destroying the very social and economic foundations of Kurdish separatism. Turkey, more radically than Iraq, has long sought to annihilate the Kurds *as a separate people or ethnic group* by forced assimilation. The events of Dersim in Turkey may be paraphrased by saying that thousands were massacred for resisting a policy of ethnocide. Does this not come close to the definition of genocide?

Iraq, while formally continuing to recognize the Kurds as a distinct nationality within Iraq, has destroyed the physical infrastructure of Kurdish society and condemned many hundreds of thousands of Kurds to lives of exile. Its use of chemical arms against the Kurds in August 1988 was, to some extent at least, also a violent reprisal for resisting ethnocide. The Iraqi regime's primary intention, however, was to deter the Kurds from further rebellion or collaboration with Iran. An appreciable number of people were killed, the massacres were deliberate, and they were meant as a message directed at the Kurds as such. Whatever the legal verdict, the moral issue is clear: this is in a class with the major crimes against humanity committed in this century.

Turkey and Iraq have at least once deliberately eliminated a significant proportion of distinct subgroups among their Kurdish population. The people of Dersim and the Barzanis had, each in their own way, come to exemplify Kurdish resistance to central government policies. In Dersim, not only rebel tribes but also tribes that had remained neutral or even cooperated with the government were partly wiped out. The disappearance of all men of the Barzani community in Iraq is an even more clear-cut case. It was not a reprisal for anything they had done themselves but an action against the spirit of resistance that the name Barzani symbolized. To all appearances, they were deliberately wiped out.

Postscript

This chapter received its final form at the time of Iraq's post–Desert Storm offensives against the Kurds and the southern Shiites, in March and April 1991. The international intervention that I was despairing of did take place after all. The allies (which by then meant the United States and its West European partners, minus Germany) first declared a no-fly zone over northern Iraq; in a later stage allied land forces entered northern Iraq from Turkey in order to create "safe havens" for the displaced Kurds. The "safe havens" gradually developed into a fragile, self-ruling, Kurdish quasi-state.

This situation made it possible for researchers, for the first time, to systematically collect information about what had really happened in the *Anfal* offensives. Truckloads of Iraqi security police and intelligence documents captured during the March 1991 uprising, lists of people who disappeared, testimonies of eyewitnesses (including several survivors of mass executions) are gradually yielding a view of the real dimensions of the 1988 massacres. Middle East Watch (a division of the New York-based Human Rights Watch), which several times sent teams of trained investigators to northern Iraq, deserves great credit for its efforts to coordinate the information-gathering process and for making the findings public in a series of reports.[59] These findings require that I revise some of the statements and conclusions I presented in the preceding article.

The *Anfal* campaigns (in which not three, as I had it, but seven distinct phases can be discerned) targeted zones declared "forbidden for security reasons," in which there were a number of guerrilla bases but also numerous inhabited villages. These villages, as I wrote, were destroyed and the inhabitants deported (apart from a number of on-the-spot mass executions). The deportees, however, were not simply resettled in desert camps in southern Iraq, as was initially believed. The evidence strongly suggests that virtually all the men and at least some of the women and children ended up in mass graves near the Saudi border, after having been processed, screened, and earmarked for execution by a well-organized bureaucratic machine.

From the evidence analyzed so far, Middle East Watch concludes that the number of victims of mass executions connected with the *Anfal* "cannot conceivably be less than 50,000, and it may well be twice that number."[60] These deaths were not the unfortunate side effects of a violent anti-insurgency campaign. The people concerned were executed and buried in mass graves at a great distance from the places where they were captured; their executions were planned and carried out on the orders of the highest authority in northern Iraq, Ali Hasan al-Majid. They had been collectively condemned to death because they were Kurds who happened to live in the wrong place.

Notes

1. The words "as such" refer to the definition of genocide according to the 1948 Convention: ". . . genocide means any of the following acts committed with the intent to destroy, in whole or in part, a national, ethnical, racial or religious group, as such: (a) Killing members of the group; (b) Causing serious bodily or mental harm to members of the group; (c) Deliberately inflicting on the group conditions of life calculated to bring about its physical destruction in whole or in part; (d) Imposing measures intended to prevent births within the group; (e) Forcibly transferring children of the group to another group." See Appendix I.

2. With the exception of the short-lived Republic of Mahabad, which existed for less than a year in a part of Iranian Kurdistan in 1946.

3. The best general historical surveys of the Kurdish national movement are: Wadie Jwaideh, *The Kurdish Nationalist Movement: Its Origins and Development* (Ph.D. thesis, Syracuse University, 1960), and Chris Kutschera, *Le mouvement national Kurde* (Paris: Flammarion, 1979). Lucien Rambout, *Les Kurdes et le droit: Des textes, des faits* (Paris: Editions du Cerf, 1947), though dated, is good on the 1920s and 1930s, as is Hassan Arfa, *The Kurds: An Historical and Political Study* (London: Oxford University Press, 1966). The author of the last-named work, a retired Iranian general, took part in a punitive campaign against Kurds.

4. Ismail Beşikçi, *Tunceli kanunu (1935) ve Dersim jenosidi* (The 1935 law concerning Tunceli and the genocide of Dersim) (Istanbul: Belge yayinlari, 1990).

5. There is not a single word about the events in the two standard texts, Bernard Lewis, *The Emergence of Modern Turkey* (London: Oxford University Press, 1968), and Stanford J. Shaw and Ezel Kural Shaw, *History of the Ottoman Empire and of Modern Turkey*, vol. 2, *The Rise of Modern Turkey 1808–1975* (Cambridge: Cambridge University Press, 1977). Turkish authors referring to the Dersim campaign prefer to gloss over the massacres. Thus, the retired general Muhsin Batur mentions in his memoirs that he took part, as a young lieutenant, in the 1938 Dersim campaign but refuses to speak out: "I beg my readers to be excused, I shall not write this page of my life." Muhsin Batur, *Anilar ve görüşler—üç dönemin perde arkasi* (Memoirs and views—behind the scene in three periods) (Istanbul: Milliyet, 1985), quoted in Musa Anter, *Anilarim* (My memoirs) (Istanbul: Doz, 1990), 44.

6. Report from the Consul in Trabzon, 27 September 1938 (Public Record Office, London, FO 371 files, document E5961/69/44).

7. This figure was given in December 1935 by then minister of the interior Şükrü Kaya (quoted in Beşikçi, *Tunceli kanunu (1935)*, 10). It referred to the province of Tunceli. The historical district of Dersim was in fact larger than Tunceli, and included parts of neighboring Sivas, Erzincan, and Elazig provinces. This may explain why another contemporary author gives the much higher population figure of 150,000, apparently referring to larger Dersim (Naşit Ulug, *Tunceli medeniyete açiliyor* [Tunceli is opened up for civilization] [Istanbul: Cumhuriyet Matbaasi, 1939], 144). The military campaigns were mainly restricted to the province of Tunceli, and therefore I prefer the former figures.

8. Interestingly (and perhaps of some political significance), many of the Dersim Kurds are partly of Armenian descent—Dersim used to have a large Armenian population. Even well before the Armenian massacres, many local Armenians voluntarily assimilated, becoming Alevi Kurds (L. Molyneux-Seel, "A Journey in Dersim," *The Geographical Journal* 44, no. 1 [1914]: 49–68). This has left traces both in the local Zaza dialects and in popular belief.

9. According to a detailed military study of the events, Dersim-born Armenians, who had survived the Armenian massacres and lived in Syria returned to the area together with Kurdish nationalists and successfully incited the tribes to rebellion. Reşat Halli, *Türkiye Cumhuriyetinde ayaklanmalar (1924–1938)* (Rebellions in the Republic of Turkey, 1924–1938) (Ankara: T. C. Genelkurmay Başkanligi Harp Tarihi Dairesi, 1972), 377.

10. Mahmut Gologlu, *Tek-partili cumhuriyet, 1931–1938* (The one-party republic, 1931–1938) (Ankara, 1974), 243.

11. Halli, *Türkiye Cumhuriyetinde ayaklanmalar,* 379.

12. Hidir Öztürk, *Tarihimizde Tunceli ve Ermeni mezalimi* (The place of Tunceli in our history and the atrocities by the Armenians) (Ankara: Türk Kültürünü Araştirma Enstitüsü, 1984), 31–36.

13. M. Nuri Dersimi, *Kürdistan tarihinde Dersim* (Dersim in the history of Kurdistan) (Aleppo, 1952). Dersimi left the area when it had become clear that the new military governor of Dersim considered him to be the major instigator of the rebellion. This was before the military operations proper had begun. Dersimi was therefore not an eyewitness of the massacres; on the whole his account seems factually correct, although his figures may be somewhat exaggerated. Possible distortions in the book concern Dersimi's own role, and his desire to depict the Dersim population as more nationalist than it actually was. The Dersim rebellion shows more the signs of traditional tribal resistance to government interference than anything so modern as the wish for a separate state.

14. Translated from Dersimi, *Kürdistan tarihinde Dersim,* 285–86. Among the girls who thus committed suicide was the author's daughter Fato (ibid., 319).

15. Dersimi, *Kürdistan tarihinde Dersim,* 286–87.

16. According to Dersimi, *Kürdistan tarihinde Dersim,* 288, the army also pretended to acquiesce in the rebels' demands, but he does not explain what these demands were.

17. The trial and executions were carried out with great haste because all had to be settled before President Atatürk, who was already on his way, visited the region. The officials in charge did not wish to embarrass the president by having the local people petition him for mercy. The events are narrated, with apparent feelings of shame, by the man who was ordered to organize the summary trial and executions, the later foreign minister Ihsan Sabri Caglayangil, in his memoirs, *Anilarim* (Istanbul: Yilmaz, 1990), 45–55.

18. Dersimi, *Kürdistan tarihinde Dersim,* 318–20. Dersimi mentions especially his own brother, who then had a clerical job at Diyarbakir air base, and who was taken away to be shot, together with two friends.

19. Dr. Şivan, *Kürt millet hareketleri ve Irak'ta Kürdistan ihtilali* (Kurdish national movements and the revolution of Kurdistan in Iraq) (Stockholm, 1975; previously published clandestinely in Turkey in 1970).

20. Şivan, *Kürt millet hareketleri,* 98.

21. Halli, *Türkiye Cumhuriyetinde ayaklanmalar,* 365–480. This important source gives a detailed, day-by-day account of the military operations, pre-

pared by the War History Department attached to the Turkish General Staff. The book is not publicly available; it was printed in a very limited edition, and most of these few copies were moreover requested back and destroyed within a short time after publication. Friends who prefer to remain anonymous provided me with photocopies of the section on Dersim. Some of the key passages are also quoted verbatim in Beşikçi, *Tunceli kanunu.*

22. Halli, *Türkiye Cumhuriyetinde ayaklanmalar,* 478.

23. Published in Beşikçi, *Tunceli kanunu,* 67.

24. When presenting a special law for Dersim in 1935, two years before the campaigns, the minister (quoted in Beşikçi, *Tunceli kanunu,* 10) declared that the people there were "a group originally belonging to the Turkish race" (*aslen Türk unsuruna mensup bir kitledir*). Destruction of Kurdish ethnic identity was paradoxically legitimated by the denial of its existence (see below).

25. Caglayangil, *Anilarim,* 47.

26. Halli, *Türkiye Cumhuriyetinde ayaklanmalar,* 390.

27. Ulug, *Tunceli,* 159 (slightly abbreviated). Naşit Hakki Ulug was a deputy for the province of Kütahya in the Grand National Assembly and had earlier written a journalistic account on "feudal" relations in Dersim and the need for their abolishment. He shows no interest in the human cost of the "civilizing" process, and mentions not a single killing.

28. When the Istanbul weekly *Ikibin'e Dogru* ("Towards 2000") published in its 6 November 1988 issue the minutes of a press meeting where Mustafa Kemal had spoken of autonomy, it created a sensation in Turkey. The magazine was immediately banned for "separatist propaganda," but a court decision later lifted the ban.

29. At the time of the common struggle for national independence, the territory to be defended was not called "Turkey" but "Anatolia and Rumelia" (the traditional names for the Asian and European parts of the present country).

30. British intelligence report on the situation in eastern Turkey after the war, Foreign Office files, series FO 371, 1919, item 44A/112202/3050 (Public Record Office, London). FO 371, 1919: 44A/112202/3050 (Public Record Office, London); A. Yamulki, *Kürdistan ve Kürd ihtilalleri* (Kurdistan and the Kurdish rebellions) (Baghdad, 1946), 70–71. The latter author mentions the case of a tribal chieftain who wished to collect his tribespeople and return with them to Kurdistan, and was prevented from doing so. Such cases were later mentioned among the major grievances leading to the first large Kurdish rebellion; see Martin van Bruinessen, "Vom Osmanismus zum Separatismus: religiöse und ethnische Hintergründe der Rebellion des Scheich Said," in *Islam und Politik in der Türkei,* ed. Jochen Blaschke and Martin van Bruinessen (Berlin: Express Edition, 1985), 109–65, at 143–44.

31. Van Bruinessen, "Vom Osmanismus zum Separatismus"; Robert Olson, *The Emergence of Kurdish Nationalism and the Sheikh Said Rebellion, 1920–1925* (Austin: University of Texas Press, 1989).

32. Bletch Chirguh, *La question kurde* (Le Caire, 1930), 52.

33. Address to the Türk Ocaklari in Ankara, 21 April 1925. Quoted in Güney Aslan, *Üniformali kasaplar* (Butchers in uniform) (Istanbul: Pencere Yayinlari, 1990), 14, after the popular history magazine *Yakin Tarihimiz.*

34. The assignment of specific areas to these three categories (of which I have reversed the order for the sake of clarity) was to be made by the Ministry of the Interior, in accordance with the spirit of this law. The law itself, its political context and implications are extensively discussed in Ismail Beşikçi,

Kürtlerin "mecburi iskan"i (The "forced resettlement" of the Kurds) (Ankara: Komal, 1977); the quoted passages from article 2 are at 133. There is a French summary of the law in Rambout, *Les Kurdes*, 32–33. The partial translation in Ute Baran, "Deportations: Tunceli Kanunlari," in *Documentation of the International Conference on Human Rights in Kurdistan* (Bremen, 1989), 110–16, is unfortunately marred by serious errors. No serious study of the implementation of the law seems to have been made; a geographer who visited Kurdistan in the late 1930s, however, observed numerous recent Turkish settlements in the area (J. Frödin, "Neuere kulturgeografische Wandlungen in der östlichen Türkei," *Zeitschrift der Gesellschaft für Erdkunde* 79, no. 1–2 [1944]: 1–20). Many of those settlers, feeling less than welcome, have migrated back to western Turkey since then.

35. Beşikçi, *Kürtlerin "mecburi iskan"i*, 142.

36. Kaya's speech before the Grand National Assembly, 25 December 1935 (quoted in Beşikçi, *Tunceli kanunu*, 10, after the parliamentary minutes).

37. Report on the situation in Dersim by Hamdi Bey, inspector of the civil service, dated 2 February 1926, reprinted in Halli, *Türkiye Cumhuriyetinde ayaklanmalar*, 375–76. This study speaks of a long-term policy of the General Staff based on the ideas in the report, suggesting that the military campaign was not simply a response to an unforeseen incident in 1937. In 1926, when Hamdi Bey wrote his report, it was still possible to mention Kurds and Kurdish political sentiment; in the 1930s, they could only be referred to in oblique terms like "tribal," "uncivilized" (i.e., lacking in modern Turkish civilization) or "originally Turkish."

38. The only figure on deportations from Dersim in the 1930s that I have seen is given by the retired general Esengin, according to whom, 3,470 persons, belonging to many different tribes, were deported to western Turkey. See Kenan Esengin, *Kürtçülük sorunu* (The problem of Kurdish nationalism) (Istanbul: Su Yayinlari, 1976), 145. The actual number may well have been higher.

39. Cf. Peter Bumke, "Kizilbaş-Kurden in Dersim (Tunceli, Türkei): Marginalität und Häresie," *Anthropos* 74 (1979): 530–48.

40. Daily *Milliyet*, 19 September 1930.

41. In January 1987, the inhabitants of 233 villages in Tunceli (out of a total of 434) were notified by the district forestry department that they had to evacuate their villages and were to be resettled in western or southwestern Turkey. See the special report in the Istanbul weekly *Ikibin'e Dogru*, 15–21 February 1987. Widespread protest occasioned by this report has apparently delayed the implementation of the evacuations.

42. A. Heyndrickx, "Clinical Toxologic Reports and Conclusions Concerning the Biological and Environmental Samples Brought to the Department of Toxicology at the State University of Ghent for Toxicologic Investigation," in *Documentation of the International Conference on Human Rights in Kurdistan* (Bremen, 1989), 210–25. I quote the conclusion of this report: "The results of blood and urine analysis of men and of environmental samples (bird, sand, stone, water and rice) confirm that at least three war gases in combination have been used: mustard gas (YPERITE), an organic phosphate which inhibits the human plasma acetylcholinesterase (Tabun, Soman, Sarin, VX or analogues) and cyanide or derivatives (cyanogen chloride, CN- or analogues). . . . The amounts found are toxic. There is no scientific doubt that the patients were injured by chemical war agents" (p. 225). The fact that cyanide was also used led a U.S. Department of Defense study later to conclude, somewhat surpris-

ingly, that many of the Kurds killed in Halabja were in fact victims of an Iranian gas attack, since the Iranians had cyanide (*Washington Post*, 3 May 1990).

43. One exception was the Dutch daily *Volkskrant* of 25 April 1987. Middle East Watch, *Human Rights in Iraq* (New Haven, CT: Yale University Press, 1990), 83, relates the events after a news bulletin of the New York-based Kurdish Program, dated 15 June 1987. An appeal by the PUK to the United Nations secretary-general dated 17 April 1987 gives the names of villages and districts attacked with chemical bombs. These reports differ in details; interviews with persons who were in the area at that time have convinced me that they are substantially correct, although the number of casualties remains unclear.

44. Middle East Watch, *Human Rights in Iraq*, 83. According to one of my informants, who was in Kurdistan at the time, the source of this report was a doctor at the military hospital, who witnessed the executions and was so disgusted that he then fled to the *peshmerga*-held area.

45. Cf. Peter W. Galbraith and Christopher Van Hollen, Jr., "Chemical Weapons Use in Kurdistan: Iraq's Final Offensive" (Staff report to the Committee on Foreign Relations, U.S. Senate, October 1988).

46. E.g., Middle East Watch, *Human Rights in Iraq*, 92–94.

47. On the eve of the Kuwait war, the vice president of Iraq's ruling Revolutionary Command Council, Izzat Ibrahim, visited the Kurdish city of Sulaimaniya and warned its inhabitants not to rebel during the coming war or their city would face a fate worse than Halabja.

48. Personal communication from Hoshyar Zibari, the representative of the KDP in Europe. See also his earlier article on this case, "The Missing Barzani Kurds," in *Documentation of the International Conference on Human Rights in Kurdistan* (Bremen, 1989), 205–9.

49. The text of the provisional constitution of 1970, with revisions of 1973 and 1974, is reproduced in Majid Khadduri, *Socialist Iraq: A Study in Iraqi Politics since 1968* (Washington, DC: The Middle East Institute, 1978), 183–98.

50. For more elaborate descriptions of the conflict between the Kurds and the government about the ethnic character of Kerkuk and Khaniqin, see Ismet Chériff Vanly, "Le Kurdistan d'Irak," in *Les Kurdes et le Kurdistan,* ed. G. Chaliand (Paris: Maspéro, 1978), 225–305, and Edmund Ghareeb, *The Kurdish Question in Iraq* (Syracuse, NY: Syracuse University Press, 1981). The former author emphasizes Kurdish grievances, the latter also presents the government's view of the problem.

51. Many more persons of alleged Iranian origins were expelled in the following years. The best discussion of this question known to me is in Samir al-Khalil, *Republic of Fear: The Politics of Modern Iraq* (Berkeley and Los Angeles: University of California Press, 1989), 18–20 and 135–38.

52. The developments were far more complicated than can be sketched here. See Martin van Bruinessen, "The Kurds between Iran and Iraq," *MERIP Middle East Reports* no. 141 (July–August 1986): 14–27.

53. Interesting observations on this process are presented in Leszek Dziegiel, *Rural Community of Contemporary Iraqi Kurdistan Facing Modernization* (Kraków: Agricultural Academy, 1981). The author is a Polish anthropologist who worked for an agricultural development project in the late seventies.

54. Since the present chapter was prepared for publication, new information on the *Anfal* campaigns has come to light, suggesting that the number of victims was still considerably higher. During the March 1991 rebellion the

Kurds seized tons of Iraqi secret police documents and started compiling lists of people who had disappeared. The first outsider to have studied this documentation, Iraqi author in exile Kanan Makiya, concluded that the number of those killed in the period of the *Anfal* campaigns was probably not less than 100,000; Kurdish leaders put forward estimates in the order of 180,000. See Kanan Makiya, "The Anfal: Uncovering an Iraqi Campaign to Exterminate the Kurds," *Harper's Magazine* (May 1992): 53–61.

55. Detailed statistics have been compiled in Shorsh Mustafa Rasool, *Forever Kurdish: Statistics of Atrocities in Iraqi Kurdistan* (N.p., 1990; distributed by the PUK foreign representation).

56. Medico International, "Deportations in Iraqi Kurdistan and Kurdish Refugees in Iran," in *The Kurdish Academy Yearbook 1990* (Berlin, 1990), 59–77.

57. Before the Iran-Iraq War, the Shiite Arabs constituted around 55 percent of the population of Iraq, the Kurds just over 20 percent, other minorities 4 to 5 percent. Sunni Arabs represented only a quarter of the total population. It is not known how the bloodshed of the past decade has affected these proportions.

58. Among this lunatic fringe one may count in Turkey the well-known nationalist author Nihal Atsiz, who in 1968 wrote in the Pan-Turkist magazine *Ötüken* that the Kurds, instead of making trouble for the Turks, had better get lost and find themselves a homeland in Iran, Pakistan, or India or, better still, somewhere in Africa. He advised them to ask the Armenians what could happen when the Turks were to lose their patience. In Iraq, the racist fringe has come to occupy center stage; it was Saddam Hussein's foster-father, uncle, and father-in-law, Khairullah Tulfa, who wrote the edifying pamphlet *Three Whom God Should Not Have Created: Persians, Jews and Flies*. The Kurds, though related to the Persians, appeared to be somewhat less offensive to Tulfa's sensibilities, however. I am not aware of similar anti-Kurdish pamphlets.

59. The most complete report to date is titled *Genocide in Iraq: The Anfal Campaign Against the Kurds* (New York: Human Rights Watch, July 1993). This well-researched and meticulously detailed report is essential reading.

60. Middle East Watch, *Genocide in Iraq*, 345.

East Timor: A Case of Cultural Genocide?

James Dunn

The term genocide has been used on occasion in connection with the tragic consequences of Indonesia's seizure of East Timor, but seldom with the specific purpose of invoking the Genocide Convention.[1] It has usually been employed as an emotive appeal for attention to the huge loss of life resulting from Indonesia's invasion and subsequent military operations, and not with any specific international humanitarian instrument in mind. The Convention is not one of the better known international instruments, and its application to this particular case has not been actively promoted. In this chapter I do not intend to address the legal definition of genocide—a task best left to international lawyers—but rather to attempt to identify and bring together the various strands of the Timor tragedy relevant to a discussion of how it might be applied to this case.

To do this, however, it has been necessary to work out an appropriate analytical framework. This approach is inevitably selective, and some important aspects of the Timor case will not be considered. At this point I ought to say something about my own credentials in relation to this matter. I first went to the Portuguese colony of East Timor in the early sixties, with only a cursory knowledge of the island and its people, Indonesia at that time being the centerpiece of my professional interest. It was, however, the beginning of a long association, which provided me with an opportunity to observe, sometimes in close quarters, the sequence of events from the last years of the colonial period up to the aftermath of the invasion.

The late fifties and early sixties were a time of changing perceptions in Canberra of Timor's importance to Australia, and during this period I worked first as an analyst of Southeast Asian affairs in the Defense

Department, and then in the Southeast Asian area of our Department of Foreign Affairs. In the postwar period—that is, in the aftermath of the war which brought Japanese forces to the islands to the immediate north of Australia, and at a time when most of Southeast Asia, including Indonesia, was in a state of turbulence—the preoccupation of the Australian governments of the time was with the search for the security of the island continent against a possible repetition of the external threat Japan had posed.

The island of Timor was at first considered important to Australia's defense, and the Portuguese colonial presence in the eastern half was perceived as preferable to the uncertainties of rule by Indonesia. In the early sixties, however, that attitude changed, our defense authorities concluding that Indonesian occupation of the eastern half would not pose an additional threat to Australia's security. It was shortly before the Dutch caved in and conceded West New Guinea to Indonesia that I took up the appointment of Australian consul in the Portuguese colony of East Timor.[2] I was to spend several years in Timor, and was there for most of the time during Indonesia's *Konfrontasi*, President Sukarno's confrontation with Malaysia.

In 1974, following the April coup in Lisbon and the subsequent announcement by the new Portuguese government that their overseas territories, including Timor, would be granted the right to determine their own future and choose full independence, the government of Prime Minister Whitlam sent another foreign affairs official and me on a fact-finding mission to East Timor, about which I subsequently wrote a report for Australian parliamentarians. In the period just before Indonesia's invasion, I was the leader of a humanitarian aid mission to the territory.[3] Early in 1977, following interviews with hundreds of refugees from East Timor, I wrote a short report based on these accounts which focused on serious allegations of atrocities committed against the civilian population by the occupying forces.[4]

East Timor is a very remote and little known territory, and most official accounts of the circumstances under which it was annexed do little justice to the subject. In order to help readers make a considered judgment of this case, it is necessary to begin with a brief profile of the country, its relationship to Indonesia, and an account of how the invasion took place and of the events that followed it. This chapter will also include a general account of the tragic and bloody events that transpired in the years following the invasion, when the invading forces set out to crush opposition from the general population as well as from the military arm of the Fretilin movement, the Falintil.[5] The result, in relative terms, was one of the greatest losses of population suffered by a people since the end of the Second World War, a loss of such dimensions to have justified consideration by an international tribunal as an act of genocide. Indeed, if the case of East Timor cannot be considered in this way it merely serves to underline the inadequacies of the existing Convention.

The Timor Problem: Some Basic Facts

The island of Timor lies at the southeastern extremity of the archipelago of Nusatenggara, which in Dutch times was called the Lesser Sundas. It is located at the opposite end of the island chain that begins with one of Asia's best-known tourist attractions, the island of Bali. The Portuguese colony of East Timor comprises the eastern half of the island. As the result of colonial expansion and rivalry, Timor was divided into two almost equal parts, a partition which began to take shape about the middle of the seventeenth century, in line with the attrition of Portugal's colonial presence in the East Indies. Boundary disputes between the two colonial powers persisted until about the late nineteenth century, that is, until the Lisbon Convention of 1893 and the subsequent signing of the *Sentenca Arbitral* in April 1913, which set the borders as they exist today.[6]

East Timor is a small country, but it is not insignificant by the standards of smallness among today's membership of the United Nations. On the eve of the Indonesian invasion in 1975 the colony had an area of about 7,300 square miles, and a population of about 680,000 people, with an annual growth rate of about 2 percent. This means that today there should be more than 900,000 people in the territory, but based on recent Indonesian statistics the population of what is now designated the twenty-seventh province of Indonesia is about 740,000 people, of whom some 140,000 are non-Timorese who have in recent years moved into the territory. It means that, in effect, the population of East Timor, eighteen years later, is 13 percent less than what it was in 1975.[7]

The ethnic and cultural pattern of life in East Timor was exceedingly complex, but, aside from some special characteristics, it resembled the patterns in the nearby islands of Eastern Nusatenggara.[8] The population was essentially Austronesian in character, but with a noticeable Melanesian influence. It reflected a long procession of migrations from the west, north, and east. But it would be simplistic to describe the territory as culturally part of Indonesia if only because of the great ethnic and cultural diversity within the sprawling archipelago. To call a Timorese Indonesian is rather like calling a Kurd an Iraqi or a Tibetan Chinese. In such cases the labels are both imprecise and resented. The Timorese were not, however, antagonistic toward people from other parts of the archipelago, until of course Indonesia began to meddle in the affairs of the island. On the other hand, they did regard visiting Indonesian fishing vessels with some suspicion, perhaps because the Timorese were not themselves a seafaring people and felt threatened by outsiders with these skills.

The nation of Indonesia was, it might be said, created not by a natural historical evolution but by colonial circumstances, determined by imperial and commercial rivalry in distant Western Europe. The legitimacy of the Indonesian state, it could therefore be argued, has its roots in Dutch colonialism and not in the natural evolution of a national political culture. As a corollary, the idea of an East Timor nation emerged spontaneously from the Portuguese colonial experience, just as Malaysia, Singapore, and the north Kalimantan states were shaped by British colonial policies and fortunes. As a political concept the idea of a nation of East Timor is surely no less valid, even taking into account the arbitrary division of the island. It is also noteworthy that a kind of natural division existed prior to the European intrusion.

Portuguese navigators first reached Timor about twenty years after Columbus completed his epic transatlantic crossing, and about fifty years later their colonial rule of the area began in earnest. Therefore for some four centuries, at least in East Timor, Portugal had been the dominant, almost exclusive, external influence—except for a brief Japanese interregnum, from January 1942 until the surrender in August 1945.

Until 1974 East Timor was apparently a subject of little concern or interest to Indonesia. In the last seven years of Sukarno's presidency Indonesia was to become one of the most aggressive anticolonial states, vigorously asserting its own claim for the "return" of West Irian. And after that objective was secured, Indonesia embarked on a costly and futile confrontation with Malaysia, which Sukarno perceived as a British neo-colonial venture. However, at no stage did Indonesia seek to bring any real pressure to bear on the Portuguese in East Timor, although the Salazar regime was at that time the only colonial power in open defiance of the postwar decolonization process, which by the early sixties was gathering momentum. While Dutch colonialism in West New Guinea was denounced in vitriolic terms, the more traditional form of colonial rule then being conducted by the Portuguese in neighboring East Timor was rarely mentioned. True, in the early sixties, at about the time of Indonesia's confrontation with Malaysia, there were occasional remarks by a few leading Indonesian political figures, who hinted that East Timor's future lay with its big neighbor, but these statements were not taken further by the government of the time, and certainly never evolved into a formal claim or political campaign.[9] And even in the two years preceding Indonesia's military intervention most official statements from Jakarta emphasized East Timor's right to self-determination.[10] Certainly, at no stage, under either Sukarno or Suharto, was a claim to East Timor ever formally made by the government in Jakarta.[11]

From Portuguese Rule to Indonesian Intervention

In the postwar years most governments of the former European powers wilted before the gathering winds of decolonization, and parted with their colonies. However, the Portuguese government led by Dr. Antonio de Oliveira Salazar ignored these winds of change, in the early sixties designating the component parts of Portugal's rambling empire "overseas provinces," a device designed to counter the international political implications of the formal UN pronouncements on decolonization.[12] It was not until after the April coup in Lisbon in 1974 that these overseas territories were granted the right to self-determination. Prior to the coup most of the African colonies were engaged in armed struggles in pursuit of independence, but in East Timor a relative calm prevailed. However, the Timorese quickly organized themselves into political parties. Two major movements emerged—Fretilin,[13] a left-wing nationalist movement, and UDT,[14] a more conservative grouping, both of which by the following September had come out in favor of independence.

The notion of joining with Indonesia was not, however, entirely absent from the thinking of some Timorese. A very small part, called Apodeti,[15] was formed with integration as its objective. In a sense Apodeti was a political contrivance, reflecting not the aspirations of an identifiable minority, but rather the opportunistic concerns of a group of Timorese.

Among the Timorese at large Apodeti attracted more ridicule than interest. Its strongest support came from the more conservative feudal chiefs, who had always been pillars of support for the Salazar regime. Independence would mean popular government and an end to the privileges they had enjoyed under the Portuguese. But even with this support Apodeti would not have existed without strong Indonesian financial and political backing, and without some support from the Portuguese administration. Some officials were of the view that the Indonesians would be more likely to accept the popular will, if the option of joining with them was openly and impartially presented to the Timorese community.[16] But the reality was that the vast majority of

Timorese preferred to continue as a Portuguese territory rather than integrate with Indonesia. Going to Indonesia was, as one put it to this writer, not decolonization but recolonization.

At this juncture it should be stressed that the independence movement in Timor in its early stages was not antagonistic toward Indonesia. It reflected the fact that, at that time, although the Timorese may have been apprehensive about Indonesia's attitude toward them, they were not hostile to Indonesians as a people. In fact, a generous response by Indonesian foreign minister Adam Malik in May 1974 deeply impressed the young Timorese leaders in the Fretilin movement.[17] At the time the Fretilin leader, José Ramos-Horta, told this writer that if Malik's magnanimous response was to prevail in Jakarta, he felt that his party would consider inviting Indonesia to be responsible for East Timor's foreign affairs and defense when the territory became independent.[18] In fact, the official Indonesian view of the changing situation in the territory subsequently moved in a very different direction.

*   *   *

At this point, let us turn to the international setting. East Timor in 1974 was no Kuwait. It was poor, undeveloped, remote, and unconnected to the global network of commercial and tourist communications. It possessed no apparent strategic value to any nation, with the possible exception of Indonesia. Its status was therefore of little consequence, in perceptions of national interest, other than to Portugal, Indonesia, and Australia. By the end of that year the Portuguese had turned to Europe and were losing interest in a distant colony of very little economic value.

In the view of the Australian political establishment East Timor was of negligible strategic and economic importance. As early as 1962 the Australian government had concluded that Indonesian rule over East Timor would not pose any additional external threat. And, significantly, in 1974 Prime Minister Whitlam, who had developed an easy relationship with President Suharto, had concluded that East Timor's integration with Indonesia was the preferred solution, a view that was conveyed to the Indonesian leader in September of that year.

However, from the Timorese point of view, Australia's position was quite critical. Many of Whitlam's statements had underlined his support for the right of self-determination, and his government was one of the first Western states to recognize the independence movement in Guinea-Bissau. Furthermore, the idea that Australia owed a debt to East Timor because of the extensive support its forces received during their commando operation against the Japanese in 1942[19] had created an unshakable belief that Australia would help out the Timorese in the end. In fact, Australia was then in a position to head off Indonesia's designs on East Timor but did not do so, although from its extensive intelligence monitoring of that country it was able to follow the development of the military's subversive activities designed to bring about integration.[20] It could indeed be argued that our responses, at the official level, strengthened the hands of the generals bent on the annexation of East Timor. Indeed, it could be said that the viability of this operation was predicated on the assumption that Australia would go along with it.

*   *   *

By the end of 1974 Indonesia was waging a kind of propaganda war against Fretilin in particular, and all Timorese in favor of independence in general. Fretilin was a party of the left and the Indonesian military chiefs were quite paranoid about left-wing activities. The Fretilin leaders were accused of being communist and of being anti-Indonesian, and falsified accounts of links between the Fretilin leadership and Peking and Hanoi were circulated. Inevitably the Timorese became increasingly hostile toward Indonesia, in reaction to the provocative propaganda outpourings from Jakarta.

In the first couple of months after April 1974, the Portuguese were rather indifferent toward the idea of independence for East Timor, with some military officers believing that joining with Indonesia made sense for such an undeveloped country. One senior official believed he had a responsibility to promote the idea of integration. However, the enormous enthusiasm for independence among the population at large eventually convinced Lisbon and the colonial authorities that the Timorese were simply not disposed to merge with Indonesia. They saw themselves as being different, culturally, politically, linguistically, and in terms of the religious disposition of East Timor.[21] The aggressive and clumsy approach of the Indonesians had, after August 1974, merely served to strengthen East Timorese national consciousness.

In the event, the Portuguese authorities commenced a decolonization program late in 1974, presenting the Timorese political elite with three options—that is, full independence, continuing with Portugal under some new and more democratic arrangement, or integration with Indonesia.

It soon became clear that the magnanimity displayed by Adam Malik was not in fact shared by Indonesia's most powerful military leaders, who had from the very outset different plans for East Timor's future.

To be fair, it was not so much a desire for additional territory that motivated them—East Timor was, in the days before the recent offshore oil discoveries, anything but an economic prize. One of their main concerns was that an independent East Timor would stimulate ambitions for independence among discontented nearby ethnic groups, such as the West Timorese and the Ambonese. Also, in the aftermath of the Vietnam War, Indonesia's military leadership was obsessed with the risk of communist infiltration and insurgency. To the military, therefore, integration was the only acceptable solution for East Timor.

As early as the end of 1974 a subversive intelligence operation was set up by a group of Indonesian generals, among them, Lieutenant General Ali Murtopo, Major General Benny Murdani, a senior intelligence officer close to the president, and Lieutenant General Yoga Sugama, then head of the intelligence services. The existence of this operation, code-named "Operasi Komodo,"[22] became known to U.S. and Australian intelligence agencies before the year was out. Its aim was to bring about the integration of East Timor at any cost, though preferably by nonmilitary means. Its first activities, which included a stream of clumsy propaganda vilifying the independence movement, the open backing of Apodeti, and some thinly disguised covert intelligence actions, had the effect not of forging divisions between the two major parties, but of bringing them together into a coalition for independence. Thus it was partly in reaction to this heavy-handed meddling that, early in January 1975, Fretilin and UDT formed a common front for independence.

The year 1975 proved to be a turbulent one for East Timor. As a result of political instability in Portugal, and the demoralization of the overseas administration, the decolonization program for Timor soon ran into difficulties. And political turmoil in Lisbon weakened the colonial power's administrative control, a deteriorating situation subtly exploited by the Indonesian generals heading Operasi Komodo.

By mid-autumn of that year, serious political differences had surfaced between the two major parties, and in an Operasi Komodo operation, guided by General Ali Murtopo himself, the Indonesians sought to divide the independence movement. Their propaganda offensive against Fretilin was intensified, while the UDT leaders were invited to Jakarta and courted. They were lectured, sometimes by Murtopo himself, on the dangers of communist subversion and were sent on subsidized tours to anticommunist political centers in Asia—to South Korea, the Philippines, and Taiwan. And fabricated evidence of links between the Fretilin leaders and Peking and Hanoi was passed on to them. At least two UDT leaders, Lopes da Cruz and Mousinho, were actually recruited by Bakin, the powerful Indonesian military intelligence agency.[23] By the middle of 1975, relations between the two Timorese parties had become so tense that talks between them broke down completely. At this time rumors were circulated by Bakin agents that Fretilin was planning a coup, encouraging UDT leaders to act hastily and rashly.[24]

Early in August 1975 Murtopo confided in UDT leaders, who were visiting Jakarta, that a Fretilin coup was imminent, and encouraged them to take preemptive action.[25] Within days of their return to Dili, these leaders, with what military support they could muster, launched an abortive coup—abortive, because in three weeks the UDT party and its followers had been overwhelmed by Fretilin, not because of any external military intervention, but because most Timorese troops in the colonial military rallied to the latter's support. In this short but intense conflict[26] the Portuguese, whose administrative apparatus had been reduced to a small number of officials and less than one hundred combat troops, withdrew to the offshore island of Atauro.

The Indonesians, however, would have no truck with the independence movement and ignored its overtures. Operasi Komodo's military commanders sought to persuade President Suharto to authorize direct military intervention, but the president, who was unenthusiastic for any actions that would undermine Indonesia's international standing as a nation without territorial ambitions, continued to hesitate until September when Generals Murtopo, Murdani, and Yoga Sugama (the intelligence chief) assured him that the governments of greatest importance to Indonesia, among them, the United States, Japan, Australia, the Netherlands, and ASEAN, were not unsympathetic to the idea of integrating East Timor. Two weeks later, Indonesia's first major military action, a covert operation, was launched: it was an attack on the border village of Balibo, which took the lives of two television teams from Australia.[27]

After its victory Fretilin set up an interim administration, tried to assuage Indonesian fears, and invited the Portuguese to return and resume decolonization. But there was no response from Lisbon, where the government was in crisis. The Indonesian response was to launch attacks over the border from West Timor; and the official news agency Antara told the world that the "anti-Fretilin forces" were counterattacking. With the Portuguese ignoring their request to return and resume decolonization, the Indonesians attacking from the west, and the international community ignoring their plight, it came as no surprise when Fretilin unilaterally declared East Timor an independent republic.

The Invasion and Its Aftermath

Having virtually provoked Fretilin's hasty decision to unilaterally declare East Timor independent, the Indonesians lost no time in mount-
ing a full-scale invasion, an amphibious attack on Dili. And so the status
of East Timor was changed abruptly on 7 December 1975,[28] when this
combined military and naval force, under the overall command of
General Benny Murdani, moved in from the sea. From the sizable
amount of evidence accumulated over the past fifteen years, it is clear
that the invasion and subjugation of East Timor, especially in the early
stages, were carried out with scant regard for the lives, let alone rights,
of the Timorese people, whose plight was virtually unknown to the
outside world. Not only was the act of aggression itself a violation of the
UN Charter: the brutal way it was carried out constituted a crime
against humanity.

In the very first days of the invasion, rampaging Indonesian troops
engaged in an orgy of indiscriminate killing, rape, and torture. There
were a number of large-scale public executions—some of the victims
women—suggesting a systematic campaign of terror. In some villages
whole communities were slaughtered, except for children of the age of
four and under.

Outraged by these atrocities the small but determined Timorese
army bitterly contested the advance of the invading forces, inflicting
heavy losses on the attackers, until the early eighties denying them
effective control outside the main towns and administrative centers.
The retaliation of the invading force to this stiff challenge to integration was the imposition of a harsh and oppressive occupation. In the
areas under Indonesian control, serious human rights violations were
daily occurrences, forcing tens of thousands of Timorese to seek refuge behind Fretilin lines.

The rugged mountainous interior of East Timor provided excellent
conditions for Fretilin's guerrilla campaign, but the resistance forces
were not in a position to provide refuge, food, and medical support for
the population, who were regularly subjected to air attacks (including
for a short period the use of napalm). The Timorese were bombed and
strafed, and once the Indonesian Air Force acquired Bronco aircraft
from the United States, these attacks intensified. For about two years
the guerrilla leaders managed to feed the people within their lines by
developing the agricultural resources available to them in the rich
mountain valleys, but according to reports from Fretilin, in 1978 these
farms were subjected to regular air attack by AURI aircraft. According
to one report, chemical substances were dropped on the crops, causing
the plants to die. By 1978 the Fretilin leaders began encouraging the

Timorese to seek refuge in the Indonesian-occupied areas, the resistance forces no longer being able to feed them, nor to provide the most basic medical treatment. In the three years following the invasion of Dili, tens of thousands of Timorese perished from starvation and disease.

Initially, the way these "refugees" were received by the Indonesians was anything but encouraging. Fretilin suspects were often summarily executed, while many were beaten or tortured at the slightest provocation. They were forced into resettlement camps, where there was precious little food and medical facilities. In 1979, even in the areas under Jakarta's control, thousands of Timorese died needlessly in resettlement camps from famine and disease.

Reports on the grim situation in East Timor began to come out of the territory as early as the end of 1976. In that year a confidential report from Catholic church sources depicted a scene of oppression and wanton killing. Its authors suggested that in the year since the invasion as many as sixty thousand Timorese might have lost their lives.[29] Was the international community aware of this very heavy loss of life and, if so, how did it react? In fact these early reports aroused very little international attention. East Timor, as previously stated, was no Kuwait: it was remote, little known, and was without any strategic or economic importance, even to the colonial power.

Here there is a more sinister aspect to this sorry tale. The gravity of the humanitarian situation in this territory could easily have been made an issue of international concern and reaction by key interested countries if they had chosen to do so.[30] Most chose to play down reports of this genocidal loss of population as being ill-founded and exaggerated. If the foreign missions in Jakarta were aware of just how serious the humanitarian situation was, they appeared to be saying precious little about it to their governments. In the case of the Australian, Canadian, and the U.S. missions, the diplomats were, I believe, inhibited by the tacit support that had been given to Indonesia at the time of the invasion.

Some of the reports that were made public could not have been arrived at honestly. For example, early in 1977 one State Department official told congressmen that only two thousand Timorese had died as a result of the invasion. A few weeks later another official, Robert Oakley, came up with a revised figure of ten thousand, which another official source later qualified with the comment that many of these deaths had occurred in the fighting between Fretilin and UDT.[31] And Australian official responses were delivered in a similar vein, that is, in a manner seemingly designed to diminish the seriousness of the situation on the ground in East Timor, to discredit reports suggesting that

Indonesian troops were responsible for serious human rights violations, and thus to deflect international concern. Indeed, early in 1978,
a year in which tens of thousands of Timorese died as a consequence of
Indonesian military operations, the Australian government, then led
by Prime Minister Fraser, took the extraordinary step of recognizing de
facto the annexation of the territory, which was by that time designated
Indonesia's twenty-seventh province.[32]

The genocidal dimensions of the loss of life in East Timor emerged
starkly in 1979, almost four years after the invasion, when Indonesian
authorities finally allowed a small number of international aid workers
to conduct a survey of the humanitarian needs of the province. The
human misery they encountered shocked these officials, whose estimates suggested that in the preceding four years Timor had lost
between a tenth and a third of its population and that 200,000 of
the remainder were in appalling conditions in "resettlement camps,"
which one official, who had previously been in Cambodia, described as
among the worst he had seen.[33] These revelations should have shocked
the world into demanding that Indonesia withdraw from the former
Portuguese colony, but that did not happen. Not one of the major
powers who were subsequently so affronted by Iraq's treatment of the
Kuwaitis and Argentina's seizure of the Falkland Islands brought any
real pressure to bear on Indonesia, in relation to the central issue of
self-determination. The best that Washington and Canberra could
come up with was to urge Indonesia to admit international humanitarian relief organizations. These requests, which elicited some response from Indonesia, resulted in the readmission to the province of
the International Red Cross, which had been forced to leave on the eve
of the invasion, in the face of Indonesia's refusal to guarantee the
necessary protection.

It was to be more than a decade after the invasion before Jakarta
could claim to exercise administrative control over most of the island.
Today, more than eighteen years after the invasion, armed resistance
continues, despite large-scale operations launched annually by Indonesian forces, who invariably outnumber the guerrillas by more than ten
to one.[34] Thanks to the intervention of international agencies, and the
work of some dedicated Indonesians, conditions in Timor improved
markedly during the eighties. However, serious human rights abuses,
mostly by the Indonesian military, have continued to occur. The most
recent of these incidents was the killing by Indonesian troops of more
than one hundred peaceful Timorese demonstrators at Santa Cruz
cemetery in November 1991.[35] The annual reports by Amnesty International have accused the authorities of summary executions, "disappearances," torture, and imprisonment on the grounds of conscience.[36]

Despite the reported decline in Fretilin guerrilla activities since Fretilin leader Xanana Gusmao's capture in November 1992, large numbers of Indonesian troops continue to remain in the territory.[37]

Some Considerations Relating to the Genocide Aspect

The Timor case is a challenging one from the point of view of evaluating the relevance of the Genocide Convention. Indonesia's military action against the Timorese was deliberate, and it resulted—by any standards—in the loss of a significant part of the population of a group. But do Indonesia's actions in East Timor since December 1975 impinge on the offenses set out in Article II of the 1948 Convention? If not, do the circumstances of this case provide us with substantive grounds for a revision of the Convention?

An obviously difficult question is whether there was any intention on the part of the Indonesian government or its military authorities "to destroy, in whole or in part, a national, ethnical, racial or religious group." This is a key element in the Convention, and, in my view, one which highlights its limitations. The Timor experience reveals some of these inadequacies, especially the notion that there must be evidence of some deliberate plan by at least a group of responsible political or military authorities.

Clearly, genocide in the form of the destruction of a significant part of a group can occur as the result of inhumane and irresponsible actions, without a formal intention being identified. Troops can be indoctrinated with hatred in what many might accept as the normal preparation for combat. In Timor, for example, in the early weeks of the fighting some of the Indonesian forces were reportedly told they were fighting Communists, who had long been the object of hatred, because of the PKI's alleged conspiracy to overthrow the government and set up a Marxist state.[38] And hatred breeds racial hatred and intolerance. The character of the invasion of Timor, with its unrestrained brutality, created an irreconcilable antagonism on the Timorese side. Antagonism therefore was mutual, causing Indonesian troops to care little about the welfare of the Timorese, whose language they did not speak and whose religion most of them did not share.

The Falintil forces fought a determined guerrilla campaign, killing thousands of Indonesian troops over the years. But a successful Fretilin operation often led to a brutal reprisal against the civilian population. In numerous incidents between 1975 and 1983, hundreds of Timorese lives were lost this way.

It might prove very difficult to unearth any evidence that the Indonesian government, or even the military leadership, sought, as a matter of policy, to destroy the Timorese people as a race or ethnic group. Yet this kind of human destruction actually took place between December 1975 and 1982. And while the carnage, or at least some of it, has been privately admitted by Indonesian authorities, until 1992 there were no reports of military commanders being charged with what were virtually violations of Indonesian law. The exception in 1992 was the sackings of senior officers and the trial of several Indonesian soldiers following the inquiry ordered by the Indonesian government after the Santa Cruz killings.

These legal processes were not, however, spontaneous. They were clearly prompted by international reaction to the Santa Cruz massacre. Moreover, in the subsequent trials and courts-martial, none of the Indonesian soldiers arraigned before the court were charged with killing Timorese demonstrators, and they received light sentences, ranging from three months to eighteen months. The leniency of these sentences stands in stark contrast to the severe punishment handed down by Indonesian courts to a number of Timorese charged with complicity in organizing the demonstration. They received stiff terms of imprisonment, ranging from six years to life.[39]

There is one aspect of intention worthy of closer scrutiny. It could be argued that when it became apparent to them that the majority of the East Timorese were opposed to integration, the Indonesian military command in the province sought to destroy the population's will for independence. This meant destroying a distinguishing characteristic of the Timorese personality, in effect changing their identity from that of a people seeking to shape their own political destiny to that of a compliant component of the Indonesian state.

If the Indonesian authorities had initially aimed to achieve this end by persuasion—by winning hearts and minds—why did their invading force behave like barbarians? Why did they torture, rape, and kill indiscriminately? Were these killings and other inhuman actions, which inevitably led to tens of thousands of deaths, not part of a plan to destroy the Timorese desire for independence and their will to resist integration? And who was ultimately responsible for these crimes against humanity?

In 1975, based on my own assessment on the ground at that time, the majority of the Timorese, while preferring independence, would have remained in the towns—in their homes, with their families—rather than flee to the interior of the island, had the invading forces shown respect for the lives, property, and rights of the civilian population. It was the Indonesians' brutal disregard for human lives, their senseless killing, their seizing and raping of girls, some of them in their early teens, which caused the mass exodus into the mountains behind Fretilin lines, where the invaders were eventually to surround them and then pursue a strategy designed to starve them into submission. This strategy had devastating consequences for the population at large, whose enormous losses have frequently been described as having genocidal proportions.

The principal targets for eradication by the occupation authorities were, if we accept the words of General Benny Murdani,[40] and probably still are, the independence movement leaders and their supporters. On the face of it the resistance to integration might be said to have diminished, because the guerrilla forces is no longer large. This is clearly not so. From the observations of those few perceptive observers who have been able to visit Timor in the past two years, the vast majority of Timorese are still openly in favor of independence, or at least remain implacably opposed to integration, even if only a few of them are prepared to take up arms.

In these circumstances, if the Indonesian military persists with the idea of eliminating support for independence, then the majority of the population is conceivably at risk.[41] In this connection, it is worth noting that although some oppressive practices may have eased in East Timor, there has been no change in the thrust of Indonesian policy and no reduction in the presence or dominant role of the military.

While it should be acknowledged that the Indonesian treatment of the Timorese population has improved markedly since the worst of the occupation ten years ago, the government's central objective remains essentially the same: to integrate the territory fully into Indonesia, and that means eradicating the desire for independence. The armed resistance from Fretilin guerrillas may no longer pose a serious threat, but the political problems created by this strategy are, if anything, more serious. The improvements in freedom of speech and assembly, which occurred in 1990, merely encouraged Timorese to speak out against integration (as the Santa Cruz affair demonstrated). In short, any attempt at modest reforms, unaccompanied by any concessions on the basic question of self-determination, serves to encourage popular opposition to integration rather than placate it. On the evidence of most recent visitors, some form of independence remains the dominant aspiration of the Timorese. It has been kept alive not only by the oppressive behavior of the military, but also by the rather patronizing attitudes of most Indonesians in Timor and by the general thrust of the development of the province which have had the effect of marginalizing the indigenous population.

It would be an exaggeration to say that Timorese aspirations have been kept alive by international support, for there has been precious little support at the governmental level. Their case has attracted attention and sympathy in the United States, Canada, Latin America, Africa, and Western Europe. It has aroused the concern of legislators in the European Parliament, the U.S. Congress, Japan, Canada, and Australia, but, so far, no appeal by parliamentarians has been able to budge those governments in a position to exert influence on the Suharto regime.

A number of recent developments have, however, given the Timorese some encouragement, if only because of the relevance of these situations to the principles at stake in East Timor, and because of the rhetoric they have aroused. These include the liberation of the Baltic States and, even more relevant, the UN response to Iraq's seizure and annexation of Kuwait. These events have given rise to unequivocal statements about the unacceptability of aggression by a big power against its small neighbor and the sacrosanct nature of that right to self-determination of which the Timorese were so cynically deprived.

The Timor situation highlights the cultural aspect of genocide. This aspect is not really dealt with by the Convention, but it remains an inseparable part of the total problem. East Timor's cultural identity was not threatened by the Portuguese in their several centuries of colonial rule. Even at the end of that period the foreign presence never amounted to more than a small percentage of the population of East Timor. The largest minority was the Chinese; the Portuguese presence, even with its military included, never amounted to more than five thousand people. Today the nonindigenous component, that is, Indonesians who have come from elsewhere in the archipelago since the invasion, amounts to as much as a fifth of the population, and their presence is dominant in most aspects of the political and economic life of the province. Their presence is in fact more intrusive and commanding than was that of the Portuguese, even in the Salazar years. The Indonesian newcomers are very much the ruling class, dominating as they do the military and the civil government.[42] Thousand of transmigrants have moved into some of the best lands, in some cases displacing the indigenous inhabitants. And a flood of informal arrivals, mostly drifters seeking to exploit any economic opportunity, has swollen the populations of the main towns. A number of observers of the Timor situation, among them diplomats, aid workers, and even the governor himself, have expressed great concern at the way the Timorese have been marginalized in their own country.

The war, the social, political, and economic restructuring of the province, the massive intrusion of outsiders, and Jakarta's efforts to change Timorese ways and attitudes—the "Indonesianizing" of East Timor—are undermining the cultural identity and life-style of the Timorese. Such a level of intervention was never contemplated under the Portuguese. The Portuguese ruled Timor as a colony but their interference in Timorese culture was minimal.

Before the annexation Timor was a world of tiny hamlets, which formed the nucleus of community life. Hundreds of these hamlets were destroyed, or their inhabitants simply were forced by the Indonesian military into resettlements, based on the concept of strategic hamlets in Vietnam. The Timorese used to study their own language and cultures, but this has been displaced by a curriculum designed to promote a sense of "Indonesianness." In the last years of rule from Lisbon many of the indigenous population spoke Portuguese, but the teaching of this language is now prohibited.[43] The intricate cultural patterns of the past, which so fascinated anthropologists, are steadily being destroyed or eroded. East Timor was the least "Indonesian" of the communities of the archipelago, its people not having shared with Irian Jaya, for example, the linking experience of Dutch colonialism.

Therefore, Indonesia's efforts to mold the character of this territory into a provincial segment of the nation in which the Timorese people are a tiny, insignificant group threatens the very survival of Timorese culture. In a sense the physical and human dismantling of the seventies and eighties is today being replaced by a different form of destruction: the dismantling of Timor's distinctive cultural identity.

Timor's economy and infrastructure have been developed considerably by the Indonesians in recent years, which impresses some outside observers. However, this development has done little for the vast majority of Timorese whose role in the economic life of their country is even weaker than the part they are playing in the politics of the province. The new economic opportunities have, in the main, been seized by intruders from elsewhere in Indonesia or by the military (who took over all the large coffee estates after the invasion).

Indonesia's annexation of their land has therefore had a devastating impact on the fortunes of the Timorese people. Their political status and culture—indeed their very identity—are today more gravely at risk than at any other time in their history. Unless the Indonesian authorities are prepared to face up to their obligations in East Timor, in accordance with internationally recognized humanitarian standards, the distinctive cultural identity of the people of this former Portuguese colony is at risk of being lost forever.

Notes

1. A notable exception is an article by Professor Roger Clark, "Does the Genocide Convention Go Far Enough? Some Thoughts on the Nature of

Criminal Genocide in the Context of Indonesia's Invasion of East Timor," *Ohio Northern University Law Review* 8, no. 1 (1981): 321–28.

2. I later served in Australian diplomatic missions in Eastern and Western Europe.

3. The mission was put together by a number of Australian aid organizations, including Catholic Relief, the Australian Council of Churches, Community Aid Abroad, and so on. I was asked to lead it and took leave from my parliamentary post to do so.

4. As a result of publicity arising from this report I was invited to testify before the congressional Sub-Committee on International Organizations of the Committee on International Relations chaired by Donald Fraser in March 1977.

5. Forcas Armadas de Libertacao Nacional de Timor-Leste—armed forces for the National Liberation of East Timor.

6. As well as the eastern half of the island, the Portuguese territory included the enclave of Oe-cussi, on the northern coast of the western sector.

7. In fact, in October 1989 Governor Carrascalao, in a briefing to visiting journalists, gave a much lower total figure—659,000—which, he said, was growing at 2.63 percent annually. If this figure was correct it gives an indication of the pace of immigration from elsewhere in Indonesia.

8. I have chosen deliberately to use the past tense, because the great upheaval caused by the invasion, especially the resettlement programs, has clearly had a significant impact on cultural and settlement patterns.

9. Curiously the strongest argument for such an outcome was advanced in 1966 by an American academic, Professor Donald Weatherbee, who concluded that "in a sense Portuguese Timor is a trust territory, the Portuguese holding it in trust for Indonesia" ("Portuguese Timor: An Indonesian Dilemma," *Asian Survey* 6, no. 12 [December 1966]): 683–95.

10. In June 1974, in contrast to most of his military colleagues (who studiously avoided uttering the word "independence"), Foreign Minister Adam Malik generously assured the Timorese of Indonesia's support for East Timor's independence. In a letter to José Ramos-Horta, a Fretilin leader, Malik wrote, *inter alia*, "The independence of every country is the right of every nation, with no exception for the people in Timor."

11. In 1957, for example, Indonesia told the UN First Committee, in a reference to Timor: "Indonesia has no claim to any territories which had not been part of the former Netherlands East Indies. No one should suggest otherwise or advance dangerous theories in that respect."

12. For example, UN General Assembly Resolution 1514 (XV), *Declaration on the Granting of Independence to Colonial Countries and Peoples*, adopted in December 1960.

13. Frente Revolutionaria de Timor-Leste Independente—the Revolutionary Front for an Independent East Timor.

14. Uniao Democratica Timorense—the Timorese Democratic Union.

15. Associacao Popular Democratica Timorense—the Timorese Popular Democratic Association.

16. Australia, too, encouraged the Portuguese to include integration as an option in the political context of decolonization.

17. For details of this letter, see James Dunn, *Timor: A People Betrayed* (Brisbane: Jacaranda Press, 1983), 108–9.

18. Conversation with the author shortly after Horta's return to Dili in June 1974.

19. Within weeks of Pearl Harbor, Australian and some Dutch forces had landed in East Timor, at that time neutral, against Portuguese protests, bringing in as a result large Japanese forces. The Timorese gave the Australians extraordinary support until their withdrawal a year later. The Japanese then imposed a harsh occupation on the local population, which cost perhaps as many as seventy thousand Timorese lives.

20. Australia was not as important to Indonesia as the United States, Japan, or the Netherlands, but a firm Australian stand on the rights of the Timorese would have influenced the policies of the other states, and almost certainly would have caused Suharto to reject military intervention.

21. East Timor is predominantly Roman Catholic.

22. Named after the dragon or giant lizard, on the nearby island of Alor.

23. Based on talks in 1975 with both of these UDT leaders.

24. An example of the provocative disinformation role of Bakin at this point was the deliberate circulation of a story by Operasi Komodo agents that a number of Vietnamese officers had been smuggled in to Timor and were training a Fretilin military force.

25. In fact at the time most Fretilin leaders were out of the country, so it was an unlikely eventuality.

26. The humanitarian consequences of this civil war were the subject of a survey by the International Red Cross and the Australian Council for Overseas Aid (ACFOA) mission, of which I was the leader, with the former insisting that the total loss of life was about 1,500.

27. There is now ample evidence that these newsmen were shot by Indonesian troops, at least three of them having been executed some time after the force entered the village.

28. As an indication of Western complicity, U.S. intelligence was informed in Jakarta by their Indonesian opposite numbers that the attack would take place on 6 December. However, the Americans were shocked to discover that President Ford and Dr. Kissinger would be in Jakarta on that day, and their hosts obligingly delayed the attack twenty-four hours.

29. A copy of this report, *Notes on East Timor,* is held by the writer.

30. Of Indonesia's major trading and aid-donor partners, the U.S., Japan, West Germany, Australia, and the Netherlands, only the last-mentioned showed concern at the governmental level.

31. Testimony of Robert Oakley in *Human Rights in East Timor and the Question of the Use of U.S. Equipment by the Indonesian Armed Forces,* before subcommittees of the Committee on International Relations, House of Representatives, 95th Cong., 28 March 1977; and letter from Edward C. Ingraham, Department of State, 13 May 1977.

32. Canberra waited only one more year before according de jure status to its recognition.

33. The confidential report, to which the author was given access, stated that, of the 200,000, about 10 percent were in such bad shape that they could not be saved.

34. The Indonesian authorities clearly hoped that the surrender of the Fretilin leader, Xanana Gusmao, in November 1992, would have led to the collapse of the resistance. In fact, a guerrilla force continues to exist, under the leadership of Santana.

35. Another one hundred or so were also reported by church authorities to have been killed by Indonesian troops, but Jakarta has merely admitted that

ninety or so Timorese are still "missing." See "East Timor: The November 12 Massacre and Its Aftermath," *Asia Watch* 3, no. 26 (12 December 1991); and "East Timor: After the Massacre," *Amnesty International*, 21 November 1991 (AI Index: ASA 21/24/91).

36. See in particular the annual reports published by Amnesty International, and also the publications of Asia Watch, especially *East Timor: Violations of Human Rights* (London: Amnesty International Publications, 1985).

37. It is noteworthy that while the Portuguese exercised control with a military force never exceeding about fifteen hundred men, the Indonesian military presence has ranged from between about ten thousand (at the present time) to more than forty thousand shortly after the invasion.

38. PKI is an acronym for the Communist Party of Indonesia. The slaughter of more than half a million "communists," including their families, in the aftermath of the 1965 Gestapu, most of them by the army, was perhaps the bloodiest episode in Indonesia's history.

39. See Amnesty International, *East Timor: "In Accordance with the Law,"* statement before the UN Special Committee on Decolonization, July 1992; and Asia Watch, *East Timor: The Courts-Martial*, vol. 4, no. 19 (23 June 1992).

40. In a speech to Timorese officials in Dili, in February 1990, Murdani warned that those who still sought to form a separate state "will be crushed by ABRI. ABRI may fail the first time, so it will try for a second time, and for a third time." In a reference to Fretilin and its sympathizers, he said: "We will crush them all . . . to safeguard the unity of Indonesian territory."

41. In 1992 the new military commander, Brigadier General Theo Sjafei, stated on more than one occasion that the aim of his command was to eradicate support for an independent East Timor.

42. The governor, Mario Carrascalao, is of course a Timorese, but, although he tries to be assertive and to do something for the rights of his people, real power rests in the hands of his "military advisers" and some technocrat specialists from Jakarta.

43. It is argued that Portuguese was the language of the colonial past, but in most former colonies study of the language of the imperial power has been permitted, if not encouraged.

The Cambodian Genocide: Issues and Responses

Ben Kiernan

During the Pol Pot period, from April 1975 to January 1979, Cambodia was subjected to what was likely the world's most radical political, social, and economic revolution. The country was cut off from the outside world; foreign and minority languages were banned; its cities were emptied; and all its neighboring countries were attacked militarily. Schools and hospitals were closed, and the labor force was conscripted. The economy was militarized, and the nation's currency, wages, and markets were abolished. Many of Cambodia's families were separated; its majority Buddhist religion, along with other religions and folk cultures, were destroyed; and 1.5 million of its nearly eight million people were starved to death or massacred.

The Toll

My estimate of the toll at 1.5 million was initially based on my own detailed interviews with five hundred Cambodian survivors, including one hundred refugees in France in 1979 and nearly four hundred inside Cambodia in 1980.[1] This estimate was supported by a survey carried out among a different sample, the refugees on the Thai-Cambodian border. In early 1980, Australian Indochina specialist Milton Osborne interviewed one hundred Khmer refugees in eight different camps. They included fifty-nine refugees of nonelite background, including forty-two former farmers and fishermen and seventeen former low-level urban workers. Twenty-seven of these people, and thirteen of the other forty-one interviewees, had lost close family members who were executed in the Pol Pot period. The one hundred refugees reported a total of eighty-eight killings of their immediate family members. Twenty of the interviewees (fourteen of them from the nonelite group) also reported losing forty immediate family members to starvation and disease during the Pol Pot period. This sample group of one hundred families (approximately five hundred people) thus lost 128 members, or about 25 percent.[2] Projected nationally, this points to a toll of around 1.5 million.[3] The thirty-nine farmers had lost twenty-five (of approximately 195) family members, which suggests a toll of 13 percent among the Cambodian peasantry.

A second study, carried out by Stephen R. Heder, surveyed 1,500 refugees on the Thai-Cambodian border in 1980–81. It provided data on the fate of 15,000 individuals, members of the immediate families of those interviewed. Breaking down Heder's sample into categories suggests the following death tolls: 33 percent of the predominantly urban "new people,"[4] around 800,000 dead, including 50 percent of the ethnic Chinese inhabitants of Cambodia, who perished in almost even numbers from starvation, disease, and execution, and 25 percent of the Khmer "new people," in similar proportions; and 15 percent of the rural Khmer "base people," or 800,000 dead, half by execution, and half by starvation and disease. The victims were thus roughly equally divided between peasants and city dwellers. This data also points to a national toll of more than 1.5 million, or about 20 percent of the population (see Table 5).[5]

Michael Vickery favors a much lower toll: 740,000 (under 10 percent). The difference is easily explained. Vickery arrives at his toll figure by using a 1975 Cambodian population figure of 7.1 million, instead of the previously accepted 7.9 million. Vickery disregards the prewar population calculations of the leading demographer of Cambodia, in favor of a much lower "guess" by the U.S. Central Intelligence Agency. His position is unsustainable.[6]

All known surveys of the toll in individual Cambodian communities also suggest a death rate well above 20 percent. The most detailed survey is probably that of anthropologist May Ebihara, author of *Svay: A Khmer Village in Cambodia*. This is the only ethnographic study of a Khmer village before the Pol Pot period, and was based on fieldwork in one hamlet of 158 people in 1959–60. In 1990, Ebihara returned to Svay, which is situated in Kandal province south of Phnom Penh, for three weeks. She found that of the 158 people she had known in 1960, nineteen had died by 1975, but no fewer than seventy-three (including thirty women) had died in 1975–79. Thus, 53 percent of the people Ebihara had known had perished under Pol Pot. Eighteen new families had formed in the hamlet after 1960; but in 1975–1979, twenty-six of the thirty-six spouses and twenty-nine of their children also perished.[7]

Similar figures were obtained from other villages in the same prov-

TABLE 5. Approximate Death Tolls under Pol Pot, 1975–79.

Social Group	1975 Population	Number who perished	Percent
"New People"			
Urban Khmer	2,000,000	500,000	25
Rural Khmer	600,000	150,000	25
Chinese (all urban)	430,000	215,000	50
Vietnamese (urban)	10,000	10,000	100
Lao (rural)	10,000	4,000	40
Total	3,050,000	879,000	29
"Base People"			
Rural Khmer*	4,500,000	675,000	15
Cham (all rural)	250,000	90,000	36
Vietnamese (rural)	10,000	10,000	100
Thai (rural)	20,000	8,000	40
Upland minorities	60,000	9,000	15
Total	4,840,000	792,000	16
Total (new and base)	7,890,000	1,671,000	21

*The rural Khmer population of 1975 included five thousand Khmer Krom (ethnic Khmers from southern Vietnam who had resettled in northwest Cambodia), two thousand—40 percent—of whom perished.

ince in 1981. The Japanese journalist Katuiti Honda surveyed the death toll in two communities in Kandal. In one group of 168 people, the death toll was seventy-seven (45 percent), including 20 who had been murdered. In another village of 728, surviving families lost 35 percent of their members, or 257 dead, including 140 murdered; this is not counting another twenty-nine households who were entirely exterminated, taking the 1975–79 death rate in that village to 41 percent.[8]

Honda also studied in detail four communities in eastern Cambodia. They comprised about 350 people in 1975. By 1979, 125 of the inhabitants (36 percent) were dead, 118 of them murdered.[9] In an eastern Cambodian village community of 220 families where Chanthou Boua and I worked for three weeks in the mid-1980s, more than two hundred people had died in the Democratic Kampuchea (DK) period, including more than a hundred murdered in 1978 alone. Among thirty-eight families we studied, the toll from 1975 to 1979 was forty-five dead, including thirty-seven murdered. Two further surveys of the toll in Cambodian villages reveal death rates of 24 percent and 35 percent. These will be discussed below.

Finally, Michael Vickery reports the testimony of two survivors of death tolls surpassing 60 percent in their cooperatives in northwest Cambodia: "They estimated that one cooperative declined from 7,000 people in 1975 to 2–3,000 in 1979, with about 15% executed, while another decreased from 8,500 in 1976 to 3,200 in 1979, with 25–30% killed."[10]

Background

Cambodia won its independence from French colonialism in 1954. Subsequently, it was ruled by Prince Norodom Sihanouk, an autocrat who tried to preserve Cambodia's independence from its neighbors and the superpowers. This became much more difficult after 1965, when the United States massively intervened in the neighboring war in South Vietnam. U.S. and Vietnamese armies soon encroached upon Cambodia's territory and integrity.

On 18 March 1969, the U.S. Air Force began a secret B-52 bombardment of Vietnamese sanctuaries in rural Cambodia.[11] One year later the neutral Sihanouk was overthrown by the U.S.-backed general, Lon Nol. The Vietnam War spilled across the border, Sihanouk swore revenge, and a new civil war tore Cambodia apart.

The U.S. bombing of the countryside increased from 1970 to 1973, when Congress imposed a halt. Up to 150,000 Cambodians were killed in the American bombardments. Nearly half of the 540,000 tons of bombs fell in the last six months of 1973. From the ashes of rural Cambodia rose the Communist Party of Kampuchea (CPK), led by Pol Pot.

Pol Pot's CPK forces (known as the "Khmer Rouge") had profited greatly from the U.S. bombardment. Contemporary U.S. government documents and peasant survivors reveal that the Khmer Rouge used the bombing's devastation and massacre of civilians as recruitment propaganda and as an excuse for their brutal, radical policies and their purge of moderate and pro-Vietnamese Khmer communists and Sihanoukists.[12] By April 1975 they were in a position of national power. The next year they proclaimed a new regime, "Democratic Kampuchea" (DK).

The Genocide and the Regime

Debate raged over the nature of the closed regime in Cambodia soon after it was established in April 1975. Persistent reports of atrocities in western Cambodia were brought out by many (not all) of the refugees escaping from there into Thailand, but little was known about events in the center of the closed country, and even less about the east.[13]

It was not clear who was in charge in Phnom Penh. "Pol Pot" was unknown until March–April 1976, when a man of that name was appointed prime minister of DK, but he stood down "for health reasons" the following October. He reappeared only in September 1977, when he visited Beijing and revealed his leadership of the previously secret Communist Party of Kampuchea. The name "Pol Pot" was soon identified by journalist Nayan Chanda as a pseudonym for Party leader Saloth Sar, but the regime never admitted this.[14] It privately considered "secrecy as the basis" of the revolution.[15]

Abroad there was also disagreement about the responsibility of the new Phnom Penh government for the killings. Grounds existed for interpreting the violence as mostly spontaneous, consisting of postwar, local revenge killings without the sanction or even against the orders of the new authorities.[16] Three independent sources reported, for instance, that the central authorities had ordered an end to the killings. According to a report in the *Bangkok Post* on 25 June 1975: "A former diplomat who escaped with 11 members of his family reported that on May 31 a Khmer Rouge official stopped him about 30 miles from the Thai border and told him: 'You are lucky. Three days ago we received instructions not to kill any more people of the old government.'" The same newspaper on 23 July 1975 reported that, according to "a Vietnamese in Phnom Penh on official business," "Khmer Rouge soldiers have been ordered to stop killing people without proper investigations and authority."[17] And a refugee who escaped from western Cambodia in January 1976 reported that he had been told by a local cadre of their executions of former government officials, but said they added that in May 1975 the regime had ordered an end to these killings.[18] At the time, these reports led me to believe that the continuing violence was largely uncontrolled and to question the view that the regime was responsible for mass exterminations. Nevertheless, throughout the Khmer Rouge period I published detailed accounts by refugees relating the killings and hardship in Cambodia.[19]

After the overthrow of the Pol Pot regime, new information threw light on the question of responsibility. In his book *Cambodia 1975–1982*, Michael Vickery reported the statement of a refugee from southwest Cambodia, whom he interviewed in Thailand in 1980: "Van, one of the most careful reporters I met among the refugees, and who was relatively positive toward life in Democratic Kampuchea, claimed that during the first six months after April 1975, orders had been issued from Phnom Penh to kill urban evacuees indiscriminately." This undercuts Vickery's contention that before 1977 there were "few excesses," but it does explain considerable regional variations in the initial violence, which was greatest in the west.[20] Vickery continues:

He had obtained this information from an elder brother, a base peasant, whose son and Van's nephew was a high-ranking DK officer who worked at the Phnom Penh airport after the war. Later, during a trip home to visit his family, he mentioned the execution order and said that it had been countermanded in October 1975 by another order forbidding lower levels of cadre to kill at all without instructions from above.[21]

This was corroborated by a village chief from another part of the country, the northwest. This "old revolutionary" reported that "in April indiscriminate killing was allowed, but in October an order came forbidding it."[22]

It should now be clear that in Phnom Penh from May to October 1975 several attempts—not entirely successful—were made to end or at least limit the killing. Either Pol Pot's "Party Center"[23] was struggling to maintain control, or it temporarily found itself outmaneuvered by different government organs or factions. But whoever issued this series of orders, their drift was clear: to limit the number of executions and the ability of lower levels to carry them out. This is true even if we assume that all political tendencies in DK were prepared to resort to political murder and that differences concerned merely the targets and scale of the violence.[24]

With Pol Pot's public emergence the next year, a green light was flashed. We now know that on 30 March 1976, a Party Center memorandum divided up what it called "The Authority to Smash People Inside and Outside the Ranks." While some political killings were held to be the prerogative of the Center, others were now delegated to the country's zones.[25] As we have seen, in 1975 Phnom Penh had proclaimed its decision-making power over executions. What was new in the 1976 directive was its partial redistribution of formal authority to determine targets, contradicting the aim of the 1975 orders. Thus the Pol Pot leadership now formally legitimized its murders of perceived opponents and those carried out by its subordinates. The Party Center established its position a year after the war; rather than order an end to the violence or make any other move to limit it, the Center instead attempted to streamline responsibility for the killings and merely avoid administrative overlap.

For subsequent months and years, there is little or no evidence of spontaneous, grass-roots violence like that of 1975; the Center had won complete control over the zone committees by 1977–78. Although it must have issued specific orders for the ever more widespread mass exterminations that occurred in that period, no further documents attesting to this appear to have survived, with the exception of the massive documentation of the arrests and murders of about 15,000 political prisoners in the capital from 1976 to 1978.[26] The existence of this prison/extermination center, known as Tuol Sleng, did not become publicly known until the regime was overthrown by Vietnamese troops in January 1979. However, the mass murders and starvation of the population had been extensively reported in the press. In my own assessment published in 1978, I noted that "refugees report widespread purges" and executions, that "Pol Pot has moved from strength to strength by largescale purges throughout 1977," and that the strength of "domestic opposition" had led to "more wide-ranging purges." I concluded that "Pol Pot is after unchallenged authority," pursuing "a chauvinism that demands big continuing sacrifices from the people to build a powerful state," while "many peasants and peasant cadres have been repressed."[27]

* * *

The 1948 United Nations Convention on Genocide can be applied to the Khmer Rouge regime's persecution and slaughter of three categories of Cambodian victims: "religious groups" like the Buddhist monks; "ethnical or racial groups" like the Cham and Vietnamese minorities; and probably at least one "part" of the majority Khmer "national" group, the eastern Khmer population from the provinces near Vietnam (and possibly the Khmer urban population too). All were targeted for destruction "as such." This does not mean that the Pol Pot regime planned to eliminate them physically or entirely, but it does mean that the regime subjected them to genocide. I will explain below how these cases have been interpreted.

Genocide Against a Religious Group

Pol Pot's government tried to eradicate Buddhism from Cambodia. Cambodia is an overwhelmingly Theravada Buddhist society, and there were about seventy thousand Buddhist monks in about three thousand monasteries throughout the country in 1975. Eyewitnesses testify to Khmer Rouge massacres of monks and the disrobing and persecution of survivors. For instance, out of a total of 2,680 Buddhist monks from eight of Cambodia's monasteries, only 70 monks were found to have survived in 1979.[28]

A self-congratulatory note on the subject also survives, in an eight-page Pol Pot "Center" document dated September 1975. Entitled "About the Control and Application of Political Leadership in Accumulating Forces for the National Front and Democracy of the Party," this document says: "Monks have disappeared from 90 to 95 per cent. . . . Monasteries . . . are largely abandoned. The foundation pillars of Buddhism . . . have disintegrated. In the future they will dissolve further. The political base, the economic base, the cultural base must be uprooted."

No longer was there to be a Cambodian Buddhist community. This clear evidence of genocidal intent was carried through. As C. Boua points out, "Buddhism was eradicated from the face of the country in just one year." In 1978, Yun Yat, who served as Pol Pot's minister for information, culture, and education, claimed that Buddhism was "incompatible with the revolution." The Cambodian people, she said, had "stopped believing" and monks had "left the temples." Yun Yat added: "The problem gradually becomes extinguished. Hence there is no problem."[29]

Genocide Against Ethnic Groups

The largest ethnic minority groups in Cambodia before 1970 were the Vietnamese, the Chinese, and the Muslim Cham ethnic group. Unlike most other communist regimes, the Pol Pot regime's view of these and the country's twenty other national minorities, who combined made up more than 15 percent of the Cambodian population, was virtually to deny their existence. The regime officially proclaimed that they totaled only 1 percent of the population.[30] Statistically, they were written off.

Their physical fate was much worse. The Vietnamese community, for instance, was entirely eradicated. More than half of the 400,000-strong community had been expelled by the U.S.-backed Lon Nol regime in 1970 (with several thousand killed in pogroms).[31] More than 100,000 others were driven out by the Pol Pot regime in the first year after its victory in 1975. The rest were simply murdered.

The exact numbers killed are unknown, but in more than a year's research in Cambodia after 1979, it was not possible to find a Vietnamese resident who had survived the Pol Pot years there. Eyewitnesses from other ethnic groups, including Khmers who were married to Vietnamese, testify to the terrible fates of their Vietnamese spouses and neighbors. This was a campaign of systematic racial extermination. It even spilled over into witch-hunts and massacres of possibly thousands of Khmer Krom, or "Lowland Cambodians," ethnic Khmers from southern Vietnam who had resettled in northwest Cambodia.

The Chinese under Pol Pot's regime suffered the worst disaster ever to befall any ethnic Chinese community in Southeast Asia. Of the 1975 population of 430,000, only about 215,000 Chinese survived the next four years.[32] Ethnic Chinese were nearly all urban, and they were seen by the Khmer Rouge as archetypal city dwellers, and therefore as prisoners of war. In this case they were not targeted for execution *because of their race,* but like other evacuated city dwellers they were made to work harder and under much more deplorable conditions than rural dwellers. The penalty for infraction of minor regulations was often death. This was systematic discrimination based on geographic or social origin.

The Chinese succumbed in particularly large numbers to hunger and to diseases such as malaria. The 50 percent of them who perished is a higher proportion than that estimated for Cambodia's city dwellers in general (about one-third). Further, the Chinese language, like all foreign and minority languages, was banned, and so was any tolerance of a culturally and ethnically distinguishable Chinese community. That was to be destroyed "as such," and this persecution could be described as genocide.

The toll among smaller ethnic minorities was also high. The Thai minority of twenty thousand was reportedly reduced to about eight thousand. Only eight hundred families survived of the eighteen hundred families of the Lao ethnic minority. Of the two thousand members of the Kola minority, "no trace . . . has been found."[33]

The Muslim Chams of Cambodia numbered at least 250,000 in 1975. Their distinct religion, language, and culture, large villages, and autonomous networks threatened the atomized, closely supervised society that the Pol Pot leadership planned. An early 1974 Pol Pot document records the decision to "break up" the Cham people, adding: "Do not allow too many of them to concentrate in one area." Cham women were forced to cut their hair short in the Khmer style, not wear it long as was their custom. The traditional Cham sarong was banned, and peasants were forced to wear only black pajamas. Restrictions were placed on religious activity.

In 1975 the new Pol Pot government turned its attention to the Chams with a vengeance. Fierce rebellions broke out. In one case, the authorities attempted to collect all copies of the Koran. The villagers staged a protest demonstration, and Khmer Rouge troops fired into the crowd. The Chams then took up swords and knives and slaughtered half a dozen troops. The retaliating armed forces massacred many and pillaged their homes. They evacuated and razed the village, and then turned to a neighboring village, massacring 70 percent of its inhabitants.

Soon the Pol Pot army forcibly emptied all 113 Cham villages in the country. About 100,000 Chams died or were massacred and the survivors were dispersed in small groups of several families. Islamic schools and religion, as well as the Cham language, were banned. Thousands of Muslims were physically forced to eat pork. Many were murdered for refusing. Of 113 Cham *hakkem,* or community leaders, only twenty survived in 1979. Only twenty-five of their 226 deputies survived. All but thirty-eight of about three hundred religious teachers at Cambodia's Koranic schools perished. Of more than a thousand who had made the pilgrimage to Mecca, only about thirty survived.[34]

In 1981 the Japanese journalist Katuiti Honda reported on the death toll in three Cham communities.[35] In Phnom Penh, Imam Him Mathot told him that in 1975 he had been evacuated from the capital to Kompong Speu province with five hundred Cham families, totaling about three thousand people. Fewer than seven hundred survived in 1979, according to the Imam: "Half the deaths were due to starvation, and the other half by execution." Mathot lost eight of the fourteen members of his own family. Across the river from Phnom Penh, he added, a Cham community of 450 families in 1975 had been reduced to fifty families, "and almost every family had lost members." Him Man, a Cham youth from Kompong Cham province, recounted in detail a Khmer Rouge massacre of two thousand Chams there, which he had personally witnessed on 12 April 1978. Man and his wife were the only survivors of five hundred Cham families of the village of Khsach So.[36]

Two surveys conducted by anthropologist Dr. Gregory Stanton and me in 1986 further illustrate the Cham death toll.[37] In Khmer Islam village, Prey Veng province, we surveyed thirty-three of the surviving forty-nine Cham households. Those families in 1975 had numbered 223 persons. By 1979 they had lost fifty-four members, including thirty-six people whom the Pol Pot forces had murdered. The death toll was 24 percent. If we include about thirty other families who had left no survivors at all, the death toll in the village as a whole seems to have been 40 to 50 percent of the population, or about 300 out of 650.

Another Cham subcommunity of twelve family groups, near the capital Phnom Penh, had comprised 111 people in 1975. Thirty-nine people—or 35 percent—died in the next four years. This sample includes one family of nine who fled to Vietnam in 1975; all survived. Of the other eleven families, only one had suffered no loss of members in the Pol Pot period.

Michael Vickery denies that the Chams suffered genocide. He does so on a statistical basis, asserting that the toll was closer to 20,000 than 100,000. He says that I underestimate the number of survivors, and that "there had never been 250,000 [Chams] to begin with," but only about 191,000 in 1975.[38] As I have shown, his figures are quite wrong.[39] Among other errors, the latter claim is based on a speculated 1936–55 Cham population growth rate that is far lower than my suggested 2.7 percent annual growth rate. The 1955 count of the adult male Cham population,[40] a minimum figure of which Vickery is unaware, points precisely to a growth rate of at least 2.7 percent since 1936. Use of accepted national growth rates from 1955 to 1970,[41] and of the 1970–75 national growth rate of 2.46 percent,[42] gives a 1975 Cham population of more than 248,000.

Genocide Against a Part of the Majority National Group

Finally, of the majority Khmers, 15 percent of the "base" population and 25 percent of the "new people" perished. The most horrific slaughter was in the very last six months of the regime, in the politically suspect Eastern Zone bordering Vietnam. My interviews with eighty-seven survivors revealed something of the toll. In just eleven villages, the Khmer Rouge carried out 1,663 killings in 1978. In another community of 350 people, there were 95 executions in 1978. In another subdistrict 705 executions occurred; in another, 1,950; in another, 400. Tens of thousands of other villagers were deported to the northwest of the country. There they were "marked" as easterners by being forced to wear a blue scarf, reminiscent of Hitler's yellow star for Jews,[43] and then eliminated en masse.

I have already noted the 1975–79 toll among thirty-eight families in one Eastern Zone village community. The forty-five deaths occurred as follows: eleven members of those families were killed in 1975, six died of disease in 1975–76, four were executed in 1977, and no fewer than twenty-four died in 1978, including twenty-two who were executed.

A total 1978 murder toll of more than 100,000 can safely be regarded as a minimum estimate.[44] The real figure is probably much higher, possibly 250,000. Yet at the height of the killings, in December 1978, the only group of American journalists to visit Democratic Kampuchea were taken along a major highway through the Eastern Zone. They reported no sign of any massacres there, revealing how successful a carefully shepherded tour can be (at least when those being guided do not speak the local language). As late as 1990, one of the American journalists on the tour, Richard Dudman, proclaimed in a column in the *New York Times*, "Pol Pot: Brutal Yes, but No Mass Murderer." Dudman claimed that "accounts of mass execution" in the Pol Pot period come from only "a few villages," and "the remains of a few hundred [sic] victims . . . certainly do not prove genocide." He recommended U.S. support for Pol Pot's Khmer Rouge.[45]

There is some disagreement among writers as to whether this clear case of mass murder in the Eastern Zone is equally clearly definable as genocide under international law. The debate about the strength of the case centers on the interpretation of the 1948 Genocide Convention. There, genocide is defined as various acts, including "killing members of the group," which are pursued with an "intent to destroy, in whole or in part, a national, ethnical, racial or religious group, as such." Does the term "as such" mean that the Convention requires an intent to destroy a whole group? Does it mean, that is, that the killings (and/or other acts of oppression) must be carried out against people *because of their membership in that entire group?* According to Gregory Stanton, the *travaux* of the Convention apparently reveal the framers deliberately inserting the phrase "as such" into the Convention to avoid its prohibiting extermination of political groups.[46] This would mean that the Eastern Zone victims would need to have been singled out because they were Khmer, which is unlikely to have been the case. On the other hand, the phrase "as such" could apply not just to the preceding word "group," but to the entire preceding clause: "in whole *or in part,* a national, ethnical, racial or religious group, as such." If this interpretation stood, the Genocide Convention would merely require the mass murder of the Eastern Zone population to have been conducted because they were members of that Eastern Zone "part" of the Khmer national group. This is what happened, but the legal case that it constitutes genocide is not as strong as the case is for the genocide against the Buddhist monks and Chams.

Varying Interpretations

Interpretations of the nature of the Pol Pot regime have varied widely and controversially, even among Marxists and neo-Marxists. Its enemy and successor regime, for instance, quickly claimed that Pol Potism had been a case of Maoism exported to Cambodia by China's leaders in the 1970s.[47] Indeed, a 1985 official Chinese publication described the Khmer Rouge rule as "the period of economic reconstruction."[48] And the pro-Chinese neo-Marxist Samir Amin had initially welcomed Democratic Kampuchea as "a correct assessment of the hierarchy of contradictions" in Cambodia, and as a model for African socialists to follow because of its "rapid disurbanisation" and its economic autarky. Amin dismissed the claim that it was "an insignificant peasant rising" as being based on "resentment."[49] But in a 1981 reflection, Amin preferred to identify a Cambodian *combination* of Stalinist orthodoxy with what he now called "a principally peasant revolution": "The excesses, which today cannot be denied, are those which we know from the entire long history of peasant revolts. They are of the same nature and represent the same character."[50]

In 1984 the historian Michael Vickery took up this very theme as a reason to *reject* Democratic Kampuchea, because, he argued, "nationalism, populism and peasantism really won out over communism." In Vickery's view, Democratic Kampuchea was no Stalinist communist regime, but "a victorious peasant revolution, perhaps the first real one in modern times."[51] Another writer, Anthony Barnett, rejects Democratic Kampuchea with a contrasting analysis. He stresses its Stalinism, its centralization and creation of "a nation of indentured labourers."[52]

Samir Amin's contribution is his analysis of Cambodian society as a relatively undifferentiated peasant society, similar to others in South Asia and Africa, and quite unlike China and Vietnam with their powerful landlord classes. His sympathy for the Khmer Rouge is based on their innovativeness in adapting a communist strategy to these particular conditions. However, "this success itself has been the origin of the tragic difficulties," including "the well known excesses and shortcomings."[53]

But Michael Vickery, in explaining the outcome of the Cambodian revolution, dismisses the very existence of the Stalinist vanguard attractive to Amin. He sees the Pol Pot leadership as not significantly influenced by foreign communist models, but "pulled along" by "the peasant element."[54] Vickery's approach combines an influential postwar intellectual trend in Southeast Asian historiography with a 1970s revisionist trend evident in the historiography of Hitler's Germany. I will outline each in turn.

In his pathbreaking 1955 work, *Indonesian Trade and Society*, J. C. Van Leur remarked that European historians of premodern Southeast Asia tended to see the region as outsiders, "from the deck of the ship, the ramparts of the fortress, the high gallery of the trading house." Yet, Van Leur argued, at least until the nineteenth century the European impact on Southeast Asia had been minimal and superficial: "The sheen of the world religions and foreign cultural forms is a thin and flaking glaze; underneath it the whole of the old indigenous forms has continued to exist."[55]

Vickery applies this analysis to Hinduism in early Cambodian history, stressing the "Indic facade" on the indigenous culture of the pre-Angkor period.[56] He also applies it to communism in modern times. In *Cambodia 1975–1982*, he writes that "foreign relations and influences are very nearly irrelevant to an understanding of the internal situation." He later explains: "We need investigations into autonomous development rather than superficial diffusionism, a change in emphasis which has become common in most of the social sciences and has led to important advances in the last 30 years." Thus, in Vickery's view, *the only way* to account for the apparent similarities between DK and the programme of Sendero Luminoso" (the Peruvian Maoist guerrilla movement) is as cases of "convergent social and political evolution out of similar backgrounds."[57] So the Cambodian and Peruvian parties' common adherence to and study of Marxism-Leninism-Mao Zedong

Thought is seen as meaningless, if not as a dangerously misleading "facade."

An exception Vickery allows to this primacy of the indigenous is the influence on Cambodia of the French colonial political prison system. But even this involved more of a "convergence" of "the colonial legal burden," inherited from the Inquisition and the French Revolution, "with attitudes and practices handed down from traditional Cambodian society . . . in which the greatest crime, punishable by the severest penalties was disloyalty to the state represented by its officials." Cambodians, Vickery emphasizes, "were more directly exposed to French thought and traditions than Soviet." After independence this influence persisted, and so the Cambodian experience of the French colonial justice system does throw light on the Khmer Rouge "security organs," unlike the Stalinist models from which Cambodia "did not need advice" to perpetrate its horrors.[58]

Vickery combines this with a separate argument. The peasantry as a mass dominated the Cambodian revolution and took it in a direction the Pol Pot leadership could not have "either planned or expected." "It is certainly safe to assume that they did not foresee, let alone plan, the unsavoury developments of 1975–79. They were petty bourgeois radicals overcome by peasant romanticism."[59] This argument is not unlike Hans Mommsen's analysis of Nazi Germany. Mommsen believes, for instance, that Hitler did not plan the extermination of the Jews early in his career, but that Nazi policy was formed on an ad hoc basis over time and under the pressure of developing circumstances. It was a case of "cumulative radicalisation." Mommsen's argument is that Hitler was no freak aberration, and that German history and society more broadly are also implicated in the genocide of the Jews.[60] Similarly, Vickery considers DK an illustration of what happens when a peasantry assumes power: "It now appears fortunate that those who predicted a predominance of agrarian nationalism over Marxism in China and Vietnam were mistaken."[61]

The Pol Pot regime, then, was made up of "middle-class intellectuals with such a romantic, idealized sympathy for the power that they did not imagine rapid, radical restructuring of society in their favour would lead to such intolerable violence." But these Khmer Rouge leaders simply discovered that "it would have been impossible to hold the support of their peasant army" unless political enemies were "punished" and a departure made from the 1917 Bolshevik model of maintaining a "normal administration" and urban "privilege."[62] And when the urban populations were deported to the countryside, "the majority base peasants" of Cambodia participated "with some glee" in the persecution of those Vickery calls "their class enemies."[63] "The violence of

DK was first of all because it was such a complete peasant revolution, with the victorious revolutionaries doing what peasant rebels have always wanted to do to their urban enemies." It "did not spring forth from the brains of Pol Pot and Khieu Samphan."[64]

A major problem with this analysis is lack of evidence. Vickery's *Cambodia 1975–1982* contributes much to our knowledge of the Khmer Rouge, but he did not consult peasant sources seriously. Among the ninety or more interviewees Vickery presents in his survey of Democratic Kampuchea,[65] only one is a peasant. This interviewee hardly supports the notion of a peasant revolution, reporting "that they were fed well, but overworked and subject to 'fierce' discipline."[66] One family which Vickery describes as "half peasant–half urban," although "most of them by 1975 had long since ceased doing field work," all survived DK, but they "said that their many cousins, aunts, uncles, etc. . . . had perished, mainly of hunger and illness, although they were peasants. . . . In the opinion of the survivors, DK mismanagement had simply been so serious that not even peasants could survive."[67]

Nearly all Vickery's oral testimony in fact comes from male urban evacuees he met in refugee camps in Thailand in 1980.[68] His account of DK's Southwest Zone, which he correctly calls "the 'Pol Pot' zone *par excellence*," is based on the testimony of four former students, a former French teacher, a former Lon Nol soldier, a medic, an agricultural engineer, "a girl from the 'new' people," and "an attractive, well-educated woman of the former urban bourgeoisie."[69] These ten accounts offer unconvincing documentation of a key zone in a "peasant revolution." Among the few inside accounts in the book are corroborating reports, already noted, of an initial order to "kill urban evacuees indiscriminately." This order went out to both the Southwest and the Northwest zones.[70] It clearly emanated from the central government—perhaps even "from the brains of Pol Pot and Khieu Samphan."

This is probably the first major controversy in the historiography of the Cambodian revolution: the question of central control. Anthony Barnett has argued that DK was "a highly centralized dictatorship," whereas Serge Thion contends that it was "a bloody mess," "riddled" with factional and regional divergence, so that "the state never stood on its feet." Vickery stands with Thion.[71] My own view is that Barnett is closer to the truth. Despite its millenarian tone, Pol Potism was not a centrifugal peasant ideology but a centralizing one.[72] As Barnett has remarked, the Khmer Rouge not only succeeded in conscripting a massive labor force to turn Cambodia's landscape into a checkerboard of irrigation works, "They even communalised people's breakfasts!"

Nor was the ideology behind this purely indigenous. It was an amalgam of various intellectual influences, including Khmer elite chauvinism, Third World nationalism, the French Revolution, Stalinism, and some aspects of Mao Zedong's "Great Leap Forward"—which DK claimed to outdo with its own "Super Great Leap Forward." The motor of the Pol Pot program was probably Khmer racist chauvinism, but it was fueled by strategies and tactics adopted from unacknowledged revolutionary models in other countries. Such syncretism is historically very common in Southeast Asia.[73]

Here lies the second most important source of disagreement among specialists on the Cambodian holocaust. Was it genocide? A range of views exists. Vickery denies the applicability of the term genocide to the Khmer Rouge record, and Thion sees the concept itself as "a political commodity," preferring not to use it at all, or to define it.[74] A more overtly political argument is made by some who see the Khmer Rouge regime as purely "communist," a child of Lenin and Stalin. David P. Chandler, for instance, ignores or downplays questions of race, and a priori rejects terms like chauvinism or genocide, which he sees as inviting "egregious" parallels with Hitler.[75] Nazi–Khmer Rouge parallels are politically uncomfortable not only for Vietnamese communists who wish to blame Pol Potism on Maoist ideology or for some Western Marxists who brook no connection between communism and genocide, but also for Western anticommunists unable to consider noncommunist influences on the Khmer Rouge.

To take another example, Stephen R. Heder's writings on the Khmer Rouge also overlook the race issue, preferring to point out merely that, under the Khmer Rouge, "foreign influences and impingements were minimized."[76] This hardly accounts for the massacres of foreign and ethnic minorities, the forced suppression of their languages and cultures, the dispersal of their communities, or the DK military attacks on three foreign countries. In a similar vein, Chandler asserts that although DK "discriminated against the Chams," and "nearly all the Vietnamese inhabitants of Cambodia" were driven from their homes, while "a central committee directive ordered the execution of [remaining] ethnic Vietnamese residents in Cambodia," nevertheless "the regime discriminated against enemies of the revolution rather than against specific ethnic or religious groups."[77] He does not make the point here that to be "discriminated against" in DK meant to suffer a higher quota of murder and destruction.

Thus, while Vickery ignores communism as a foreign influence on DK, Chandler's explanations consider few others. Both writers, however, reject the case for genocide. Chandler asserts that most of the deaths "were never intended by DK," whose goal was a "utopian program of total and rapid social transformation." He also follows Vickery's underestimation of the toll, offering an unsubstantiated figure of one million despite the evidence for a much higher toll presented at the start of this chapter.[78] Such scholarship has its counterpart in the policymaking world.

War and Forgetting: The Failure of International Action

Despite its record, some Chinese and Western governmental circles saw an anti-Vietnamese, geopolitical use in the Khmer Rouge movement. A 1980 U.S. Central Intelligence Agency report on the "Demographic Catastrophe" in Cambodia blamed it largely on the Vietnamese intervention of 1979, and it even claimed that the Pol Pot regime had committed its "final executions" in 1976.[79] That is, it denied that the Khmer Rouge mass murders of half a million people in 1977 and 1978 had ever happened. In December 1980, news leaked out that Dr. Ray Cline, former deputy director of the CIA, had made a secret visit to a Khmer Rouge camp.[80]

Along with China, which supplied arms, and Thailand, which supplied sanctuary, the United States was instrumental in rescuing the Khmer Rouge army after its 1979 defeat by Hanoi. From 1979 to 1981, the United States led Western nations in voting for the Khmer Rouge to represent their Cambodian victims in the United Nations. In 1982, Washington helped prod two small pro-American groups into a Khmer Rouge-dominated alliance,[81] and for more than a decade the United States has rejected all opportunities to take individual or collective action against the Khmer Rouge. Former U.S. national security adviser Zbigniew Brzezinski says that in 1979: "I encouraged the Chinese to support Pol Pot. . . . Pol Pot was an abomination. We could never support him but China could."[82] They both did. The United States, Brzezinski says, "winked, semi-publicly" at Chinese and Thai aid for the Khmer Rouge.

Washington also pressured UN humanitarian organizations to aid the Khmer Rouge. In *Rice, Rivalry and Politics,* the major study of the relief effort for Cambodian refugees in Thailand, Linda Mason and Roger Brown, graduates of the Yale School of Management, revealed: "The U.S. Government, which funded the bulk of the relief operation on the border, insisted that the Khmer Rouge be fed." They add: "When World Relief started to push its proposal for aid to the Khmer Rouge, the U.S. was supportive, though behind the scenes . . . the US preferred that the Khmer Rouge operation benefit from the credibility of an internationally-known relief organization." Under U.S. influence, the World Food Program alone handed over $12 million worth of food to the Thai army to pass on to the Khmer Rouge. According to former Assistant Secretary of State Richard Holbrooke, "20–40,000 Pol Pot guerrillas benefited."[83] Mason and Brown note that the health of the Khmer Rouge army "rapidly improved" throughout 1980. "The Khmer Rouge had a history of unimaginable brutality, and having regained their strength, they had begun fighting the Vietnamese."[84]

In the U.S. public arena, the cause was taken up by Douglas Pike, author of *Viet Cong* and a prominent Indochina War hawk. Pike claimed in 1979 that Pol Pot was a "charismatic" and "popular" leader, under whom "most" Cambodian peasants "did not experience much in the way of brutality."[85] Ten years later, Pike argued in the *New York Times* for sharing "political power" with Pol Pot's forces. Although entitled "Khmer Rouge: Not the Threat It Was," his article threatened that "exclusion of the powerful Khmer Rouge . . . would only invite civil war." Their *inclusion* would invite peace. Pike opposed "forcing a shotgun wedding" between the non-Khmer Rouge parties, favoring the existing one between Pol Pot and the U.S.-backed noncommunists. He expressed no opinion on a possible machine-gun marriage between Pol Pot and the Khmer people.[86]

In Britain, the journalist William Shawcross, author of *Sideshow*, has assumed a fairly similar role. In 1979, he alleged that Hanoi's invasion to overthrow Pol Pot meant "genocide" by enforced starvation—"two million dead by Christmas." But four years later, in his second book on Cambodia, *The Quality of Mercy*, Shawcross had to concede that "there is no evidence that large numbers of people did . . . starve to death" at the hands of the Vietnamese or their Cambodian allies.[87]

The Quality of Mercy was a critique of the international aid program that helped save Cambodia from the threat of famine in 1979–80. Shawcross concluded that even though it "helped millions of ordinary Cambodians . . . overall its results were not a cause for great rejoicing."[88] He apparently considers that the aid program's aims had little to do with "ordinary Cambodians." Sharing this view, the Conservative British government voted for the Khmer Rouge in the UN and supported an international embargo on Cambodia. In 1990 London's Charity Commission began an investigation of Oxfam, the leading force in the successful aid program to Cambodia. The next year the Charity Commission criticized Oxfam for having "prosecuted with too much vigour" its public education campaign concerning the Pol Pot regime and the threat of its return.[89] Few "ordinary Cambodians" would be likely to agree. Only in 1991 did British government officials admit that despite repeated denials, for most of the 1980s elite SAS military teams had been training forces allied to the Khmer Rouge.[90]

In July 1990, after eleven years of diplomatic support for the Khmer Rouge, Washington pledged it would vote to end Khmer Rouge representation at the UN. (As of 1993, however, Pol Pot's ambassador and his coalition partners still operated from the Cambodian UN Mission in New York.[91]) In August 1990, a U.S.-sponsored Cambodian peace plan was promulgated by the United Nations; the Khmer Rouge were to be included in the proposed settlement. Within days, the UN's Human Rights Subcommission decided to *drop from its agenda* a draft resolution on Cambodia. This resolution had referred to "the atrocities reaching the level of genocide committed in particular during the period of Khmer Rouge rule," and it called on all states "to detect, arrest, extradite or bring to trial those who have been responsible for crimes against humanity committed in Cambodia," and "prevent the return to government positions of those who were responsible for genocidal actions during the period 1975 to 1978." But the resolution was dropped when "several speakers said it would render a disservice to the United Nations after the five permanent members of the UN Security Council issued a joint plan this week."[92] The November 1991 version of the UN plan attempted to give Pol Pot's Khmer Rouge "the same rights, freedoms and opportunities to take part in the electoral process" as any other Cambodian.[93] The plan would also have dismantled or disarmed the only forces opposed to the Khmer Rouge, and while proclaiming UN neutrality, could well have left the Khmer Rouge army in a position of practical military superiority. The threat of a second Cambodian genocide provoked no warnings, let alone action, from the superpowers. Indeed, the United States and China are primarily responsible for the threat.[94]

Others share responsibility. In late November 1989, Australia's foreign minister Gareth Evans launched his peace proposal for Cambodia, which was adopted by the UN the next year. But Evans refused to take any initiative against the Khmer Rouge, insisting on a solution acceptable to China. He was played for a sucker. The effect of his kowtow was revealed by China's ambassador in London: "from the beginning of January" 1990, Beijing began sending tanks to the Khmer Rouge, for the first time in twelve years.[95]

The UN is condoning what its own special rapporteur on genocide, Benjamin Whitaker, has described as "genocide . . . even under the most restricted definition."[96] (And in 1989 the U.S. Department of State concurred.) The first round of Cambodian negotiations, held in Indonesia in 1988, had produced a provision against "a recurrence of the genocidal policies and practices of the Pol Pot regime." The UN, on the other hand, mentions only "the policies and practices of the past." Its Human Rights Commission, having refused to discuss the genocide, now deals with Cambodia under the agenda item favored by the perpetrators, "the rights of the people to self-determination."

As part of a new effort to break the Cambodian deadlock, Japan made three new proposals in early 1991: UN monitoring from the start of a cease-fire, expulsion from the settlement process of any group which violates the cease-fire, and establishment of a special commission to investigate the Khmer Rouge. In Bangkok on 18 March 1991, Richard Solomon, U.S. assistant secretary of state, criticized Tokyo's proposals as potentially complicating the international peace efforts.

China described the overthrow of democracy in Thailand in February 1991 as "correct and just."[97] In April the new strongman in Bangkok, Army commander Suchinda Krapayoon, told a visiting U.S. senator that he considered Pol Pot a "nice guy."[98] (In 1985 Marshal Siddhi Savetsila, foreign minister of the former military regime, had described Pol Pot's deputy, Son Sen, as "a very good man.")[99] The prime minister of Thailand, Anand Panyarachun, pointedly told Khmer Rouge leader Khieu Samphan: "Sixteen years ago, I was also accused of being a communist and now they have picked me as Prime Minister. In any society there are always hard-liners and soft-liners, and society changes its attitude to them as time passes by."[100]

Meanwhile, readers of the *Bangkok Post* were treated to a new angle on the Khmer Rouge genocide:

Pol Pot, the infamous leader of the Khmer Rouge, has called on Cambodians to protect endangered species. He means, of course, Cambodia's diminishing wildlife, though during the period of Khmer Rouge rule from 1975 to late 1978, the most endangered species here was the human species. An estimated one million Cambodians died of starvation or murder at that time.

But now, Western intelligence sources along the Thai-Cambodian border say that Pol Pot recently issued a directive calling on Cambodians not to poach birds and animals, and to refrain from killing them for any reason. . . .

Anyone contravening Pol Pot's "green" directive . . . is brought before a jungle court and is *normally* sentenced to four days' labour on constructing fencing for animal sanctuaries, the sources add.[101]

This report was soon disproved,[102] but it does contain the real story: its source. "Western intelligence along the Thai-Cambodian border," which most likely means the CIA, apparently wished to "greenwash" the Red Khmer. It invited us to believe that Pol Pot was building up a healthy body of environmental case law—suggesting that some unusual offenders get, say, five-day and some three-day "sentences" for poaching rare birds.

The disinformation was specific. The same "Western intelligence sources" claimed that even Pol Pot's military commander, the notorious Mok, was also "hot on ecology issues and protection of endangered species." Mok's jungled area of northern Cambodia is where the conservationist courts held hearings. In fact, Mok is Pol Pot's most brutal general. In 1975–79, he slaughtered hundreds of thousands in rolling purges throughout Cambodia. Inside the country he is known as "The Butcher," though Western journalists routinely refer to him as *Ta* ("Grandfather") Mok.[103]

The claim that the Khmer Rouge use prisoners in the jungle to build fences for endangered animal species was no flash in the pan. According to the *Far Eastern Economic Review*, an "analyst at a Western embassy in Bangkok" has even described the Khmer Rouge as "much more respectful of civilians than the other three factions," while "diplomats say that the Khmer Rouge would not have signed an agreement it did not intend to follow."[104] Such claims make for extraordinary reading, in the light of the Khmer Rouge's record by that time, let alone its behavior since: Khmer Rouge violations quickly destroyed the very agreement it signed.[105]

We may expect more doublespeak if the Khmer Rouge army approaches power, and Washington is obliged to defend its twelve-year policy of diplomatic, economic, and other support for the Khmer Rouge genociders. In a 1991 article in the *Washington Quarterly*, Nate Thayer, an Associated Press reporter, filed away the 1975–79 Khmer Rouge genocide among Cambodia's last "20 years of continuous warfare, displacement, and foreign intervention that have killed millions."[106] Apparently, 1.5 million Cambodians were "displaced" somewhere. Using the official euphemism, Thayer distinguished "the policies and practices of the Khmer Rouge" from what he calls the "*violence and misery that preceded and succeeded them.*"[107]

Thayer laments the difficulty of erasing "the 20 years of distortion concerning the Khmer Rouge." Pol Pot's people are not "historically skilled or interested in molding world opinion," and have never made a "serious" attempt to "defend themselves."[108] So, "the view of the Khmer Rouge as a fanatical band of neo-Maoist or Marxist killers who engineered a bizarre campaign of auto-genocide will probably never be altered, even though the reality of what happened . . . is much more complex." Pol Pot's regime did implement some "more objectionable policies" and "abuses of human rights." But these were "largely perpetrated only on a certain sector of the population. It is this sector to which journalists, scholars and other foreign observers have had access." In Thayer's view, the "good news" still struggles for a hearing above the din of the "tales of horror" and of "killing of family members," which though "accurate," merely come from "the vast majority" of city dwellers. Urban Cambodians, he asserts, have received "disproportionate" attention, for they are "only the victims" (!), or even treacherous "defectors," that is, from the Khmer Rouge.

But "the Cambodian peasantry" reveals to Thayer an "objective national reality." Having visited "the rural areas" dominated by the Khmer Rouge and their allies, he claims unique "access" to the peasantry.[109] He stumbles upon the fact that "it is rare to hear of complaints of execution or violence perpetrated by the Khmer Rouge on the peasants" in areas "where the guerrillas are strongest." And the consequences of voicing such complaints in areas controlled by the Khmer Rouge alliance? Thayer prefers to accuse *others* of relying on "methodologically unacceptable" sources. Again a Western journalist returns from a guided tour to speak for the peasantry. It is an old story in Indochina, one which French scholar Paul Mus once described as "the monologue of colonialism."

The Khmer Rouge, according to Thayer, enjoy "considerable support among the population." Thayer estimates that support at "perhaps 20 percent." The original source is impeccable: Pol Pot himself. Thayer quotes him ruminating: "Suppose there are 100 seats in the Kampuchean National Assembly, it would not be bad if we had 20 persons." Pointing out that the by now familiar "analysts" are inclined to "agree" with this, Thayer follows suit.[110]

Forget for a moment about the 20 percent of Cambodians already "displaced," as Thayer's euphemism has it, by the "policies and practices of the past." Why support any Cambodian army with one-fifth, or much less, of the surviving population on its side? (Some rare species apparently do need protection, from Cambodian public opinion.) Of this, Washington needed little convincing. U.S. Assistant Secretary of State Richard Solomon described Nate Thayer's piece as "an outstanding analysis," "the most soberminded and well-informed assessment of that issue I've seen." Congressman Stephen J. Solarz of New York, an architect of U.S. Cambodia policy, found Thayer to be "a brilliant young journalist." He added: I've met with him and I have the highest regard for his judgment.[111]

Thayer was later appointed Phnom Penh correspondent of the *Far Eastern Economic Review.* When the Khmer Rouge leader Khieu Samphan returned to Phnom Penh after the October 1991 Paris Agreement to be greeted by a crowd of vengeful demonstrators who nearly lynched him, Thayer's coverage of the event in the *Review* relied heavily on Khmer Rouge sources, and unlike all other eyewitness reports, it included no interviews with any member of the crowd.[112]

In January 1992, Khmer Rouge troops made a concerted attack on twenty-five villages in Kompong Thom province. They mortared and burned "whole villages," killed thirteen people, wounded eighteen, and drove ten thousand from their homes. Diplomats conceded that "the Khmer Rouge apparently mounted the attacks." Their former allies Ieng Mouly of the KPNLF and Prince Sihanouk also suggested that they held the Khmer Rouge responsible. Nate Thayer was alone in laying no blame on the Khmer Rouge, alleging in the *Review* that "government forces clashed with Khmer Rouge guerrillas, causing the worst ceasefire violations since the signing of the peace accord in November." On 26 February, Khmer Rouge forces fired on a UN helicopter in the area, wounding the commanding officer of the Australian contingent in Cambodia.[113]

As of 1992, the perpetrators of genocidal massacres were running their country's mission at the United Nations, represented there by Pol Pot's handpicked ambassador. Ironically, while still a member of the UN, *the Pol Pot regime could be held accountable* for its crimes in the World Court. And its overthrow in 1979 has meant that the evidence could be gathered against it. Fellow members of the UN, who have signed the Convention without reservations, could take the case to the World Court. None has done so even though the Pol Pot forces remain the major obstacle to peace in Cambodia. Negotiations have consistently broken down over their role and because of Chinese and U.S. demands for the ouster of their only Cambodian opponent, the Hun Sen regime.[114]

The chance is unique in the annals of mass murder. Failure to seize it undoubtedly encourages future genociders in the knowledge that the Convention will never be applied. The long delay has buoyed Pol Pot's forces, which are now pursuing a war to retake power.

In the Saudi Arabian video version of the television series "War and Remembrance," which covers the Holocaust in some detail, all references to Jews were "blanked out" before broadcasting. "You could see the characters mouthing the word "Jew," one viewer commented, "but no sound was coming out." The *Wall Street Journal* reports that "references to Jews are often censored" in Saudi Arabia. Saudi radio has even called Saddam Hussein "a Jew."[115]

In 1989 I wrote an article for a Saudi-based journal about Pol Pot's massacres of Muslims in Cambodia in the late 1970s. One hundred thousand Muslims had been killed or starved to death in four years. One point I made was that the Pol Pot regime had marked victims by making them wear distinctive blue Cambodian neck scarves. These scarves, I wrote, were "the grim equivalents of the Yellow Star, used by Hitler to mark Jews for slaughter during World War Two." I wrote that Pol Pot had called his revolution the only "clean" one in history, just as the Nazis boasted that areas they occupied had been "cleaned" of Jews. The journal printed my critique of Saudi diplomatic support for the Pol Pot regime, but none of my statements mentioning the Jews or their plight appeared in the published version.[116]

Could something like this happen in the *New York Times?* In November 1988 I was commissioned by the *New York Times Magazine* to write a story about the "blue scarves." I submitted the piece, detailing how hundreds of thousands of innocent peasants were targeted and identified for slaughter. I noted the Yellow Star precedent, and mentioned in passing some additional parallels: "Like Hitler's regime, Pol Pot's 'Democratic Kampuchea' staged military attacks against all of its neighbours. It forcibly deported its citizens en masse, and it brutally persecuted and exterminated the country's ethnic minorities." After reading this, the editor spoke to me and insisted: "We just won't go into the issue of Nazi Germany." I could mention only the 1948 Genocide Convention.[117]

In this case the notion of the uniqueness of the Jewish experience under Hitler seems to have blocked free exploration of the nature of genocide. In the reverse of the Saudi regime's racism, it is a kind of positive discrimination that places the Holocaust in a category apart from all other cases. As Richard Evans has pointed out, there is much truth to this: only the Nazis made such a systematic attempt at "killing in its entirety a whole racial group."[118] The genocide of the Pol Pot regime, for example, did not involve an attempt to *murder all* Chams or Buddhist monks. But it apparently did set out to murder all Eastern Zone Cambodians. Limiting discussion of possible parallels between the Nazis and the Khmer Rouge to the single point of the blue scarf and yellow star distorts the context and serves the interest of neither group of their victims. And there is more to the comparison than meets the eye. During World War II in occupied Croatia, the Nazi puppet regime ordered Serbs to wear blue armbands as a sign of their alien status.[119] Pol Pot, who visited Croatia in 1950, not long after the war ended, was surely apprised of this fact.

The American-Saudi coalition in the Middle East includes Egypt, another Muslim country that has long supported the Pol Pot regime. In 1988 I sent a lengthy piece on the genocide of the Cambodian Muslims to an American publisher. The publisher referred the manuscript to an outside reader, one of Egypt's ambassadors, for review. The ambassador's response was thoughtful, but evinced little concern for his fellow Muslims in Cambodia. He did not question the facts of the case, although he doubted it qualified as genocide. Further, he voiced reservations about publishing the book in the current climate, warning that such material might serve only to heighten the level of frustration among Islamic fundamentalists.

The ambassador added that, if the book were published by an American publisher, it might invoke America's involvement in Vietnam. The late Beverly Jean Smith once demolished this argument: "But fear of moral blackmail is scarcely a basis for a foreign policy. Nor is a conspiracy of silence between two established orders."[120] Surely citizens, too, are justified in calling attention to injustice at home and abroad.

Human Rights Organizations and the Cambodian Genocide

We have noted how in 1990, the UN's Human Rights Subcommission dropped from its agenda a draft resolution that had noted "the atrocities reaching the level of genocide committed in particular during the period of Khmer Rouge rule" and had called for action to be taken against the perpetrators. The UN's failure is yet to stir any scandal in the international human rights community. The extraordinary fact is that in the decade and more since Pol Pot's overthrow, many reputable legal organizations have dismissed proposals to send delegations to Cambodia to investigate the crimes of his regime, which caused the deaths of 1.5 million out of a population of 8 million in four years. The International Commission of Jurists, the American Bar Association, and LawAsia have all refused such opportunities[121] to report on what the UN's special rapporteur on the matter described in 1985 as "genocide."

Amnesty International has also rejected suggestions that it publish a serious report on the genocide, limiting itself over the past fifteen years to a few pages here and there. Amnesty has preferred to publicly document in detail only post-1979 human rights violations by Pol Pot's opponents, the successor regime that ended the genocide. The New York-based Lawyers Committee for Human Rights, too, has focused on post-genocidal violations, starting with those of the anti-Khmer Rouge Cambodian government. In a 1984 preliminary report, the Lawyers Committee even asserted that the Khmer Rouge had adopted "a policy of restraint with respect to violations of physical security."[122]

To its credit, however, the Lawyers Committee did not repeat this error in its 1985 report, which recognized that Phnom Penh's human rights violations in the 1980s "pale in comparison to the mass murders of recent memory" (1975–79). In later reports, the Lawyers Committee documented in detail the continuing crimes of the Khmer Rouge and their noncommunist allies against refugees in Thailand since 1979.[123] Though it has produced no report on the 1975–79 Khmer Rouge genocide, the Committee stated: "The bestiality that roamed large throughout Kampuchea in the 1970s remains unpunished. Violations of the nearly unprecedented scale practiced in the Pol Pot years demand a full historical and legal accounting. Under the supervision of David Hawk, the Cambodia Documentation Commission is working toward that objective."[124]

The Cambodia Documentation Commission (CDC) had adopted this goal in 1982, and by 1987 there was good reason to hope it would be successful. It managed a creditable campaign to persuade one or more Western nations to take the case against the Pol Pot regime to the World Court, under the 1948 Genocide Convention.[125] The campaign failed due to Chinese and U.S. opposition, not to any lack of a legal basis, evidence, or effort. However, David Hawk also failed to fulfill commitments to publish research he had commissioned on the genocide.[126] He opposed alternative initiatives and declined to join others, such as the Cambodian Genocide Project and the Campaign to Oppose the Return of the Khmer Rouge, who were working toward the same goal. From 1988, his CDC progressively downgraded the issue,[127] and in 1990, Hawk threw his support behind a "comprehensive settlement" proposal that would include the Khmer Rouge, preferring such a settlement to none or to challenging those insisting on inclusion of the Khmer Rouge. Like William Shawcross, he has preferred to target the critics of the Khmer Rouge, rather than the supporters of their role in the UN process.[128]

A few voluntary organizations around the world have pressed on, unaided by the major league human rights lobby. These include the U.S. Cambodia Genocide Project, which in 1980 had conceived the proposal for a World Court case; the Australian section of the International Commission of Jurists, which in January 1990 called for "international trials" of the Pol Pot leadership for genocide; the Minnesota Lawyers International Human Rights Committee, which in June 1990 organized a one-day mock trial of the Khmer Rouge following the procedures of the World Court, with testimony by a dozen surviving victims of the genocide; and the Washington-based lobby group Campaign to Oppose the Return of the Khmer Rouge, which has the support of forty-five U.S. organizations, a former Cambodian prime minister, a former minister of information, and survivors of the Khmer Rouge period.

In mid-1991 the UN Human Rights Subcommission reversed its position. It passed a resolution noting "the duty of the international community to prevent the recurrence of genocide in Cambodia" and "to take all necessary preventive measures to avoid conditions that could create for the Cambodian people the risk of new crimes against humanity."[129] However, the bureaucratization of human rights discussion persisted. On 30 November 1992, an international seminar was organized in Phnom Penh by the Human Rights Component of the

UN Transitional Authority in Cambodia (UNTAC). At the seminar the Component's deputy director (a former official of Amnesty International) deterred the circulation of material detailing the Khmer Rouge genocide and war crimes. The opening speech by the director of the Human Rights Component could have been written by Nate Thayer: it referred to the 1975–79 genocide only as part of "decades of conflict, upheaval and confrontation."[130] But the UN's special representative in Cambodia, Yasushi Akashi, actually twisted on a double euphemism, describing "the policies and practices of the past" as "a euphemism for the gross human rights violations which Cambodia has experienced in recent decades."[131] All this was equivalent to describing only "the social disruption and confrontation in Germany between 1920 and 1950," eliding the Weimar Republic and Konrad Adenauer, along with the atrocities of the Nazi regime. That elision would hardly be tolerated by human rights groups anywhere. Yet in Cambodia it was their handiwork. The three-hour opening public session of the Human Rights Component's seminar saw no reference to the specific years 1975–79, to genocide, to mass murder, nor even to killings by the Khmer Rouge. No action was to be taken either. The Human Rights Component's director pointed out that despite "UNTAC's complete inability to work in one of the zones of Cambodia"—a euphemism for the Khmer Rouge zone—"we must take all steps to avoid the gross violations of the past by dealing with the present." This appears to mean preventing human rights violations only by the parties that allow a UN presence in their zones. While the Khmer Rouge's past crimes are consigned to the past, their current human rights violations are quarantined and thus out of UN control. The director stretches credulity in proclaiming that "the UNTAC human rights mandate . . . is unparalleled in its comprehensiveness and its ambition."[132]

In the fourteen years since the Pol Pot regime's occupation of Cambodia's UN seat was first challenged, not a single Western country has voted against its right to represent the victims of its genocide. Some international human rights organizations also deferred to the political agenda of the U.S. and Chinese governments, which was to focus attention on the human rights violations of the opponents of the Khmer Rouge, not on the Khmer Rouge genocide. For many years, U.S. policy appeared to require a Vietnamese withdrawal from Cambodia, which was completed in 1989. But Washington then attempted to replace the government of the State of Cambodia, the only force resisting the Khmer Rouge genociders, with a more pliable regime led by longtime allies of Pol Pot—Prince Sihanouk and KPNLF leader Son Sann. By its own complicity, the UN Security Council signaled to future genocidists that the worst they can expect is to have their opponents partially disarmed, if not removed from office, and to face them in unarmed combat with immunity from prosecution. Washington and Beijing forced Cambodia to accept a Khmer Rouge return and to risk a Khmer Rouge seizure of power due to the predictable UN failure to disarm them. As of early 1993, the Khmer Rouge return to Cambodia appeared irreversible. The Cambodian conflict continues.

Notes

1. For my figure of 1.5 million deaths, see Barry Wain, *The Refused—The Agony of the Indochina Refugees* (Hong Kong: Dow Jones, 1981), 272, n. 8; or Ben Kiernan, "Kampuchea Stumbles to Its Feet" (December 1980), in *Peasants and Politics in Kampuchea, 1942–1981,* ed. Ben Kiernan and Chanthou Boua (London: Zed Books, 1982), 380.

2. Milton Osborne, "Pol Pot's Terrifying Legacy," *Far Eastern Economic Review* (6 June 1980): 20–22. Thirty-three of the interviewees, nearly half of them from nonelite background, reported another two hundred or more nonimmediate family members executed. Forty-two of the one hundred reported having witnessed executions take place, particularly in the latter years of the regime.

3. If Osborne's sample was representative, the 25 percent death rate would suggest a national toll of two million. Despite Osborne's efforts his sample does underrepresent the peasantry, who make up 80 percent of the population (not 42 percent). But it also overrepresents Khmer Rouge supporters, as the survey was partly conducted in camps dominated by them. This data therefore points to a possible toll of around 1.5 million.

4. The terms "new people" and "base people" were used by the Khmer Rouge in 1975 to describe those who had lived under enemy control until then, and those who had lived in the Khmer Rouge "bases" in the countryside.

5. See Ben Kiernan, "Kampuchea's Ethnic Chinese Under Pol Pot: A Case of Systematic Social Discrimination," *Journal of Contemporary Asia* 16, no. 1 (1986): 18–29, 29 for the full reference. A New Zealander working for an international agency carrying out a census of Phnom Penh's population, whom I met there in February 1975, told me that the population of Phnom Penh at that time was 1.8 million. My estimate of the number of "new people" at 3,050,000 is based on this figure plus an estimate of 1,250,000 for the population of other towns and rural areas then under the control of Lon Nol's Khmer Republic. This second figure is comprised as follows: Battambang province's population in 1968 was 685,000 (Migozzi, *Cambodge,* 228); for 1975 I have estimated 700,000, both in rural areas and the swollen towns of Battambang, Sisophon, Nimit, Poipet, Pailin, and Maung Russei. The twelve other Cambodian urban centers under Lon Nol control in 1975 had totaled 231,000 inhabitants in 1968 (Migozzi, *Cambodge,* 228), but population increase as well as rural refugee influx greatly increased these numbers by 1975. For instance, Kompong Thom in 1968 had 14,000 inhabitants, but the figure rose to 60,000 in 1974 (a 76 percent increase; Donald Kirk, "The Khmer Rouge: Revolutionaries or Terrorists?," unpublished paper, 9); Kompong Chhnang had 19,000 in 1968, and 50,000 in 1975 (a 62 percent increase). An average increase of 50 percent from 1968 to 1975 would give nearly 350,000. I have estimated the rural population controlled by Lon Nol's regime outside Battambang (mostly in Kandal prov-

ince) at another 200,000 people. (With about 400,000 rural Khmers in Battambang, these comprised the 600,000 rural Khmer "new people" [Table 5].)

6. The 1970 population was estimated at 7,363,000 by Jacques Migozzi in *Cambodge: Faits et problemes de population* (Paris: CNRS, 1973), 226, 212. A mid-1974 UN estimate, corroborated by an independent Western statistician then working with the Cambodian government, put the population at 7,890,000. In a radio broadcast on 21 March 1976, the Pol Pot government gave its own count of the population as 7,735,279. The number of survivors in 1979 is thought to have been 6.2 to 6.7 million. See Ben Kiernan, "The Genocide in Cambodia, 1975–1979," *Bulletin of Concerned Asian Scholars (BCAS)* 22, no. 2 (1990): 35–40, for the evidence for the April 1975 population figure of 7,894,000 (I have rounded this down to 7,890,000 in Table 5). For Vickery's 7.1 million figure for 1975 (the word "guess" is his), see Michael Vickery, *Cambodia 1975–1982* (Boston: South End, 1984), 185; Vickery, "How Many Died in Pol Pot's Kampuchea," *BCAS*, 20, no. 1 (1988): 70–73; Vickery, "Comments on Cham Population Figures," *BCAS*, 22, no. 1 (1990): 31–33.

7. May Ebihara, "A Cambodian Village under the Khmer Rouge," in *Genocide and Democracy in Cambodia,* ed. Ben Kiernan (New Haven, CT: Yale University Southeast Asia Council/Schell Center for International Human Rights, 1993), forthcoming.

8. Katuiti Honda, *Journey to Cambodia: Investigation into Massacre by Pol Pot Regime* (Tokyo: Committee for Publication of Journey to Cambodia, 1981), 48–50, 56–62.

9. Honda, *Journey to Cambodia*, chaps. 3, 5.

10. Vickery notes that these two informants "had high school or university education, were accustomed to dealing with figures, and were sober and nonsensational in their accounts." Vickery, *Cambodia, 1975–1982*, 118, 320, n. 195.

11. William Shawcross, *Sideshow: Kissinger, Nixon and the Destruction of Cambodia* (London: Deutsch, 1979), 21–23, 31.

12. Ben Kiernan, *How Pol Pot Came to Power* (London: Verso, 1985), chap. 8, and Kiernan, "The American Bombardment of Kampuchea, 1969–1973," *Vietnam Generation*, 1, no. 1 (1989): 4–41.

13. My view in early 1976 was as follows: "Many tell of sporadic executions of people by the victorious Khmer Rouge, and although there are few eyewitnesses to such incidents, some of these reports are believed to be true." *Tharunka* (Sydney), 3 March 1976.

14. For a brief biography of Pol Pot, see Ben Kiernan, "Medieval Master of the Killing Fields," *Guardian Weekly* (London), 12 August 1990.

15. Chanthou Boua, David P. Chandler, and Ben Kiernan, eds., *Pol Pot Plans the Future: Confidential Leadership Documents from Democratic Kampuchea, 1976–77* (New Haven, CT: Yale University Southeast Asia Studies Monograph No. 33, 1988), 346, 214–20.

16. At this stage, as I wrote later in the *Bulletin of Concerned Asian Scholars* 11, no. 4 (1979) and 12, no. 2 (1980), I misjudged the nature of the Khmer Rouge program.

17. The Vietnamese official, whose identity remains unknown, added that "thousands had been shot dead by the Cambodian communist soldiers," and that some killings continued even after the order to stop. *Bangkok Post*, 23 July 1975.

18. David P. Chandler, Ben Kiernan, and Muy Hong Lim, *The Early Phases of Liberation in Northwest Cambodia: Conversations with Peang Sophi* (Clayton, Vic-

toria: Monash University Centre of Southeast Asian Studies, 1976), working paper no. 11, 9. I cited this and the two 1975 *Bangkok Post* accounts, in "Social Cohesion in Revolutionary Cambodia," *Australian Outlook* 30, no. 3 (1976): 34, n. 13, as evidence for my view at the time that the violence was mostly spontaneous, consisting of postwar, local revenge killings.

19. In November 1976, two colleagues and I published the story of Peang Sophi, a Khmer refugee from the Khmer Rouge, whom Hong Lim and I had interviewed at length. Sophi reported that the Khmer Rouge maintained control partly by "the threat and collective memory of force," and he told of a number of executions and disappearances and of the circulation of "a macabre jingle, 'the Khmer Rouge kill, but never explain'" (Chandler, Kiernan, and Lim, *The Early Phases of Liberation*, 3–4, 9). In an article I published in December 1976, based in large part on refugee accounts I had collected in Thailand, I wrote that the Khmer Rouge had "often executed local authorities, money-lenders and landlords" and that "there is little doubt that high-ranking army officers and some officials of the Lon Nol regime were executed after the war . . . on orders from the Khmer Rouge provincial or central leadership." I also wrote that "on the exodus from Phnom Penh" in April 1975, "eyewitnesses reported seeing female Khmer Rouge troops ask several men if they were Lon Nol soldiers, then take them aside and execute them. . . . For many months after that, refugees reported that Lon Nol soldiers were hunted down . . . a few refugees were eyewitnesses to executions." I described "the harshness of the evacuation as witnessed by Westerners": "The trek into the country, and the hard work in the fields that was to follow, were very tough going for people unused to manual work. . . . Some starved in the countryside. . . . Many of them fled to Thailand with tales of starvation, hardship, and forced labour. In one village . . . 1,500 out of 2,000 people are said to have died of starvation," while in the area "much of the rice they grew was taken away" by the Khmer Rouge. "It is little wonder that several thousand peasants have fled. . . . Many ordinary Khmer peasants have been the victims" of "continued violence and hardship." Kiernan, "Social Cohesion in Revolutionary Cambodia," 371–86. See also note 13, above, and Ben Kiernan, "Why's Kampuchea Gone to Pot?" *Nation Review* (Melbourne), 17 November 1978.

20. Vickery, *Cambodia 1975–1982*, 60. See Ben Kiernan, *Cambodia: Eastern Zone Massacres* (New York: Columbia University, Center for the Study of Human Rights, Documentation Series No. 1, 1986), see 4–6, for considerable evidence of "relative tranquility in the East in 1975 and 1976 at least."

21. Vickery, *Cambodia 1975–1982*, 98–99.

22. Ibid., 112.

23. While the term "Center" technically invokes the authority of the Central Committee of the CPK, there is no evidence that such a body ever met, in plenary session or as a body on any other occasion, during the DK period. In reality the term "Party Center" therefore refers to those members of the Standing Committee of the Central Committee who had national responsibility and were not specifically responsible for a *regional* area, such as one of the zones of the country. The Party Center included: Pol Pot, Nuon Chea, Vorn Vet (executed 1978), Ieng Sary, Son Sen, and Khieu Samphan.

24. I am grateful to Stephen Heder for putting this view to me in a personal communication, April 1991.

25. Boua, Chandler and Kiernan, *Pol Pot Plans the Future*, 3.

26. See Chanthou Boua, Ben Kiernan, and Anthony Barnett, "Bureaucracy

of Death: Documents from Inside Pol Pot's Torture Machine," *New Statesman* (London), 2 May 1980, 669–76.

27. Kiernan, "Why's Kampuchea Gone to Pot?"

28. Chanthou Boua, "Genocide of a Religious Group: Pol Pot and Cambodia's Buddhist Monks," in *State-Organized Terror: The Case of Violent Internal Repression*, ed. V. Schlapentokh, C. Vanderpool, T. Bushnell, and J. Sundram (Boulder, CO: Westview, 1991).

29. Karl Jackson, ed., *Cambodia 1975–1978: Rendezvous with Death* (Princeton, NJ: Princeton University Press, 1989), 191.

30. *Democratic Kampuchea Is Moving Forward*, August 1977, 6, claimed a Khmer majority of "99 percent."

31. See for instance Robert Sam Anson, *War News: A Young Reporter in Indochina* (New York: Simon and Schuster, 1989), chaps. 8–9.

32. Kiernan, "Kampuchea's Ethnic Chinese Under Pol Pot," pp. 18–29.

33. Ben Kiernan, "The Survival of Cambodia's Ethnic Minorities," *Cultural Survival*, 14, no. 3 (1990): 64–66.

34. Ben Kiernan, "Orphans of Genocide: The Cham Muslims of Kampuchea under Pol Pot," *Bulletin of Concerned Asian Scholars*, 20, no. 4 (1988): 2–33.

35. Katuiti Honda, *Journey to Cambodia*, 132–39.

36. These two accounts published by Honda were overlooked in my study, "Orphans of Genocide," 2–33.

37. Kiernan, "Orphans of Genocide," 17, 27.

38. Vickery, "Comments on Cham Population Figures," 32–33.

39. Kiernan, "The Genocide in Cambodia, 1975–1979."

40. "Les Khmers Islam...," *Angkor* (Phnom Penh), 30 June 1956, p. 4. I am grateful to Justin Corfield of Monash University for drawing my attention to this reference. The minimum figure it gives for Cham adult male voters on the Cambodian electoral roll is 29,786. (Females did not vote until 1958: see *La femme cambodgienne de l'ère du Sangkum* [Phnom Penh, Ministry of Information, July 1965], 5: "Les citoyennes cambodgiennes votèrent pour la première fois le 21 mars 1958.") This must be doubled to include Cham females over twenty-one, and then projected to include Chams of both sexes under twenty-one. (I use the national proportion: the number on the 1958 national electoral roll was 39.16 percent of the Cambodian population at that time, noted in J. Delvert, *Le paysan cambodgien* [Paris: Mouton, 1961], 305.) Thus the Cham population in Cambodia *as early as 1955* already numbered around 150,000.

41. National growth rates of 2.65 percent for 1955–60, 2.83 percent for 1960–65, and 2.95 percent for 1965–70. See Jacques Migozzi, *Cambodge*.

42. Kiernan, "The Genocide in Cambodia, 1975–1979," 38.

43. Ben Kiernan, "Blue Scarf/Yellow Star: A Lesson in Genocide," *Boston Globe*, 27 February 1989. And Kiernan, "Genocidal Targeting: Two Groups of Victims in Pol Pot's Cambodia," in Schlapentokh et al., *State-Organized Terror*.

44. Kiernan, *Cambodia: Eastern Zone Massacres*.

45. Richard Dudman, "Pol Pot: Brutal Yes, but No Mass Murderer," *New York Times*, 17 August 1990. According to John Pilger, Dudman has been used by the U.S. Public Broadcasting Service as an "expert" on issues such as whether to screen Pilger's 1979 film *Cambodia Year Zero*, which was highly critical of the Khmer Rouge. Pilger says that Dudman opposed screening it. *Year Zero* and Pilger's two subsequent award-winning Cambodia documentaries (*Year One* and *Year Ten*) were not shown on PBS, except in San Francisco where *Year Ten*

was shown in 1990. In 1991, PBS station WNET (New York) did broadcast the next Pilger-David Munro film, *Cambodia: The Betrayal*, on 11 February. The other films have been screened in more than thirty countries.

46. Dr. Gregory Stanton, Cambodia Genocide Project, personal communication. Diane Orentlicher of the International League for Human Rights shares this view; personal communication.

47. For a presentation of this case, see Vladimir Simonov, *Kampuchea: Crimes of Maoists and Their Rout* (Moscow: Novosti, 1979), 21: "Each act of the Kampuchean tragedy was staged according to a Chinese blueprint."

48. *Cambodia* (Guangxi: People's Publishing House, 1985). I am grateful to Penny Edwards for her translation of this material.

49. Samir Amin, "The Lesson of Cambodia," in *Imperialism and Unequal Development* (Sussex: Harvester Press, 1977), 147–52, at 147, 150. See note 50, however.

50. Samir Amin, paper presented under the title "The Lesson of Cambodia" at the Conference on Kampuchea, Tokyo, 31 May–3 June 1981, 4, 8–9, where he first credits the Khmer Rouge with "the honour of having defined a strategy of anti-imperialist struggle," and then claims that "the revolution had been carried out by the peasants themselves." On page 15, Amin credits, "Stalin, who in his time was a better Marxist than his successors." Amin's paper presents the Chinese government's view of the world at that time.

51. Vickery, *Cambodia 1975–1982*, 289–90, and 66.

52. Anthony Barnett, "Democratic Kampuchea: A Highly Centralized Dictatorship," in *Revolution and Its Aftermath in Kampuchea: Eight Essays*, ed. David P. Chandler and Ben Kiernan (New Haven, CT: Yale Southeast Asia Studies Monograph No. 25, 1983), 211–29, and remarks at the August 1981 Chiangmai colloquium on Cambodia that led to that book.

53. See note 50, above.

54. Vickery, *Cambodia 1975–1982*, 287.

55. J. C. Van Leur, *Indonesian Trade and Society* (The Hague: van Hoeve, 1955), 95.

56. Michael Vickery, *Cambodia Before Angkor*, forthcoming from the Centre of Southeast Asian Studies, Clayton, Australia.

57. Vickery, *Cambodia 1975–1982*, xii; and "Violence in Democratic Kampuchea: Some Problems of Explanation," paper distributed at a conference on State-Organized Terror: The Case of Violent Internal Repression, Michigan State University, East Lansing, MI, November 1988, 23, at 17. Emphasis added.

58. Vickery, "Violence in Democratic Kampuchea," 15–16.

59. Ibid., 17, and Vickery, *Cambodia 1975–1982*, 287.

60. For a summary of this argument, see Richard J. Evans, *In Hitler's Shadow* (New York: Pantheon, 1989), 74–76, and references cited.

61. Vickery, *Cambodia 1975–1982*, 290.

62. Vickery, "Violence in Democratic Kampuchea," 14, 20, 5.

63. Michael Vickery, "Cambodia (Kampuchea): History, Tragedy and Uncertain Future," *Bulletin of Concerned Asian Scholars* 21, no. 2–4 (1989): 35–58, at 47.

64. Vickery, "Violence in Democratic Kampuchea," 17; *Cambodia 1975–1982*, 286.

65. Vickery states in his preface: "I have made no attempt to count the number of people with whom I talked. . . . Interested readers can do that for them-

selves" (*Cambodia 1975–1982*, xi.). I counted ninety-two interviewees, including seventeen teachers, thirteen former students, six former Khmer Rouge, four people described as "bourgeois," "intellectual," or "elite," three "businessmen," three engineers and a doctor, seven former Lon Nol officers and three soldiers, six carpenters, a radio mechanic, a truck driver, and twelve others of backgrounds clearly identified as urban. The remainder, unidentifiable by background, were not peasants. Vickery concedes that "bourgeois refugees . . . have provided most of the information used here" (p. 85).

66. Vickery, *Cambodia 1975–1982*, 112.

67. Ibid., 106.

68. Nine of Vickery's ninety-plus informants are identified as female. See note 65, above.

69. Vickery, *Cambodia 1975–1982*, 98, 91, 97.

70. Ibid., 98, 112.

71. Chandler and Kiernan, *Revolution and Its Aftermath in Kampuchea*, 211–29, esp. 213; 10–33, esp. 28; and 99–135, respectively.

72. See Ben Kiernan, "Wild Chickens, Farm Chickens, and Cormorants," in Chandler and Kiernan, *Revolution and Its Aftermath in Kampuchea*, 136–211.

73. For some examples of Southeast Asian cultural eclecticism, see Jayne Susan Werner, *Peasant Politics and Religious Sectarianism: Peasant and Priest in the Cao Dai in Viet Nam* (New Haven, CT: Yale University Southeast Asia Studies Council Monograph No. 23, 1981); and David Mitchell, "Communists, Mystics, and Sukarnoism," *Dissent* (Autumn 1968): 28–32.

74. See Vickery, "Comments on Cham Population Figures," 31–33; and Serge Thion, "Genocide as a Political Commodity," forthcoming in Kiernan, *Genocide and Democracy in Cambodia*.

75. David P. Chandler, *The Tragedy of Cambodian History* (New Haven, CT: Yale University Press, 1991), 3. Chandler overlooks the case for genocide altogether. He briefly notes the abolition of religion (263–65) but not the ban on minority languages and cultures nor the enforced dispersal of communities, and he offers no estimates of any death toll among either monks or minorities. He concedes that "the party seems to have . . . discriminated against the Chams, a Muslim minority unsympathetic to the revolution"—a false imputation until the genocide began in 1975. He avers that DK, as he puts it, treated the Chinese "poorly," but that China may have helped protect them (285).

76. Stephen R. Heder, *From Pol Pot to Pen Sovan to the Villages* (Bangkok: Chulalongkorn University Center of Asian Studies, May 1980), 1.

77. Chandler, *The Tragedy*, 285; 375, n. 36. He reveals no basis beyond DK's own for regarding ethnic victims such as the Chams as "enemies of the revolution." Chandler's anti-Vietnamese bias is clear in his 1984 statement: "*Unfortunately*, the imposition of foreign control, however humiliating it is, particularly to people serving in the government itself, does not seem to arouse emotions as intense as the possibility that 'Pol Pot' might at some stage return to power" (David P. Chandler, "Cambodia in 1984: Historical Patterns Re-asserted?" in *Southeast Asian Affairs* 1985 [Singapore: Heinemann, 1985], 177–86, 182, emphasis added). He also describes the 1975 DK ethnic cleansing campaign against longtime Vietnamese residents of Cambodia as a "repatriation" (*The Tragedy*, 285).

78. Chandler, *The Tragedy*, 1.

79. *Kampuchea: A Demographic Catastrophe* (National Foreign Assessment Center, U.S. Central Intelligence Agency, May 1980), Appendix C. For cri-

tiques of this document, see Michael Vickery, "Democratic Kampuchea: CIA to the Rescue," *Bulletin of Concerned Asian Scholars (BCAS)* 14, no. 4 (1982): 45–54; and Kiernan, "The Genocide in Cambodia, 1975–1979," 35–40, and references cited.

80. "Thais Furious at Cambodians for Disclosing Visit by Reagan Aide," *Los Angeles Times,* 5 December 1980. I am grateful to Jack Colhoun for this reference.

81. Both Norodom Sihanouk and Son Sann reported being pressured by the United States to join this coalition with Pol Pot. See Ben Kiernan, "Kampuchea 1979–81: National Rehabilitation in the Eye of an International Storm," *Southeast Asian Affairs 1982* (Singapore: Institute of Southeast Asian Studies/ Heinemann, 1982), 167–95, at 187 (citing the *Age* [Melbourne], 29 April 1981), and David J. Scheffer, "Arming Cambodian Rebels: The Washington Debate," *Indochina Issues,* no. 58 (June 1985): 4.

82. Elizabeth Becker, *When the War Was Over* (New York: Simon and Schuster, 1986), 440.

83. William Shawcross, *The Quality of Mercy: Cambodia, Holocaust and Modern Conscience* (New York: Deutsch, 1984), 289, 395, 345. Omang and Ottoway, writing in the *Washington Post* on 27 May 1985, also report that the U.S. government provided food aid to the Khmer Rouge in 1979, but they say this was stopped by Congress in 1980.

84. Linda Mason and Roger Brown, *Rice, Rivalry and Politics: Managing Cambodian Relief* (Notre Dame, IN: University of Notre Dame Press, 1983), 136, 159, 135.

85. Douglas Pike, *St. Louis Post-Dispatch,* 29 November 1979, and *Christian Science Monitor,* 4 December 1979.

86. Douglas Pike, "Khmer Rouge: Not the Threat It Was," *New York Times,* 5 August 1989. For Pike, Pol Pot's command of the 25,000 armed Khmer Rouge is no great "threat," because (Pike claims to know) their "average age" is twenty-two! He also fantasizes that, on the other hand, "about 80 percent of the present cadre structure of the Phnom Penh Government are ex-Khmer Rouge." The real figure is the reverse, less than 20 percent; see Michael Vickery, "Cambodia and the Khmer Rouge," *Far Eastern Economic Review,* 30 November 1989, 4–5. In 1990, Pike added his view that "we on the sidelines lament the sad state of Cambodian scholarship" (*Indochina Chronology,* 9, no. 3 [July–September 1990]: 12).

87. William Shawcross, *Sunday Telegraph,* 26 September 1979; "The End of Cambodia," *New York Review of Books,* 24 January 1980; and *The Quality of Mercy,* 370. For a more extended discussion of Shawcross and the Cambodia issue, see Ben Kiernan, "The Cambodian Genocide, 1975–1979: A Critical Review," in *Genocide in the Twentieth Century: Critical Essays and First-Person Accounts,* ed. Israel Charny, William Parsons, and Samuel Totten (New York: Garland Publishing, 1994).

88. Shawcross, *The Quality of Mercy,* 415.

89. Nick Cohen, "Oxfam Activities Censured as Too Political," *Independent,* 10 May 1991, and John Pilger, "In Defence of Oxfam," *New Statesman and Society,* 17 May 1991, 8. I am grateful to Paul Donovan for drawing my attention to this issue.

90. See John Pilger, "West Conceals Record on Khmer Aid," *Sydney Morning Herald,* 1 August 1991, and "Culpable in Cambodia," *New Statesman and Society,*

27 September 1991. A report by Asia Watch and Physicians for Human Rights notes that "China and the United Kingdom are, or have been, involved in training Cambodian resistance factions in the use of mines and explosives against civilian as well as military targets." Asia Watch, *Land Mines in Cambodia: the Coward's War* (September 1991), see 25–27, 59, emphasis added.

91. See for instance, "Permanent Mission of Cambodia, Press Release No. 023/91, April 18, 1991," republished in *Cambodian Press* (Lowell, MA), 1 May 1991.

92. *Agence France Presse* report from Geneva, 30 August 1990.

93. UN Security Council statement on Cambodia, released 11 January 1991, 24, 27 (UN Doc. A/46/61/S/22059.

94. For a detailed analysis of the negotiations that led to the promulgation of the UN Peace Plan, see Ben Kiernan, "Deferring Peace in Cambodia: Regional Rapprochement, Superpower Obstruction," in *Beyond the Cold War: Conflict and Cooperation in the Third World*, ed. George W. Breslauer, et al. (Berkeley: University of California, Berkeley, International and Area Studies Research Series No. 80, 1991), 59–82; and Ben Kiernan, "The Cambodian Crisis, 1990–1992: The UN Plan, the Khmer Rouge, and the State of Cambodia," *Bulletin of Concerned Asian Scholars* 24, no. 2 (1992): 3–23.

95. *Parliamentary Debates* (Commons), 26 October 1990, 674. A witness interviewed by journalist David Feingold reported that five Chinese T-59 tanks were handed over to the Khmer Rouge near the Thai province of Trat on 21 June 1990. A total of twenty-four had arrived in Cambodia by October, according to *Jane's Defence Weekly*, which described them as "the most significant increase in firepower the resistance to the Vietnamese-installed government has ever received." (Nate Thayer, "Khmer Rouge Receive Chinese Tanks," Associated Press, 7 October 1990; *Indochina Digest*, 6–12 October 1990.) Gareth Evans denied this, claiming "there is no evidence available to the Australian government that the Khmer Rouge have recently received tanks from China. Indeed, the consensus among the experts is to the contrary" (Ministerial Statement, 6 December 1990). No such consensus ever existed. While some debated whether Thai forces had yet delivered all of the tanks to the Khmer Rouge, the Chinese definitely dispatched them in January 1990, and the Khmer Rouge received at least five and possibly as many as twenty-eight tanks. Thai intelligence on the Cambodian border reported in March 1991 that in a nearby engagement the Khmer Rouge were "backed by T-62 tanks" (*Nation* [Bangkok], 23 March 1991). At least one Khmer Rouge tank (possibly "four or five") was captured by Cambodian government forces and was displayed for foreign observers (*Bangkok Post*, 21 April 1991).

96. Benjamin Whitaker, Report to the UN Economic and Social Council, 2 July 1985, UN Doc. 4/SUB, 2/1985/6, at 10, n. 17.

97. *Indochina Digest*, no. 91–10, 8 March 1991.

98. Senator Bob Kerrey, testimony before the U.S. Senate Foreign Relations Committee, 11 April 1991.

99. Reuter, *Age* (Melbourne), 3 September 1985.

100. "Khmer Factions Pleased with Anand," *Nation* (Bangkok), 10 May 1991.

101. James Pringle, "Pol Pot Calls on Cambodians to Protect Wildlife," *Bangkok Post*, 31 January 1991 (emphasis added).

102. See for instance, Charles-Antoine de Nerciat, "The Green Khmer Rouge?" AFP, *Nation* (Bangkok), 17 February 1991.

103. Pringle, "Pol Pot Calls on Cambodians to Protect Wildlife."

104. Nate Thayer, "A Khmer Ruse," *Far Eastern Economic Review,* 7 March 1991; and 7 November 1991, 28.

105. See Kiernan, "The Cambodian Crisis, 1990–1992," 3–23.

106. Nate Thayer, "Cambodia: Misperceptions and Peace," *Washington Quarterly,* Spring 1991, 179–91.

107. Ibid., 179, 190, emphasis added. This is no mistake. Again on 186, Thayer omits Khmer Rouge killings from his characterization of the last "20 years of war, starvation, displacement and stagnation."

108. Ibid., 181, 5.

109. Thayer asserts that, himself excepted, "journalists, scholars and other foreign observers have had access . . . only" to "a certain sector of the population," because "the rural areas and population . . . [remain] largely inaccessible to independent observers." (See "Cambodia: Misperceptions and Peace," 185, and "A Khmer Ruse.") This assertion is absurd.

110. Thayer, "A Khmer Ruse"; and "Cambodia: Misperceptions and Peace."

111. Asian and Pacific Subcommittee of the House Foreign Affairs Committee, Hearings on Cambodia, Washington, DC, 10 April 1991.

112. Nate Thayer, "Tactics of Silence," *Far Eastern Economic Review,* 12 December 1991, 10–11.

113. *New York Times,* 21 January 1992, and "Peace Accord Violation Leaves 13 Dead: Khmer Rouge Forces Attack Villages," *Financial Times,* 21 January 1992; David Brunnstrom, "UN to Send Units to Disputed Cambodia Provinces," Reuter, Phnom Penh, 24 January 1992; Nate Thayer, "Unsettled Land," *Far Eastern Economic Review,* 27 February 1992, 26; "Khmer Rouge Said to Shoot UN Officer," *Washington Post,* 27 February 1992.

114. With breathtaking hypocrisy, demands for removal of the Hun Sen regime are often accompanied by allegations that it is made up of former Khmer Rouge who, in the words of U.S. congressman Stephen J. Solarz, were once "part of the Pol Pot killing machine" (*Far Eastern Economic Review,* 22 March 1990). As I pointed out in the *New York Review of Books* (27 September 1984), "after five years this has yet to be demonstrated." In September 1990, Stephen R. Heder also concluded that, "after careful examination of all the available evidence, I have seen no evidence that any of the ex-Khmer Rouge in positions of high political authority in today's Cambodia were involved in large-scale or systematic killing of Cambodian civilians." ("Recent Developments in Cambodia," paper presented at the Australian National University on 5 September 1990.) See note 86, above, for evidence that contrary to further allegations, only 20 percent of the present Cambodian leadership have any ties at all to the Khmer Rouge, unlike the longterm allies of Pol Pot whom Congressman Solarz vigorously supports. Prince Sihanouk, for instance, alleged in 1989 that Cambodian foreign minister Hor Nam Hong had once been a Khmer Rouge official. Hor Nam Hong sued for libel, and in January 1991 a French court convicted Sihanouk of defamation, ordering the prince and the newspaper *Journal du Dimanche,* which had published the libel, to pay fines of $10,000, plus damages of $20,000 to Hor Nam Hong. Sihanouk, for his part, remained in his alliance with the Khmer Rouge (Associated Press, 23 January 1991).

115. *Wall Street Journal,* 9 November 1989; *Atlantic,* February 1991, 26.

116. Kiernan, "Blue Scarf/Yellow Star."

117. Nor could I incorporate other material, even a few paragraphs of my

own unpublished work on the subject. This was ironic. On 20 December 1981, the *New York Times Magazine* had published a report on Cambodia by Christopher Jones, which was later discovered to have been fabricated (see [Melbourne] *Age,* 25 February 1982). In it, Jones had passed off as his own material from some of my published work, from copies I had given him personally in Phnom Penh the previous year. The editor seemed unaware of this. Given the political nature of the cuts that were now required, I declined to submit another version, and the magazine declined to pay me a kill fee. The piece was published in abbreviated form in the *Boston Globe* (Kiernan, "Blue Scarf/Yellow Star").

118. Evans, *In Hitler's Shadow,* 91.

119. Mark Aarons, *Sanctuary! Nazi Fugitives in Australia* (Melbourne: Heinemann, 1989), 61.

120. Beverly Jean Smith, "White Nomad," in *Burchett: Reporting the Other Side of the World, 1939–1983,* ed. Ben Kiernan (London: Quartet, 1986). Smith was referring to those Australians who chided critics of the Indonesian invasion of East Timor on the grounds that Jakarta "could have a lot to say about our treatment of the aborigines."

121. Gregory Stanton, personal communication.

122. Lawyers Committee for Human Rights, "Human Rights in Kampuchea: Preliminary Summary of Findings and Conclusions," New York, December 1984, 18.

123. These two excellent reports by the Lawyers Committee for Human Rights are entitled *Seeking Shelter: Cambodians in Thailand* (New York: Lawyers Committee for Human Rights, 1987), and *Refuge Denied* (New York: Lawyers Committee for Human Rights, 1989).

124. *Kampuchea: After the Worst* (New York: Lawyers Committee for Human Rights, 1985), 7, 8.

125. See the Cambodia Documentation Commission's excellent survey of the human rights and legal questions involved in Hurst Hannum, "International Law and Cambodian Genocide: The Sounds of Silence," *Human Rights Quarterly,* 11, no. 1 (February 1989): 82–138.

126. I was an adviser to the Cambodia Documentation Commission from 1984 to 1991. Its director David Hawk had commissioned me to write studies of the Eastern Zone massacres, and of the genocide of the Chams; he also commissioned Chanthou Boua to gather evidence on the genocide against the Buddhist monks. My 100-page *Cambodia: Eastern Zone Massacres* was published by the CDC and Columbia University's Center for the Study of Human Rights in 1986. Despite my request, Hawk declined to advertise it, and no American library obtained a copy until I donated one to Yale University Library in 1991. In 1987, I sent Hawk an eighty-page monograph on the Cham genocide, for publication as agreed. Hawk took no action, and I sought publication elsewhere (*BCAS,* 20, no. 4 [1988]). When Boua completed her research on the genocide of the Buddhist monks, she sent the material to Hawk, offering to write it up. He asked her to wait for two others to coauthor the study. They never did, so she went ahead alone (Chanthou Boua, "Genocide of a Religious Group: Pol Pot and Cambodia's Buddhist Monks," in Schlapentokh, et al., *State-Organized Terror*).

127. In April 1990 the CDC distributed an appeal to UN member states. "An International Court case against the Khmer Rouge genocide" was now listed number four in the CDC's ranking of issues. Priority was given to "complete

Vietnamese withdrawal under UN verification," and two other demands targeting not the Khmer Rouge but their opponents. The UN continued to seat the Khmer Rouge-dominated coalition in its General Assembly, and the CDC appeal *followed* the actual Vietnamese withdrawal of September 1989. On 3 December 1990, Australian foreign minister Gareth Evans replied to the CDC's first point by noting, "It is Australia's assessment that all Vietnamese formed military units have been withdrawn from Cambodia. However there are claims and counter-claims about residual Vietnamese advisers and small groups of Vietnamese troops." The CDC gave such a problematic issue much higher priority than its previously proclaimed goal—that of bringing genocidists to justice.

128. See for instance David Hawk's 23 January 1991 criticism of Raoul Jennar's assessment of the UN Plan (and Jennar's reply of 18 April 1991, entitled "Because Only the Cambodians Will Pay the Price of Our Mistakes"); and Hawk's attack on John Pilger and David Munro's film, *Cambodia: The Betrayal*, on WNET television on 11 February 1991. On William Shawcross, see Kiernan, "The Cambodian Genocide, 1975–1979: A Critical Review."

129. "1991/8 Situation in Cambodia," Resolution passed by the UN Human Rights Subcommission, 23 August 1991, text in Raoul Jennar, *The Cambodian Gamble*, report dated 13 September 1991, 35–36.

130. Statement by Dennis McNamara, director of UNTAC Human Rights Component, at the International Symposium on Human Rights in Cambodia, 30 November–2 December 1992, 2.

131. Statement by Yasushi Akashi, special representative of the secretary general for Cambodia at the opening session of the International Symposium for Human Rights in Cambodia, 30 November 1992, 1.

132. Dennis McNamara, statement on 30 November 1992, 1–2.

Appendix 1: Text of the 1948 Genocide Convention

CONVENTION ON THE PREVENTION AND PUNISHMENT OF THE CRIME OF GENOCIDE

The Contracting Parties

Having considered the declaration made by the General Assembly of the United Nations in its resolution 96 (1) dated 11 December 1946 that genocide is a crime under international law, contrary to the spirit and aims of the United Nations and condemned by the civilized world;

Recognizing that at all periods of history genocide has inflicted great losses on humanity; and

Being convinced that, in order to liberate mankind from such an odious scourge, international cooperation is required;

Hereby agree as hereinafter provided

Article I

The Contracting Parties confirm that genocide whether committed in time of peace or in time of war, is a crime under international law which they undertake to prevent and to punish.

The Convention was signed on 11 December 1948 and entered into force on 12 January 1951.—ED.

Article II

In the present Convention, genocide means any of the following acts committed with intent to destroy, in whole or in part, a national, ethnical, racial or religious group, as such:

(a) Killing members of the group;
(b) Causing serious bodily or mental harm to members of the group;
(c) Deliberately inflicting on the group conditions of life calculated to bring about its physical destruction in whole or in part;
(d) Imposing measures intended to prevent births within the group;
(e) Forcibly transferring children of the group to another group.

Article III

The following acts shall be punishable:

(a) Genocide;
(b) Conspiracy to commit genocide;
(c) Direct and public incitement to commit genocide;
(d) Attempt to commit genocide;
(e) Complicity in genocide.

Article IV

Persons committing genocide or any of the other acts enumerated in article III shall be punished, whether they are constitutionally responsible rulers, public officials or private individuals.

Article V

The Contracting Parties undertake to enact, in accordance with their respective Constitutions, the necessary legislation to give effect to the provisions of the present Convention and, in particular, to provide effective penalties for persons guilty of genocide or any of the other acts enumerated in article III.

Article VI

Persons charged with genocide or any of the other acts enumerated in article III shall be tried by a competent tribunal of the State in the territory of which the act was committed, or by such international penal tribunal as may have jurisdiction with respect to those Contracting Parties which shall have accepted its jurisdiction.

Article VII

Genocide and other acts enumerated in article III shall not be considered as political crimes for the purpose of extradition.

The Contracting Parties pledge themselves in such cases to grant extradition in accordance with their laws and treaties in force.

Article VIII

Any Contracting Party may call upon the competent organs of the United Nations to take such action under the Charter of the United Nations as they consider appropriate for the prevention and suppression of acts of genocide or any of the other acts enumerated in article III.

Article IX

Disputes between the Contracting Parties relating to the interpretation, application or fulfilment of the present Convention, including those relating to the responsibility of a State for genocide or any of the other acts enumerated in article III, shall be submitted to the International Court of Justice at the request of any of the parties to the dispute.

Article X

The present Convention, of which the Chinese, English, French, Russian and Spanish texts are equally authentic, shall bear the date of 9 December 1948.

Article XI

The present Convention shall be open until 31 December 1949 for signature on behalf of any Member of the United Nations and of any non-member State to which an invitation to sign has been addressed by the General Assembly.

The present Convention shall be ratified, and the instruments of ratification shall be deposited with the Secretary-General of the United Nations.

After January 1950, the present Convention may be acceded to on behalf of any Member of the United Nations and of any non-member State which has received an invitation as aforesaid.

Instruments of accession shall be deposited with the Secretary-General of the United Nations.

Article XII

Any Contracting Party may at any time by notification addressed to the Secretary-General of the United Nations, extend the application of the present Convention to all or any of the territory for the conduct of whose foreign relations that Contracting Party is responsible.

Article XIII

On the day when the first twenty instruments of ratification or accession have been deposited, the Secretary-General shall draw up a procès-verbal and transmit a copy of it to each Member of the United Nations and to each of the non-member States contemplated in article XI.

The present Convention shall come into force on the ninetieth day following the date of deposit of the twentieth instrument of ratification or accession.

Any ratification or accession effected subsequent to the latter date shall become effective on the ninetieth day following the deposit of the instrument of ratification or accession.

Article XIV

The present Convention shall remain in effect for a period of ten years as from the date of its coming into force.

It shall thereafter remain in force for successive periods of five years for such Contracting Parties as have not denounced it at least six months before the expiration of the current period.

Denunciation shall be effected by a written notification addressed to the Secretary-General of the United Nations.

Article XV

If, as a result of denunciations, the number of Parties to the present Convention should become less than sixteen, the Convention shall cease to be in force as from the date on which the last of these denunciations shall become effective.

Article XVI

A request for the revision of the present Convention may be made at any time by any Contracting Party by means of a notification in writing addressed to the Secretary-General.

The General Assembly shall decide upon the steps, if any, to be taken in respect of such request.

Article XVII

The Secretary-General of the United Nations shall notify all Members of the United Nations and the non-member States contemplated in article XI of the following:

(a) Signatures, ratifications and accessions received in accordance with article XI;
(b) Notifications received in accordance with article XII;
(c) The date upon which the present Convention comes into force in accordance with article XIII;
(d) Denunciations received in accordance with article XIV;
(e) The abrogation of the Convention in accordance with article XV;
(f) Notifications received in accordance with article XVI.

Article XVIII

The original of the present Convention shall be deposited in the archives of the United Nations.

A certified copy of the Convention shall be transmitted to all Members of the United Nations and to the non-member States contemplated in article XI.

Article XIX

The present Convention shall be registered by the Secretary-General of the United Nations on the date of its coming into force.

Appendix 2: Chronologies of the Case Studies

The Armenian Question Since 1878

1878   February–July: The "Armenian Question" relating to
                security and administrative reforms for the Armenians
                of the Ottoman Empire becomes an international ques-
                tion by the treaties of San Stefano and Berlin.

1894–96   The Hamidian pogroms and massacres claim between
                100,000 and 200,000 Armenian lives; widespread
                forced religious conversion, economic ruin, and flight
                from the Ottoman Empire occur.

1908   Liberal "Young Turk" revolution creates a constitu-
                tional regime limiting the authority of the sultan and
                offering the promise of liberty, equality, and fraternity
                among all people of the Ottoman Empire.

1909   Counterrevolution is attempted in Constantinople,
                resulting in widespread massacres of Armenians in
                Adana and other parts of Cilicia. Sultan Abdul-
                Hamid II is dethroned and exiled.

1912–13   Balkan Wars result in the loss of nearly all Ottoman
                possessions in Europe.

1913   The chauvinist wing of Young Turks stages a coup
                d'état and establishes a dictatorship under Enver, Tal-
                aat, and Jemal.

1914   February: Final European-imposed Armenian reform
                plan creates two inspectorates and European inspec-
                tors-general in the Armenian provinces.

July: World War I begins.

August: Secret German-Turkish military alliance forms.

November: Ottoman Empire joins German Empire against Entente (Great Britain, France, Russia).

December: Turkey invades Russian Caucasus.

1915   January: Turkish military fails and retreats from the Caucasus front.

February: Armenian soldiers in the Ottoman army are segregated into unarmed work battalions and subsequently killed.

March: Limited deportation of Armenians begins in parts of Cilicia.

April: Armenian political, intellectual, and religious leaders are arrested; the Armenian Genocide begins.

May: Allies officially protest and pledge to hold Turkish government and perpetrators responsible, individually and collectively.

May–October: The entire Ottoman Armenian population, except for those in Constantinople (Istanbul) and Smyrna (Izmir), are subjected to systematic deportations and massacres. More than a million Armenians—the majority of the Armenians in the Turkish Empire—perish, their homes and lands looted, historical and cultural monuments destroyed. The Armenians' existence in their ancestral homelands ends after three millennia.

1916   Russian imperial armies and Russian Armenian volunteers occupy Armenian provinces. Americans stage fund-raising and relief activities for refugees and survivors scattered throughout the Near East.

1917   March: Russian "democratic" revolution forces abdication of Czar Nicholas II.

April: United States declares war on Germany; Turkey severs diplomatic relations with the United States.

Summer: Russian armies disintegrate on the Caucasus front. Russian Armenians attempt to defend the front.

November: The "Bolshevik" revolution is staged in Russia; the Russian civil war begins. Armenians, Georgians, and Azerbaijanis attempt to form a local anti-Bolshevik administration.

1918   February–May: Turkey stages an offensive, reoccupying Turkish Armenian provinces, invading Russian Armenia, and renewing massacres.

April–May: Georgians, Azerbaijanis, and Armenians form "Transcaucasian Federated Republic."

May 26: Federated Republic disintegrates.

May 28: Russian Armenian leaders declare "Republic of Armenia" around Erevan.

June 4: Turkish government recognizes small Russian Armenian republic and annexes the other half of Russian Armenia.

September 15: Turkey occupies Baku on the Caspian Sea and massacres 30,000 Armenians—the last major massacre of World War I.

October 30: Turkey capitulates and signs the Mudros Armistice.

November 11: Germany capitulates; World War I ends.

December: Turkish armies evacuate most of Transcaucasia and Russian Armenia.

1919   January: Paris Peace Conference opens.

February–July: Turkey holds courts-martial of Young Turk ministers and perpetrators of Armenian Genocide. Death sentences are issued *in absentia* for Young Turk dictators who had taken refuge in Germany and Soviet Russia.

Summer: Turkish "Nationalist" resistance movement is organized under Mustafa Kemal.

Winter and Summer: Two hundred thousand Armenian refugees die of starvation, exposure, and epidemic. United States raises private and public charity to assist the "Starving Armenians."

1920   January: Republic of Armenia is granted de facto recognition by Allied Powers.

February: Massacres of Armenians are renewed in Cilicia.

February–April: Turkish Peace Treaty is drafted with provisions for an independent Armenia combining Russian Armenia and Turkish Armenia.

April: Mustafa Kemal leads the organization of a Turkish countergovernment in Ankara.

August: Turkey signs the Treaty of Sèvres by which the Turkish government recognizes a united Armenian state and pledges to cooperate in the punishment of the perpetrators of the Armenian Genocide and to liberate Armenian women and children who had been forcibly converted and kept in domestic captivity.

August: Turkish Nationalists and Soviet Russians draft a treaty of friendship; Soviet war material and gold are shipped to the Nationalists.

September–November: Turkish Nationalists invade the Republic of Armenia beyond the old Russo-Turkish frontier of 1914.

December: The remnant of the Armenian republic is Sovietized; Turkish Nationalist forces continue to occupy all of Turkish Armenia and half of Russian Armenia. Soviet Azerbaijan cedes disputed districts of Kazabagh, Zangezuz, and Nakhichevan to Soviet Armenia.

1921 March: Soviet-Turkish treaty of Moscow recognizes the Turkish annexation of half of Russian Armenia and the retention of all of Turkish Armenia. The treaty also stipulates that the disputed district of Nakhichevan must be awarded to Soviet Azerbaijan.

March–June: Conflicting decisions are issued relating to Nagorno-Karabagh.

1922–23 The allied Powers and the United States make peace with the new Turkish government of Mustafa Kemal and revise the Treaty of Sèvres through several Treaties of Lausanne, in which "Armenia" and "Armenians" are not mentioned. The Armenian Question is abandoned internationally.

1923 Nagorno-Karabagh is awarded to Azerbaijan SSR as an "Autonomous Region."

1924 U.S. immigration law virtually stops flow of Armenian refugees to the United States.

1927–65 Armenians and their supporters continue to petition, write letters, and stage protests regarding the status of Nagorno-Karabagh and pleading for its reunion with Armenia.

1965 Armenian communities throughout the world activize on the fiftieth anniversary of the Armenian Genocide. Major demonstrations erupt in Soviet Armenia.

1965–88   More active national expression emerges in Soviet Armenia, with more aggressive protests and petitions regarding Karabagh.

1988   January: One hundred thousand Karabagh Armenians petition for a referendum in Karabagh. Gorbachev appoints a special commission to study the question.
             February: Demonstrations are staged in Karabagh, as well as democratic movement marches and meetings in Erevan. Up to a million people participate in peaceful demonstration.
             February: Soviet of People's Deputies of Karabagh appeals to the Supreme Soviet for the transfer of Mountainous Karabagh to Armenia.
             February–March: Massacres of Armenians and anti-Armenian riots occur in Sumgait and other parts of Azerbaijan.
             March–December: Tensions continue, and thousands of Armenians flee from Azerbaijan and Azerbaijanis from Armenia.
             December: Disastrous earthquake destroys one-third of Soviet Armenia and claims at least fifty thousand lives.
             December: Leaders of the "Karabagh Movement" are arrested in Armenia.

1989   A special administration under central government is created for Karabagh. Tensions and killings continue. Azerbaijan fully blockades Armenia.

1990   Armenians in Baku; many thousands of Baku Armenians flee to all parts of Soviet Union and abroad.
             Soviet military forces occupy Baku with bloodshed.
             The special administration in Karabagh ends, and Gorbachev insists on rule of law, respect for the constitution, and return of the status quo.
             Soviet armed forces and Armenians clash on the eve of the Armenian national Independence Day (28 May). The blockade continues.
             August: First freely elected Parliament of Soviet Armenia declares the process for establishing sovereignty of the Republic of Armenia. The declaration includes as an underlying objective international recognition of the Armenian Genocide of 1915.

United States Senate tables vote on recognizing 24 April as a day of commemoration of Armenian Genocide, amid strong intervention from the Department of Defense, the Department of State, and the White House.

Turkish government, Turkish agencies, and associated individuals and scholars continue their active campaign to deny the reality and scope of the Armenian Genocide. The Armenian trauma continues through the denials and renewed bloodshed in the Caucasus.

Major Events in Modern Kurdish History

1514	In the battle of Chaldiran, the Ottomans definitively push the rival Safavids eastward into what is now Iran. Most of the local Kurdish rulers opt for incorporation into the Ottoman Empire; a minority allies itself with Iran.
1639	The treaty of Qasr-i Shirin establishes a stable border between the Ottoman and Safavid (Persian) empires, that has remained virtually unchanged ever since. The boundary divides Kurdistan into an Ottoman part and a smaller Iranian part. In both, local Kurdish rulers maintain a high degree of autonomy.
1820–30s	The last autonomous Kurdish principalities in the Ottoman Empire are abolished. Henceforth all of Kurdistan is administered by centrally appointed governors.
1880	The Shaikh ʿUbaidullah (Turkish-Persian) frontier region rebels, marking the first rebellion in which at least the leader appears to hold modern nationalist ideals.
1915	The Ottoman Empire enters into World War I. Armenians are deported and massacred; some Kurds take part in the killings, while others protect their Armenian neighbors.
1918	The Ottomans are defeated, the Empire is cut up, and Allied administrations are established in Mesopotamia and Syria. The Allies occupy Istanbul. Kurdish nationalists in the capital and in Iraq, most of whom lack a firm popular base, begin feverish activities.

1919–21   Kemalists (Kurds as well as Turks) fight Turkey's "National War of Liberation" against Greeks, Armenians, and occupation forces.

1919   Shaikh Mahmud, one of the most influential Kurdish leaders, rebels against the British in Mesopotamia and demands Kurdish independence. He seeks cooperation with the Kemalists, perceiving parallel interests.

1920   The peace treaty signed at Sèvres (between the Allies and Turkey's *ancien régime*) leaves open the possibility of an Armenian and a Kurdish state in the eastern provinces of the former empire.

1923   After the Kemalists' victory, Turkey becomes a republic. The Lausanne treaty replaces that of Sèvres, giving recognition to the Kemalists' territorial claims, and no longer referring to possible Armenian or Kurdish states. The status of Mosul province (oil-rich and with a Kurdish population majority), contested by Turkey and the British administration in Mesopotamia, remains undecided until a future referendum.

1925   Shaikh Said rebels in Turkey, followed by severe military reprisals and repressive legislation banning the expression of religious sentiment and Kurdish ethnicity. The first deportations of Kurds to western Turkey begin.

1926   Mosul province joins Iraq. Turkey officially gives up all claims but will always maintain a special interest in northern Iraq because of its important oil deposits, its sizable Turkish minority, and the potential impact of events there on its own Kurdish population.

1929–30   The Ararat rebellion in eastern Turkey, the largest and most unambiguously nationalist Kurdish revolt, is suppressed with much bloodshed, and followed by a new wave of deportations from the rebellious areas to western Turkey.

1934   Turkey adopts a law regulating forced resettlement of its non-Kurdish population.

1935   A special law places the province of Tunceli (Dersim) under military rule and gives the military governor extraordinary powers.

1937   Minor incidents trigger a punitive military action against the Dersim tribes, resulting in wholesale slaughter. Seyyit Riza, charismatic nationalist leader, is captured and executed.

1938   Second Dersim campaign results in even more indiscriminate bloodshed than the previous year. Dersim is pacified; many of the survivors are sent into exile to western Turkey.

1946   Iranian and Iraqi Kurds, profiting from a temporary power vacuum in Iran, establish a short-lived semi-independent republic in the region of Mahabad. By the end of the year Iranian troops reestablish central control over all of Iranian Kurdistan.

1958   Left-wing army officers overthrow the monarchy in Iraq and establish a populist regime. Colonel Qassem invites Mulla Mustafa Barzani back from exile in the Soviet Union and promises the Kurds equal political rights and autonomy.

1961   Relations between Qassem and the Kurds rapidly deteriorate. A guerrilla war breaks out that will continue throughout the decade in spite of several (violent) changes of regime in Baghdad.

1968   The Baath regime comes to power in Baghdad.

1970   The Kurds and the central government conclude a peace agreement promising the Kurds autonomy and representation in the central government.

1971   Iraq nationalizes the Iraqi Petrol Company.

1972   Iraq signs a treaty of friendship with the Soviet Union. Barzani meets Henry Kissinger in Tehran and is promised substantial American support.

1974   Baghdad unilaterally declares a severely curtailed autonomy, which is rejected by the Kurdish nationalists. Armed hostilities are resumed on an unprecedented scale. Iraq bombs the town of Qal 'a Diza. Tens of thousands flee their homes to the mountains of northern Iraq or to Iran. Iran covertly sends troops (artillery) into Iraq to support the Kurds.

1975   At an OPEC conference in Algiers, the Shah signs an agreement with Saddam Hussein. In exchange for Iraqi concessions in an old border conflict, he gives up his support of the Kurds. Within weeks, the Kurdish movement in Iraq collapses; the rebels surrender to the Iraqi army or take refuge in Iran.

1976   Iraq begins evacuating a zone along the Iranian border in order to prevent infiltration of guerrillas. A modest new Kurdish resistance movement emerges.

1979   The Iranian revolution overthrows the Shah's regime. Strong movement for autonomy grows among the Iranian Kurds. Many pro-Shah officers and politicians flee to Iraq. Baghdad gives financial, logistic, and arms support to various Iranian opposition groups, including the major Kurdish parties. The new Iranian regime renews support to the (Iraqi) Kurdistan Democratic Party (KDP) led by Barzani's sons.

1980   Iraq invades Iran, beginning a war that will last eight years and cost more than a million lives.

1983   Iran opens a front in the north and penetrates a few miles into Iraqi Kurdistan, aided by KDP *peshmergas.* Iraq first hints at its possession of chemical arms.

1988   March: Iraq bombs the Kurdish town of Halabja with chemical warheads after it has been captured by Iranian troops supported by Iraqi Kurds.
              August: A cease-fire is called in the Iran-Iraq War. A final offensive is launched against the Kurdish guerrillas in northernmost Iraq. Villages are bombed with chemical warheads. Tens of thousands flee into Turkey.

1990   August 2: Iraq invades and occupies Kuwait. An anti-Iraqi alliance is formed to protect Saudi Arabia from a hypothetical Iraqi invasion and to expel Iraq from Kuwait.

1991   January–February: "Operation Desert Storm" is launched. Iraq is expelled from Kuwait and much of its military and civilian infrastructure destroyed. Shiites in the south, and later Kurds in the north, believing Saddam's military might has been destroyed, rebel.

End March: Iraqi troops attack the Kurdish towns, wreaking massive destruction. Hundreds of thousands flee in panic toward the Turkish and Iranian borders.

The Timor Affair

Circa 1512   The Portuguese make their first visit to the island of Timor and nearby islands.

1859   Border negotiations begin with the Dutch (and are finally settled by the Sentenca Arbitral of 1913).

1941   Ten days after the bombing of Pearl Harber, Allied forces, mainly Australians and Dutch, land near Dili against Portuguese protests.

1942   February: Japanese invade and are resisted by an Australian commando force. The Australian force is evacuated in early 1943. The Japanese impose a harsh occupation regime.

1945   August: Japan surrenders. Timor is in a devastated state. Deaths from the war are estimated at between forty and seventy thousand people. Portugal resumes colonial rule.

1963   Timor is declared an "overseas province" of Portugal, a move designed to counter decolonization pressures.

1974   April: A coup is staged in Lisbon. The new regime extends to all overseas territories the right to self-determination. East Timor's population is assessed at about 680,000 and growing at 2 percent per year.
May: The two main Timorese political parties form.
June: José Ramos-Horta visits Jakarta and has talks with Foreign Minister Adam Malik, who supports Timor's right to self-determination and independence and offers Indonesian support. However, this gesture is opposed by leading generals, including Murdani (now defense minister), Ali Murtopo, and Yoga Sugama.
September: Major parties come out in favor of independence. Meanwhile in Java, visiting Australian prime minister Whitlam reportedly tells the Indonesian president that the best solution would be for Timor to become part of Indonesia.

December: Meeting of top-ranking Indonesian generals establishes Operasi Komodo, a covert subversive operation designed to bring about integration of East Timor.

1975   August: Attempted coup by UDT leads to a brief but intense civil war, during which a depleted Portuguese administration retreats to the offshore island of Atauro. War ends early in September with UDT remnants retreating across the border to Indonesian Timor. The International Committee of the Red Cross (ICRC) mission estimates casualties of about fifteen hundred.

September: Fretilin extends peace feelers to Indonesia. Operasi Komodo generals persuade Suharto to authorize military intervention, first, in the form of covert operations. Australian ambassador Woolcott reports the comment of his U.S. colleague (Newsom) that if Indonesia intervened militarily he hoped they would do so "effectively, quickly and not use our equipment." Fretilin leadership requests that the Portuguese return and complete decolonization. First major Indonesian military attack (on Balibo) claims the lives of five Australian newsmen.

Faced with continuing Indonesian attacks and no outside help, Fretilin declares unilateral independence with leaders Xavier do Amaral and Nicolau Lobato.

December: Immediately after a brief visit by President Ford and Secretary of State Kissinger to Jakarta, Indonesians launch (on the 7th) a major assault on Dili. The Timorese make desperate appeals for help, claiming indiscriminate killing.

December 12: A UN General Assembly resolution calls on Indonesia to withdraw its forces at once and asks the Security Council "to take urgent action to protect territorial integrity of East Timor and the inalienable right of its peoples to self-determination." Indonesian general declares that "no power on earth will take East Timor away from Indonesia." UN officials are warned that any attempt to get to Fretilin-controlled territory by air will result in the aircraft being shot down.

1976   UN Security Council special envoy makes a brief visit to Timor, in the face of an orchestrated reception. His report is inconclusive. Widespread killing by rampaging troops is reported from Timor. ICRC is denied access.

July: The territory is formally annexed as the "twenty-seventh province" following the hastily stage-managed "election" of a local assembly; members are selected by the Indonesian military command.

October: The Timor issue comes before the UN General Assembly with a resolution of the kind to resurface annually.

December: The Catholic church issues the first of its reports describing the grim humanitarian situation, and referring to a death toll as high as sixty thousand. The report claims that Fretilin is maintaining stiff resistance and controls 80 percent of the country.

1977　　Author Dunn's report on the grim humanitarian conditions in East Timor attracts UN and Congressional interest, but the facts are denied by the U.S. State Department.

November: A church source in Timor reports intensive oppression and widespread executions, and claims intense fighting throughout the island.

1979　　A few international humanitarian aid officials are at last allowed into Timor, where they report that the situation is desperate. According to one of these reports, between one-tenth and one-third of the population has perished while 200,000 remain in dire straits in resettlement camps.

1980　　Timorese armed resistance continues with Fretilin now under the leadership of Gusmao (Xanana), following the killing of Lobato and capture of Xavier do Amaral in late 1978.

1981　　Local Indonesia-appointed assembly protests to Indonesian President regarding the misbehavior of the military.

1982　　Present governor, Mario Carrascalao—a former UDT leader—is appointed.

UN General Assembly Resolution 37/30 calls on the secretary-general to initiate consultations with all parties to the conflict, with a view to achieving a comprehensive settlement.

1986   April: A former bishop of Timor tells U.S. Catholics that East Timor has lost "perhaps one third of its population as a direct result of Indonesian invasion and occupation."

1988   International interest increases significantly. The Portuguese government reaffirms its commitment to "bring about the decolonization of East Timor." In a petition to a UN committee of twenty-four members, Lord Avebury, chairman of the British Parliament's Human Rights Group, announces the formation of a new group, Parliamentarians for East Timor, with the support of forty-five parliamentarians around the world. Resolution of the European Parliament by a large majority supports Timorese self-determination. A letter signed by 182 bipartisan members of the U.S. House of Representatives and 47 senators calls on Secretary of State Schultz to give more attention to the situation in East Timor.

1989   Bishop Belo of Timor writes to the UN secretary-general stating that "the process of decolonization of Portuguese Timor has still not been resolved by the UN" and calls for a referendum to allow the Timorese to express their choice.

1990   February: General Murdani tells a meeting of Timorese officials in Dili that the Indonesian armed forces will crush any attempt to set up an independent state so the Timorese should stop dreaming of it.

1991   Amnesty International reports (the latest in February 1991) speak of continuing human rights violations, including summary executions by the military. A large influx of Indonesians is reported. Population is stated officially at 710,000, but includes more than 100,000 Indonesians.

Cambodian Events Since 1950

1950   Cambodian communists join forces with Vietnamese against French colonialism.

1954   Geneva Conference: French withdraw from Cambodia, Vietnam, and Laos.

1954–70	Kingdom of Cambodia, under Prince Norodom Sihanouk, establishes an autocratic monarchy, nonaligned in foreign policy and neutral in the Vietnam War.
1962	Cambodian communist leader disappears. Pol Pot takes his place and makes plans for a rebellion. (In 1964–65 Pol Pot visits China and Vietnam.)
1965	United States escalates the Vietnam War; Vietnamese communist forces increasingly seek sanctuary in Cambodia. Sihanouk breaks relations with the United States, while continuing to crack down on domestic communists and other dissenters.
1967	Pol Pot group of Cambodian communists ("Khmer Rouge") launches an insurgency against Sihanouk in northwest Cambodia, leading to brutal government repression.
1969	U.S. B-52 bombardment of Vietnamese sanctuaries in Cambodia begins.
1970–75	Coup against Sihanouk establishes General Lon Nol as president of a U.S.-backed regime, the Khmer Republic. Sihanouk, in exile in China, joins forces with the Vietnamese and the Cambodian communists (the "Khmer Rouge"). Lon Nol's rule initially wins the support of the urban classes, but becomes increasingly dictatorial.
1973	U.S. B-52 bombardment of the Cambodian countryside in support of Lon Nol forces reaches its peak. Two hundred fifty thousand tons of bombs are dropped in seven months, before the U.S. Congress calls a halt to the bombing on 15 August. From 1969 to 1973, the bombing resulted in 50,000 to 150,000 civilian deaths. Pol Pot forces use the bombing's killing and destruction as recruitment propaganda and as an excuse for the abandonment of moderate socialist policies in the insurgent zones. Moderate communists suspected of disloyalty to Pol Pot are purged.
1975–79	Khmer Rouge forces led by Pol Pot defeat Lon Nol's army and take Phnom Penh on 17 April 1975. Democratic Kampuchea (DK) is formed. Cities are immediately evacuated, and the country is cut off from the

outside world. Surrendered Lon Nol officers, soldiers, and officials are killed. All Cambodians are forced into unpaid agricultural labor.

1976 — Massive starvation in parts of northwest Cambodia follows the deportation there of hundreds of thousands of evacuated urban dwellers.

1977 — A second wave of bloody purges convulses Cambodia, centrally directed by the Pol Pot group which attempts to eliminate all dissident communists and other moderates and recalcitrants. The purges spread to the mass of the peasantry as well as to the persecuted urban evacuees. Cambodia also launches military attacks across all three of its borders, massacring civilians in Thailand, Vietnam, and Laos.

1978 — Cambodia declines to negotiate with Vietnam over the border war. Domestically, massive purges spark an uprising in the Eastern Zone of Cambodia in opposition to the Pol Pot regime. Rebels are defeated and regroup across the Vietnamese border, where they call for help from Hanoi.

1979 — Vietnamese troops invade and overthrow the Pol Pot regime. The People's Republic of Kampuchea is formed. Former Eastern Zone rebel Heng Samrin is proclaimed president; and Hun Sen is named foreign minister (later prime minister).

1989 — First Paris Conference on Cambodia fails. Vietnamese troops withdraw from Cambodia. Pol Pot's Khmer Rouge and their allies (including Sihanouk) resume their attempt to retake power from Hun Sen's newly proclaimed State of Cambodia (SOC).

1990 — Supreme National Council (SNC), composed of six SOC members and two from each of the three opposition factions, including former DK president Khieu Samphan and deputy prime minister Son Sen, is formed.

1991 — Paris Agreement on Cambodia is signed on 23 October by the four Cambodian factions and eighteen foreign ministers of interested countries.

Selected Bibliography

I. GENERAL

Bazyler, Michael. "Reexamining the Doctrine of Humanitarian Intervention in Light of the Atrocities in Kampuchea and Ethiopia." *Stanford Journal of International Law* 23, no. 2 (1987): 547–619.

Chalk, Frank, and Kurt Jonassohn. *The History and Sociology of Genocide: Analyses and Case Studies.* New Haven, CT: Yale University Press, 1990.

Charny, Israel, ed. *Genocide: A Critical Bibliographic Review.* London: Mansell, 1988.

Dadrian, Vahakn N. "A Typology of Genocide." *International Review of Modern Sociology* 5 (Fall 1975): 201–12.

Drost, Pieter N. *The Crime of State.* 2 vols. Leyden: A. W. Sythoff, 1959.

Fein, Helen. "Genocide: A Sociological Perspective." *Current Sociology* 38, no. 1 (1990).

———, ed. *Genocide Watch.* New Haven, CT: Yale University Press, 1992.

Ginsburgs, George, and V. N. Kudriavtsev, eds. *The Nuremberg Trial and International Law.* Netherlands: Martinus Nijhoff Publishers, 1990.

Harff, Barbara, and Ted Gurr. "Toward Empirical Theory of Genocides and Politicides: Identification and Measurement of Cases since 1945." *International Studies Quarterly* 37, no. 3 (1988): 359–71.

———. "Victims of the State: Genocides, Politicides and Group Repression since 1945." *International Review of Victimology* 1 (1990): 1–19.

Horowitz, Irving Louis. *Genocide: State Power and Mass Murder.* New Brunswick, NJ: Transaction Books, 1976.

———. *Taking Lives: Genocide and State Power.* New Brunswick, NJ: Transaction Books, 1980.

Kuper, Leo. *Genocide: Its Political Use in the Twentieth Century.* New Haven, CT: Yale University Press, 1982.

———. *The Prevention of Genocide.* New Haven, CT: Yale University Press, 1985.

Lemkin, Raphael. *Axis Rule in Occupied Europe.* Washington, DC: Carnegie Endowment, 1944.

———. "Genocide as a Crime under International Law." *American Journal of International Law* 41 (1947): 145–71.

Porter, Jack Nusan, ed. *Genocide and Human Rights: A Global Anthology.* Washington, DC: University Press of America, 1982.

Wallimann, Isidor, and Michael Dobkowski, eds. *Genocide and the Modern Age.* Westport, CT: Greenwood Press, 1987.

Walzer, Michael. *Just and Unjust Wars.* New York: Basic Books, 1977.

Whitaker, Ben. *Revised and Updated Report on the Question of the Prevention and Punishment of the Crime of Genocide.* UN Economic and Social Council, Commission on Human Rights, UN Doc. E/CN.4/Sub.2/1985/6 (1985).

II. CASE STUDIES

A. THE ARMENIANS

Dadrian, Vahakn N. "The Structural-Functional Components of Genocide." In *Victimology*, edited by I. Drakpin and E. Viano, 3 (Lexington, MA: D. C. Heath, 1974): 123–35.

———. "Genocide as a Problem of National and International Law: The World War I Armenian Case and Its Contemporary Legal Ramifications." *Yale Journal of International Law* 14, no. 2 (1989): 221–334.

———. "The Documentation of the World War I Armenian Massacres in the Proceedings of the Turkish Military Tribunal." *International Journal of Middle East Studies* 23, no. 4 (1991): 549–76.

Guroian, Vigen. "Post-Holocaust Political Morality: The Litmus of Bitburg and the Armenian Genocide Resolution." *Holocaust and Genocide Studies* 3, no. 3 (1988): 305–22.

Hovannisian, Richard G. "The Allies and Armenia, 1915–18." *Journal of Contemporary History* 3 (January 1968): 145–55.

———. *The Armenian Holocaust: A Bibliography Relating to the Deportations, Massacres, and Dispersion of the Armenian People, 1915–1923.* Cambridge, MA: Armenian Heritage Press, 1980.

———, ed. *The Armenian Genocide: History, Politics, Ethics.* London: Macmillan, and New York: St. Martin's Press, 1992.

Melson, Robert F. *Revolution and Genocide: On the Origins of the Armenian Genocide and the Holocaust.* Chicago: University of Chicago Press, 1992.

Trumpener, Ulrich. *Germany and the Ottoman Empire, 1914–1918.* Princeton, NJ: Princeton University Press, 1968.

Walker, Christopher J. *Armenia and Karabagh.* London: Minority Rights Publication, 1991.

B. THE KURDS

Arfa, Hassan. *The Kurds: An Historical and Political Study.* London: Oxford University Press, 1966.

Chaliand, G., ed. *Les Kurdes et le Kurdistan.* Paris: Maspéro, 1978.

Ghareeb, Edmund. *The Kurdish Question in Iraq.* Syracuse, NY: Syracuse University Press, 1981.

al-Khalil, Samir. *Republic of Fear: The Politics of Modern Iraq.* Berkeley and Los Angeles: University of California Press, 1989.

Kutschera, Chris. *Le mouvement national Kurde.* Paris: Flammarion, 1979.

Middle East Watch. *Human Rights in Iraq.* New Haven, CT: Yale University Press, 1990.

Olson, Robert. *The Emergence of Kurdish Nationalism and the Sheikh Said Rebellion, 1920–1925*. Austin: University of Texas Press, 1989.

Rambout, Lucien. *Les Kurdes et le droit: Des textes, des faits*. Paris: Editions du Cerf, 1947.

Van Bruinessen, Martin. "The Kurds in Turkey." *MERIP Middle East Reports*, no. 121 (February 1984): 6–12.

———. "The Kurds between Iran and Iraq." *MERIP Middle East Reports*, no. 141 (July–August 1986): 14–27.

C. EAST TIMOR

Amnesty International. *East Timor: "In Accordance with the Law."* Statement before the United Nations Special Committee on Decolonization, July 1992.

Asia Watch. *East Timor: Violations of Human Rights*. London: Amnesty International Publications, 1985.

Budiardjo, Carmel, and Liem Soei Liong. *The War against East Timor*. London: Zed Books, 1984.

Clark, Roger. "Does the Genocide Convention Go Far Enough? Some Thoughts on the Nature of Criminal Genocide in the Context of Indonesia's Invasion of East Timor." *Ohio Northern University Law Review*, 8, no. 1 (1981): 321–28.

Cultural Survival. *East Timor: Five Years after the Indonesian Invasion: Testimony Presented at the Decolonization Committee of the United Nations General Assembly, October 1980*. Cambridge, MA: Cultural Survival, 1981.

Dunn, James. *Timor: A People Betrayed*. Brisbane: Jacaranda Press, 1983.

Jolliffe, Jill. *East Timor: Nationalism and Colonialism*. St. Lucia: University of Queensland Press, 1978.

Ramos-Horta, José. *Funu: The Unfinished Saga of East Timor*. Trenton, NJ: Red Sea Press, 1987.

D. CAMBODIA

Boua, Chanthou, David P. Chandler, and Ben Kiernan, eds. *Pol Pot Plans the Future: Confidential Leadership Documents from Democratic Kampuchea, 1976–77*. New Haven, CT: Yale University Southeast Asia Studies Monograph No. 33, 1988.

Chandler, David P. *The Tragedy of Cambodian History: War, Politics and Revolution Since 1945*. New Haven, CT: Yale University Press, 1991.

Hannum, Hurst. "International Law and Cambodian Genocide: The Sounds of Silence." *Human Rights Quarterly* 11, no. 1 (February 1989): 82–138.

Jackson, Karl, ed. *Cambodia 1975–1978: Rendezvous with Death*. Princeton, NJ: Princeton University Press, 1989.

Kiernan, Ben. *How Pol Pot Came to Power*. New York: Routledge, Chapman and Hall, 1985.

———. *Cambodia: Eastern Zone Massacres*. New York: Columbia University, Center for the Study of Human Rights, Documentation Series No. 1, 1986.

———. "Orphans of Genocide: The Cham Muslims of Kampuchea under Pol Pot." *Bulletin of Concerned Asian Scholars*, 20, no. 4 (1988): 2–33.

Mason, Linda, and Roger Brown. *Rice, Rivalry and Politics: Managing Cambodian Relief*. Notre Dame, IN: University of Notre Dame Press, 1983.

Ponchaud, François. *Cambodia Year Zero.* Harmondsworth: Penguin, 1978.
Shawcross, William. *Sideshow: Kissinger, Nixon and the Destruction of Cambodia.* London: Deutsch, 1979; New York: Simon and Schuster, 1979.
———. *The Quality of Mercy: Cambodia, Holocaust and Modern Conscience.* New York: Simon and Schuster, 1984.
Vickery, Michael. *Cambodia 1975–1982.* Boston: South End, 1984.

Contributors

George J. Andreopoulos, lecturer and former associate director of the Orville H. Schell Center for International Human Rights at Yale, has written on diplomatic history, international relations, and international human rights. Forthcoming publications include *The Laws of War: Constraints on Warfare in the Western World* (with Michael Howard and Mark Shulman), and *Recovery from Defeat* (with Harold Selesky). He is currently working on a book on humanitarian intervention.

Frank Chalk, associate professor of history at Concordia University, and chairman of the Executive Committee of the Montreal Institute for Genocide Studies, is the coauthor (with Kurt Jonassohn) of *The History and Sociology of Genocide: Analysis and Case Studies* (1990). His essays have appeared in a number of books, including *Genocide in the Modern Age,* edited by Isidor Wallimann and Michael N. Dobkowski, and *Genocide: A Critical Bibliographic Review,* edited by Israel Charny.

Israel W. Charny, executive director of the Institute on the Holocaust and Genocide, Jerusalem, is the author of *How Can We Commit the Unthinkable? Genocide, the Human Cancer* (1982); editor, with Shamai Davidson, of *The Book of the International Conference on the Holocaust and Genocide* (1983); editor of *Toward the Understanding and Prevention of Genocide* (1984); and editor of *Genocide: A Critical Bibliographic Review,* (two vols., 1988, 1991).

James Dunn, a foreign affairs and human rights specialist, has been a diplomat and senior adviser to the Australian Parliament and served in East Timor as consul. He is the author of *Timor: A People Betrayed,* and has testified before a Congressional committee on the subject. He is a foreign affairs columnist for *The Bulletin.*

Helen Fein, executive director of the Institute for the Study of Genocide and currently a Visiting Scholar at the Human Rights Program at Harvard Law School, is the author of "Genocide: A Sociological Perspective," *Current Sociology* 38:1 (Spring 1990), and *Accounting for Genocide: National Responses and Jewish Victimization during the Holocaust* (1979). She was the recipient of the 1979 Sorokin Award of the American Sociological Association.

Richard G. Hovannisian, professor of Near Eastern History, holder of the Armenian Educational Foundation Chair in Modern Armenian History, and associate director of the von Grunebaum Center for Near Eastern Studies at the University of California, Los Angeles, is the author of *Armenia on the Road to Independence, 1918* (1967) and the multivolume study *The Republic of Armenia* (1971, 1982). He is the editor of and a contributor to *The Armenian Genocide: History, Politics, Ethics* (1992).

Ben Kiernan, associate professor of history at Yale University, is author of *How Pol Pot Came to Power* (1985) and coauthor of four other books on modern Cambodia, including *Pol Pot Plans the Future* (with Chanthou Boua and David P. Chandler, 1988), a collection of internal documents of the Khmer Rouge regime. He is now working on a new history of that regime.

Leo Kuper, emeritus professor of sociology at UCLA, is the author of many books and articles on genocide, including *Genocide: Its Political Use in the Twentieth Century* (1982) and *The Prevention of Genocide* (1985).

Martin van Bruinessen, research fellow at the Royal Institute of Linguistics and Anthropology in Leiden, Netherlands, has written extensively on the Kurdish question as well as on Ottoman history and politics. Among his writings are *Agha, Shaikh and State: On the Social and Political Organization of Kurdistan, The Kurds between Iran and Iraq,* and *The Ethnic Identity of the Kurds.*

Index

University of Pennsylvania Press
Pennsylvania Studies in Human Rights

Bert B. Lockwood, Jr., Series Editor
Professor and Director, Urban Morgan Institute for Human Rights, University
of Cincinnati College of Law

Advisory Board

Marjorie Agosin
Philip Alston
Kevin Boyle
Richard P. Claude
David Weissbrodt